THE CONCISE JEWISH BIBLE

Books by Philip Birnbaum

A BOOK OF JEWISH CONCEPTS

THE NEW TREASURY OF JUDAISM

FLUENT HEBREW

MAIMONIDES' MISHNEH TORAH

THE BIRNBAUM HAGGADAH

ETHICS OF THE FATHERS

DAILY PRAYER BOOK

PRAYER BOOK FOR SABBATH AND FESTIVALS

HIGH HOLYDAY PRAYER BOOK

THE CONCISE JEWISH BIBLE

EDITED AND TRANSLATED BY

PHILIP BIRNBAUM

Sanhedrin Press

NEW YORK • LONDON

SANHEDRIN PRESS,
a division of Hebrew Publishing Company,
New York, N.Y.

Library of Congress Cataloging in Publication Data

Bible. O. T. English. Birnbaum. 1976.
  The concise Jewish Bible.

  I. Birnbaum, Philip. II. Title.
BS895.B57   221.5'2   76-49108
ISBN 0-88482-450-0
ISBN 0-88482-451-9 pbk.

PRINTED IN THE UNITED STATES OF AMERICA

Contents

Introduction

The Bible is the best-selling book of all time. In one form or another, the Bible has served as a source of comfort and inspiration to mankind for untold centuries. Yet surprisingly few seem to be familiar with its contents. It should be read regularly; it should have a real bearing upon the life of those who use it. The aim of this edition is to provide a short version of the Bible which is easy to read, a joy to handle, and intelligible to many people.

The Bible is the classical book of noble ethical sentiment. When read intelligently, it reveals itself as the immortal epic of a people's indomitable struggle after a nobler life in a happier world. Heinrich Heine referred to the Bible as "that great medicine chest of humanity . . . sunrise and sunset, promise and fulfillment, birth and death, the whole human drama, everything is in this book . . . it is the book of books, *Biblia* . . . He who lost his God may find him again in this book, and he who has never known him will inhale here the breath of God's word . . ."

The Bible has been the Magna Carta of the poor and of the oppressed. Down to modern times no state has had a constitution in which the interests of the people are so largely taken into account as that drawn up for Israel in the books of Leviticus and Deuteronomy. Nowhere is the fundamental truth so strongly laid down that the welfare of the state in the long run depends on the uprightness of the citizen.

The Ten Commandments, unrivalled by any other code for simplicity and comprehensiveness, represent a summary of universal duties that are binding upon the entire human species. They cover the whole religious and moral life, affirming the existence of God and stressing the observance of the Sabbath and the reverence due to one's parents; and forbidding murder, adultery, theft, false testimony, and predatory desires. The Hebrew prophets vividly realized that tomorrow is inherent in today. Foreseeing the outcome of national crises and evil practices, they fearlessly criticized the morals of their own day while teaching a nobler way of living. Their message was usually one of warning and exhortation, including a prediction of coming events in the near or distant future. Their boldness could have been possible only in a country where freedom of speech was a fact. Their severe judgment of the moral condition of the people of Israel resulted from their lofty ethical conception of the God of Israel. Addressing themselves to the people of their own time on things of spiritual importance, they always sought to arouse in them a feeling against social suffering and injustice, urging them to relieve the oppressed, to champion the cause of the weak and defenseless, to hate the evil and love the good. They never stood aloof from their people, whom they loved intensely; they never failed to plead for human mercy, justice and uprightness.

Over one-sixth of the Bible is written in poetic form. The Psalms have been on the lips of more people throughout the centuries than any other written compositions. They represent the highest product of the religious poetry of all the nations, and stand out unique among the prayers of the whole world by the majesty of their language and their simplicity. In the poetry of the Bible, we find the human heart in all its moods and emotions—in penitence, in danger, in desolation and in triumph.

The Structure of the Bible

The three divisions of the Hebrew Bible, which is commonly referred to as the Old Testament, are called in Hebrew *Tanakh* (a word formed from the initial letters of *Torah, Neviim, Kethuvim*). *Torah* (Pentateuch) consists of the Five Books of Moses which are contained in the *Sefer Torah* as well as in the printed editions known as *Hummashim* (fifths). The framework of history in the

6

Pentateuch extends from the creation of the world to the death of Moses. The first book, Genesis (*Bereshith*) opens with the story of creation; Exodus (*Shemoth*) tells of the exodus from Egypt; Leviticus (*Vayyikra*) contains laws which relate to the priests, members of the tribe of Levi; Numbers (*Bemidbar*) derives its English name from the census of the Israelites in the wilderness; Deuteronomy (*Devarim*) contains a restatement of the Mosaic laws.

The second part of the Bible, the Prophets (*Neviim*), has eight books that are subdivided into Former Prophets (*Neviim Rishonim*) and Latter Prophets (*Neviim Aharonim*). The Former Prophets comprise four historical books: Joshua, Judges, Samuel, and Kings. The Latter Prophets are also made up of four books: Isaiah, Jeremiah, Ezekiel, and the *Tré-Asar*, Twelve Minor Prophets, so called because of their comparatively short length. The Twelve Minor Prophets are: Hosea, Joel, Obadiah, Jonah, Micah, Nahum, Habakkuk, Zephaniah, Haggai, Zechariah, and Malachi. The books of Isaiah, Jeremiah and Ezekiel are the Major Prophets, books much greater in size. Isaiah, for example, has sixty-six chapters, whereas the book of Obadiah consists only of one chapter.

The third part of the Bible, known as Hagiographa (*Kethuvim,* Sacred writings), is made up of the remaining eleven books: Psalms, Proverbs, Job, Song of Songs, Ruth, Lamentations, Ecclesiastes, Esther, Daniel, Ezra-Nehemiah, and Chronicles. Forming a class by themselves, the Five Scrolls (*Hamesh Megilloth*) are arranged in the Hebrew Bible according to the sequence of the occasions on which they are recited in the synagogue as part of the liturgy: Song of Songs on *Pesah,* Ruth on *Shavuoth,* Lamentations on *Tishab b'Av,* Ecclesiastes on *Sukkoth,* and Esther on *Purim.*

Apocrypha

Originally, the Hebrew Bible included only the Pentateuch, but later the Prophets, and finally the Hagiographa were added. The Song of Songs was one of the last books to be included, when Rabbi Akiva of the second century declared it to be the holiest of all the sacred poetical writings.

The Apocrypha consists of those books that are found in the Greek version of the Bible, the Septuagint, but not in the Hebrew Bible itself. They represent a remarkable ethical literature that was inspired by the Hebrew Bible during the period of the Second Temple. In Hebrew, the books of the *Apocrypha* are known as the "hidden books" (*Sefarim Genuzim*). They are also called *Sefarim Hitzonim* (outside books) or *Kethuvim Aharonim* (latter writings.) Originally written in Hebrew, Aramaic or Greek, they were produced after the time of Ezra the Scribe, when direct revelation had ceased with the ending of the prophetic era. If not for the Septuagint, they would have disappeared entirely from our knowledge. And yet they include such important works as *Ben Sira* (Ecclesiasticus), the *Wisdom of Solomon,* the *First Book of Maccabees,* and the stories of *Judith* and *Tobit.* The book of *Ben Sira* contains an admirable collection of proverbs covering a wide range of subjects concerning practical affairs, physical health and good manners. The *First Book of Maccabees* describes the rise of the Maccabean revolt. The *Second Book of Maccabees* is filled with stories of defiant martyrdom during the Maccabean struggles, which proved decisive in forming the character of subsequent generations. In the book of *Tobit* are enshrined lofty Jewish ideas concerning pure family life and the duty of kindness to the poor. The book of *Judith* tells of the flight of a besieging enemy after a daring act performed by a pious and beautiful widow named Judith, who succeeded in slaying the foe's general, Holofernes. The courage of the besieged was roused to the point that they rushed out and put the enemy to complete rout.

Though the books of the Apocrypha are for the most part akin to those which constitute the Bible, they were not admitted to the Holy Scriptures for a variety of reasons. With the exception of *Ben Sira,* the books of the Apocrypha gradually disappeared and were discredited by Jews, mainly because they were held under suspicion as being affected by later sectarian interpolations.

Use of the Bible in the Synagogue

The prayer life of the Jew is saturated with the contents of the Bible. The daily prayer book abounds in biblical quotations; it includes almost half of the book of Psalms, the entire Song of Songs, and lengthy excerpts from each of the Five Books of Moses, and other biblical books.

The public reading of the Torah in the synagogue has been one of the most powerful factors in Jewish education through the centuries. Originally, the reading was accompanied by translation and interpretation, so that the contents of the Torah became known to all the people of Israel. Writing in the first century, historian Flavius Josephus states that Moses showed the Torah to be the best and the most necessary means of instruction by enjoining the people to assemble not once or twice or even just frequently, but every week, on the Sabbath, while abstaining from all other work, in order to hear the Torah and learn it in a thorough manner—a thing which all other lawgivers seem to have neglected. The additional Torah readings on Sabbath afternoons, when people have leisure, and on Mondays and Thursdays, the market days in early times, are attributed to Ezra the Scribe, who organized Jewish life after Israel's return from the Babylonian captivity. In Eretz Yisrael, it was the practice to read the Torah on Sabbath mornings in a triennial cycle. Today, the universal custom is to complete the public reading of the Torah once each year.

The prophetical section recited after the Torah reading on Sabbaths and festivals is known as *Haftarah* (conclusion). Usually, though not always, the *Haftarah* contains some reference to an incident mentioned in the assigned Torah reading. On the three Sabbaths preceding the fast of *Tishah b'Av,* which commemorates the destruction of the Temple, prophecies of rebuke are recited, whereas on the seven Sabbaths after *Tishah b'Av* the *Haftarah* consists of prophetic utterances of comfort and consolation.

Rabbi David Abudarham of fourteenth-century Spain traces the custom of reading from the Prophets after the Torah reading back to the period of religious persecutions

9

preceding the Maccabean revolt. According to his theory, the *Haftarah* was introduced originally as a substitute for the Torah reading, when the latter was prohibited under the severe decrees of Antiocus Epiphanes, who reigned over Syria (165–163 BCE).

Some authorities suggest that the *Haftarah* readings were instituted to emphasize the great value of the Prophets, in order to oppose the Samaritans, who strictly observe the precepts of the Pentateuch, but reject not only the rabbinic tradition but also the prophetical writings.

Masoretic Text

The text of the Hebrew Bible, known as the Masoretic Text, has been transmitted from generation to generation with scrupulous uniformity and unparalleled accuracy of transcription, thus protecting it against any misunderstanding or interpolation. As early as the second century, Jewish tradition had established the consonantal text and its pronunciation so firmly that no change is known to have occurred in it since.

When Hebrew had ceased to be a spoken language, it became imperative to devise a system of vowels, in the form of dots and dashes, so as to enable anyone to learn the mechanics of reading and pronouncing Hebrew correctly. This was accomplished by the Masorites, whose activity extended from the sixth to the tenth centuries, chiefly in Tiberias. Addressing themselves to careful watchfulness over the received text of the Bible, the Masorites counted every word and letter. They drew up lists of irregular or unusual spellings, and built up the safeguards for the preservation of the sacred teachings. The last and most renowned Masorite scholar was Aaron ben Asher of the tenth century.

The collection of critical Masoretic notes is found either in separate works or in the form of marginal notations. The notations on the side margins of the Rabbinic Bible *(Mikraoth Gedoloth)* are referred to as *Small Masorah*; those on the upper and lower margins of the biblical books are called *Large Masorah*. The *Masorah Finalis,* found in nearly all the printed editions at the end of the various books, indicates the number of chapters, verses, the middle point of the book, full and defective spellings, and abnormally written letters. On account of its obscure terminology, consisting of numerous abbreviations, the Masoretic sign language is a study in itself.

Bible Accents

The primary purpose of the special signs of cantillation, which are placed both above and under the words of the Hebrew Bible, is to regulate even more minutely the reading of the holy text. They serve, in fact, a threefold purpose: 1) as musical notes; 2) as marks of the tone-syllables; and 3) as marks of punctuation, to indicate the logical relation of words to one another. This system of musical notation facilitates a deeper penetration into the meaning of the component parts of biblical verses.

The understanding of the biblical text is readily aided by the signs of accentuation, though it is not always easy to tell why certain modes of cantillation were chosen. A knowledge of the accents is indispensable to the study of the Hebrew Bible. Rabbi Abraham ibn Ezra of twelfth-century Spain, best known for his penetrating Bible commentaries, declared that one should not accept an interpretation of a biblical passage if it does not follow the guiding accents.

As marks of punctuation, the accents are divided into *disjunctive,* indicating various degrees of pause, and *conjunctive,* serving to connect words. A special system, musically more significant than the common system, is used in the books of Psalms, Proverbs and Job.

During the Middle Ages it was generally believed that the signs of cantillation as well as the signs of vocalization had been originated by Ezra the Scribe and the members of the Great Assembly (*Anshé Kneseth ha-Gedolah*), who flourished several centuries before the common era. Aaron ben Asher, the tenth-century masoretic scholar,

11

speaks of the accents as the contribution of the prophets to whom the interpretation of every word was revealed. Elijah Levita (1468–1549) was the first to prove the post-talmudic date of the vowels and the accents.

Bible Translations

The name *Bible* is derived from the Greek word *biblion* for a book written upon the byblus or papyrus reed. The British and Foreign Bible Society alone has published complete Bibles in well over two hundred languages and translations of individual biblical books in about one thousand languages.

The earliest version of the Hebrew Bible in another language is the Septuagint, a Greek translation produced in Egypt between the third and first centuries before the common era. The first translation into a language of western Europe is the Latin version, the Vulgate, completed in 405 c.e. The first English version is that of John Wyclif, about 1382.

The Septuagint derived its name, meaning seventy, from the legend preserved in the letter of Aristeas, that the Torah was translated into Greek in Alexandria, Egypt, by 72 emissaries from Jerusalem, six from each tribe of Israel, at the request of Ptolemy II (278–270 b.c.e.). Subsequently, the rest of the Bible was also translated. Scholars regard this as a fanciful story of the origin of the Septuagint, which they usually refer to by the symbol LXX.

Those who have made a study of the vocabulary, idioms and syntax used in the Septuagint, have been led to believe that the work gradually developed through the practice of oral translation in the synagogues of Alexandria, though some of the twenty-four books of the Bible were translated and edited by individuals. The Torah was the first and foremost part of the Bible that had to be made accessible to the Greek-speaking Jewish community.

It has been suggested that if the initiative proceeded from the Alexandrian Jews themselves, royal sanction was obtained for the translation and a copy presented to the library. The various books of the Bible, other than the

Torah, were translated gradually. By the end of the second century before the common era, all the books of the Hebrew Bible existed in Greek. The various books are generally judged separately as to their individual worth in terms of authentic renderings. Some of them, like the Torah, are faithful to the Hebrew text; others, like Jeremiah, vary constantly from the original Hebrew and are paraphrastic, a restatement of passages in other words. The Septuagint abounds in misreadings, mistranslations, and internal corruptions. Hence, there is no single Septuagint version, but every ancient manuscript presents a different text, departing in its own way from the Hebrew text.

While the Septuagint was originally intended for the use of the Greek-speaking Jews, at the same time it transmitted Jewish teachings to the non-Jewish world and attracted many proselytes to Judaism. But the Jews of the Roman empire had to be provided with a substitute Greek version to take the place of the Septuagint, marred as it was by blunders and interpolations. In Psalm 96:10, for example, the phrase "from the cross" was added to the sentence "The Lord reigns." The word *almah* (young woman), in Isaiah 7:14, was retranslated "virgin" for sectarian reasons. Three new versions were produced—Aquila, Symmachus and Theodotion. Considerable portions of the translation of Aquila, a disciple of Rabbi Akiva, survive. They demonstrate its faithfulness to the Hebrew original, even at the expense of the Greek idiom.

These three Greek versions were used simultaneously by scholars who sought authentic information about the contents of the Hebrew original: Aquila served as a dictionary, Symmachus as a commmentary, and Theodotion as a translation. Origen (185–254) of Alexandria compiled the Hexapla, a polyglot Bible containing the original Hebrew in square characters, a Greek transliteration enabling the student to pronounce every Hebrew word, and the Greek translations of Aquila, Symmachus, the Septuagint, and Theodotion. The six texts appeared in six parallel columns, hence the name *Hexapla*. Only fragments were found in the Cairo Genizah of some columns copied from Origen's Hexapla; a few leaves of a copy containing the Psalms were discovered in Milan.

The Targum

The name of *Targum Onkelos* has been given to the Aramaic translation of the Five Books of Moses. Like Aquila, Onkelos is spoken of as a proselyte and a disciple of Rabbi Akiva. *Targum Onkelos* has continued to be read and studied to this day, when Aramaic is no longer spoken by the Jewish people. It became customary to review the weekly *sidrah* (portion) twice in the original Hebrew and once in the *Targum* (*shenayim mikra v'ehad Targum*).

Though remarkably faithful to the original Hebrew text as a whole, *Targum Onkelos* occasionally expands somewhat in poetic passages, in order to introduce ethical ideas derived from the talmudic sages. Avoiding anthropomorphic expressions which represent God with human attributes, *Targum Onkelos* uses circumlocutions, as when "the mouth of the Lord" is rendered "the *memra* (word, command) of the Lord." In Genesis 20:3, "God came" is rendered "a word from the Lord came." When God says that he will meet the people (Exodus 25:22), *Targum Onkelos* translates: "I will cause my word to meet you and I will speak with you."

The biblical modes of speech, accommodating the human ear, are thus toned down. God does not smell the sweet savor of an offering, but rather accepts it with delight; he does not pass over the people of Israel on the Passover night, but rescues them; he does not go before the people, but leads them. The *Targum* also avoids anything that may appear derogatory at the expense of the patriarchs of the Jewish people. Jacob does not "steal Laban's heart," but merely hides from him his going away; Rachel does not steal her father's household gods, but only takes them. Jacob does not flee, but simply departs. Similarly, Leah's eyes were not weak, but pretty. Moses married a beautiful woman, not a Kushite.

The same characteristic applies to the Aramaic version of the prophetical books of the Bible, the *Neviim*. Known as *Targum Yonathan,* it was composed by Hillel's most distinguished disciple, Jonathan ben Uzziel, who lived one century before the destruction of the Second Temple. The third division of the Bible, *Kethuvim* (Hagiographa), has *Targums* to the various books which differ in character from one another. The *Targum Sheni* to the book of Esther is additional to the ordinary *Targum,* more midrashic and replete with legend. Unlike all other Aramaic paraphrases of biblical books, *Targum Onkelos* to the Torah has long enjoyed a sanctity second only to the Hebrew text itself.

Archaic Renderings

Many English-speaking Jews of recent generations have been hindered from gaining a wholesome appreciation of the Hebrew Bible by "Bible English." The antiquated English versions of the Bible abound in phrases like "yielded up the ghost" instead of died. If translation is to facilitate a proper understanding of the original, it must be freed from archaic forms like: "Thou sawest the affliction of our fathers . . . and heardest their cry . . . and shewedst signs and wonders." Unquestionably irritating are such expressions as "He gathereth the outcasts of Israel"; "He hath lifted up a horn for His people"; "and redeemed him from the hand of him that was stronger than he." Many forms of expression have become archaic, for example: howbeit, aforetime, must needs, would fain, behooved. Other words have changed in meaning and are no longer understood by the average reader. The King James Version uses the word "let" in the sense of "hinder," "wealth" for "well-being." The King James Version, the basis of most subsequent English translations, was completed in 1611 by a team of fifty-four scholars. It was itself based upon a Greek text that was marred by mistakes, containing the accumulated errors of fourteen centuries of manuscript copying. These scholars lacked a thorough knowledge of the Hebrew language and a close acquaintance with the commentaries written in Hebrew by medieval Jewish scholars.

The Jewish commentators of the Bible, who regarded the Book of Books as an inexhaustible storehouse of wisdom to which one can always resort for guidance and inspiration, frequently read into the text the knowledge which they derived from a variety of sources. They made use of Talmud and Midrash, philosophy and mysticism, for a deeper understanding of the biblical message. The fourfold method of Bible interpretation, known as *Pardes,* consisted of the literal, allegorical, homiletical and mystical construction ascribed to the scriptural text by expositors of various bents. The general rule, however, was not to admit any interpretation that was incompatible with the plain meaning of the passage.

The Concise Jewish Bible

Since the present work is intended for readers of all ages, it is composed throughout in lucid, simple style. In translating the contents of *The Concise Jewish Bible* direct from the original Hebrew text, I have chosen to follow the wise counsel of Maimonides to the effect that whoever wishes to translate each word literally, "and at the same time adheres slavishly to the order of the words and sentences in the original, will meet with much difficulty. The translator should first try to grasp thoroughly the sense of the subject, and then state the theme with perfect clarity. This, however, cannot be done without changing the order of the words, substituting many words for one word, or one word for many words, so that the subject is perfectly intelligible in the language into which it is translated" (Rambam's letter to Samuel ibn Tibbon).

It has been my aim to include in this volume biblical portions to suit everyone's taste in terms of enlightenment, guidance and interesting reading, and to make it all intelligible to young and old without the aid of footnotes and marginal comments. Books like Job and Ecclesiastes, which are scarcely read by the majority of people, by reason of the difficult passages, have been made accessible and instructive by eliminating whatever is unclear and of doubtful meaning. In this manner, the average reader is enabled to concentrate on that which captures the imagination and stirs the heart. A brief general introduction has been provided for each book.

It remains to urge that a useful book as this does not become the real property of its owner unless, through thorough reading, its contents enter his mind, his thinking, and his practice in everyday life. It is sincerely hoped that a large number of readers will find in *The Concise Jewish Bible* much to awaken their interest and stimulate their thinking. They may well be induced to delve further into the teachings of the entire Bible and its commentaries. May this book enlighten the minds of all those who strive to make this world a better place to live in.

PHILIP BIRNBAUM

September, 1976
New York City

Genesis   בְּרֵאשִׁית

Genesis contains the early history of mankind, describes the lives of the forefathers of Israel, and ends with the death of Joseph. Its records, covering a period of more than two thousand years from the creation, go back to remote antiquity. The narratives in Genesis were handed down, through many generations, by word of mouth before they were ever written down; and these stories became the vehicle for countless ethical and spiritual lessons.

Throughout the book there is a noble conception of man, what he was created to be and what he has the power to become. The statement that man was made in the image of God strikes the keynote of all that follows. The moral grandeur and depth of meaning, as well as the simplicity and sublimity of the story of creation, are universally recognized. All men are descended from Adam and Eve, all men are related; hence the unity of all mankind. This is said to be the most fundamental teaching in the entire Bible: *all* men are created in the image of God.

Israel's ancestors are represented here in their family relations: as husband and wife, parent and child, brother and sister. Here are illustrations of truthfulness, grace and loveliness, with a wealth of instructive example.

Great moral truths are woven into the texture of the narratives of Genesis. Indeed, there is no more impressive book in the Bible than Genesis. Its charm and power are inherent in the personal portraits of Abraham, Jacob and Joseph, breathing and alive in the freshness of the world's dawn.

Like the rest of the Torah, Genesis is primarily a book of instruction; it conveys the idea that the Creator of the universe forever guides those who trust in him. Its language is adapted to the understanding of young and old alike. Children can grasp the outline of its story, while erudite scholars continue to discover fresh meanings in it.

When God first created the heavens and the earth, the world was waste and void; darkness lay over the deep; and the spirit of God moved above the waters.

God said: "Let there be light," and there was light. God saw that the light was good, and he separated the light from the darkness. God called the light Day, and the darkness he called Night. There was evening and there was morning, the first day.

God said: "Let there be an expanse between the waters." And so God made the expanse, and called it Heaven. There was evening and there was morning, the second day.

God said: "Let the waters under the heaven be gathered into one place, and let the dry land appear." And so it was. God called the dry land Earth, and the gathered waters he called Seas. God saw that it was good. Then God said: "Let the earth bring forth plants yielding seed and trees bearing fruits of every kind." And so it was. God saw that it was good. There was evening and there was morning, the third day.

God said: "Let there be lights in the sky, to separate day from night and to mark days and years." And so it was. God made the two great lights, the greater light to rule the day and the lesser light to rule the night, and the stars. God saw that it was good. There was evening and there was morning, the fourth day.

God said: "Let the waters abound in life, and let birds fly above the earth across the sky." And so God created the great sea-monsters and every kind of living creature and every kind of winged bird. God saw that it was good. God blessed them, saying: "Be fruitful, multiply, and fill the waters of the seas; and let the birds multiply on the earth." There was evening and there was morning, the fifth day.

God said: "Let the earth bring forth every kind of living creature, cattle, reptiles, and wild beasts." And so it was. God saw that it was good. Then God said: "Let us make man in our image, after our likeness; let him have dominion over the fish in the sea, the birds of the air, the cattle, every wild beast of the earth, and every reptile that crawls on the earth." So God created man in his own image; male and female he formed them. God blessed them and said: "Be fruitful, multiply, fill the earth and subdue it; have dominion over the fish in the sea, the birds of the air and every living thing that moves upon the earth."

Thus the heavens and the earth were finished, and all their host. By the seventh day God had completed the work which he had made, and he rested on the seventh day from all his work. Then God blessed the seventh day and hallowed it, because on it he rested from all the work which he had done.

The Lord God formed man from the dust of the ground and breathed into his nostrils the breath of life. He planted a garden in Eden, where he put the man to till it and look after it. And the Lord God commanded him, saying: "You are free to eat from any tree in the garden, but you shall not eat from the tree of knowledge, for you shall die the day you eat from it."

Then the Lord God said: "It is not good for man to be alone; I will make a helpmate for him." So the Lord God caused a deep sleep to fall upon the man; he took one of his ribs, shaped it into a woman and brought her to the man. The man said: "This, at last, is bone of my bones and flesh of my flesh; she shall be called woman because she was taken from man."

Now the serpent said to the woman: "Did God say that you must not eat fruit from any tree in the garden?"

The woman replied: "We may eat fruit from the trees of the garden; but, as to the tree in the middle of the garden, God said: 'You shall not eat from it, you shall not touch it, lest you die.'"

"No," said the serpent, "you shall not die; God knows that on the day you eat from it your eyes will be opened and you will be like gods knowing good and evil."

The woman saw that the tree was good for food; she took some of its fruit and ate it; she also gave some to her husband, and he ate. Then the eyes of both were opened and they realized that they were naked, so they hid themselves among the trees of the garden.

The Lord God called to the man: "Where are you?" And he said: "I heard thy voice in the garden and I was afraid, because I was naked, so I hid myself." God said: "Who told you that you were naked? Have you eaten from the tree of which I forbade you to eat?" The man said: "The woman thou gavest me as a companion, she gave

21

me some fruit of the tree, and I ate." Then the Lord God said to the woman: "What is this that you have done?" The woman said: "The serpent misled me, and I ate."

The Lord God said to the serpent: "Because you have done this, cursed are you above all cattle; dust you shall eat all the days of your life." To the woman he said: "In pain you shall bear children, yet your desire shall be for your husband." To the man he said: "Because you have listened to your wife, in the sweat of your brow you shall eat bread till you return to the ground from which you were taken; you are dust, and to dust you shall return."

The man called the name of his wife Eve (Life), because she was the mother of all living beings. Eve bore Cain, and later she bore his brother Abel. Abel was a shepherd, while Cain was a farmer.

In the course of time Cain brought some fruit of the ground as an offering to the Lord, while Abel brought some fat firstlings from his flock. The Lord favored Abel and his offering, but had no regard for Cain and his offering. So Cain was very angry and downcast.

"Why are you angry?" the Lord said to Cain; "why are you downcast? If you do well, you will be accepted; if you do not well, sin is lying in wait for you, eager to be at you, but you must master it."

Cain said to his brother: "Let us go into the field." When they were in the field, Cain rose up against his brother Abel and killed him. And the Lord said to Cain: "Where is your brother Abel?" He said: "I do not know; am I my brother's keeper?" And the Lord said: "What have you done? Your brother's blood cries to me from the ground! And now, cursed shall you be; you shall be a fugitive and wanderer on the earth." And the Lord put a mark on Cain to prevent anyone from killing him.

Now when men began to multiply over the earth, the Lord said: "My spirit shall not remain in man forever, for he is flesh; his days shall be one hundred and twenty years." When the Lord saw that the wickedness of man on earth was great, and that man's impulse is never anything but evil, he said: "I will blot out man from the face of the

22

earth—man and beast and reptile and bird; I am indeed sorry that I have made them."

Noah, however, was an upright man and found favor with the Lord. So God said to Noah: "I have resolved to put an end to all flesh; the earth is filled with violence on account of them; I will destroy them together with the earth. Make yourself an ark, for I am about to bring a flood upon the earth; everything that is on the earth shall perish. You shall enter the ark, you and your sons and your wife and your sons' wives along with you. You shall take into the ark two of every living creature of every kind, to keep them alive with you; they shall be male and female. Store up every sort of food for you and for them." Noah did all that God had commanded him.

After seven days the waters of the flood came upon the earth; all the fountains of the great deep burst forth, and the windows of the heavens were opened. Rain fell upon the earth forty days and forty nights. Whatever was on the dry land died; the Lord blotted every living creature from the earth; only Noah and those inside the ark were left. For a hundred and fifty days the waters swelled over the earth. Then God made a wind blow, and the waters subsided steadily till they dried off the earth.

Noah came out of the ark along with his sons and his wife and his sons' wives. God blessed Noah and his children and said to them: "Be fruitful and multiply, and fill the earth. Whoever sheds the blood of man, by man shall his own blood be shed, for God made man in his own image."

When the whole world had one language, one vocabulary, there was a migration from the east; men came upon a plain in the land of Shinar and settled there. Then they said to one another: "Come, let us make bricks; let us make a name for ourselves by building a city and a tower reaching to heaven; it will keep us from being scattered upon the face of the whole earth."

"They are one people," said the Lord, "and they have one language. Come, let us go down and confuse their language, that they may not understand one another's speech." So the Lord dispersed them over the face of all the earth, and they gave up building the city. Hence it was called Babylon, because there the Lord confused the language of the whole earth, and from there the Lord dispersed them over the face of the whole earth.

Abraham was the son of Terah who was a descendant of Noah's eldest son Shem. Now the Lord said to Abraham: "Leave your country and go to the land which I will show you. I will make a great nation of you; all the nations of the earth shall be blessed through you." So Abraham left Chaldea, taking his wife Sarah and his nephew Lot with all the property they had acquired, and reached the land of Canaan. Then the Lord appeared to Abraham and said: "I give this land to your descendants." He built an altar to the Lord who had appeared to him, and he traveled on toward the Negev.

Abraham was very rich in cattle, silver and gold; and Lot, who went with Abraham, also had flocks and herds and tents. The land could not support them both; their possessions were so large that they could not dwell together. So Abraham said to Lot: "Let there be no strife between you and me, between your herdsmen and my herdsmen. Separate yourself from me; if you go to the left, I will go to the right; or if you go to the right, I will go to the left."

They parted company, and Lot moved toward Sodom. Then the Lord said to Abraham: "Look around now from where you are, northward and southward and eastward and westward; all the land you see I give to you and your descendants for all time. I will make your descendants as numerous as the dust of the ground. Arise, walk through the length and the breadth of the land, for I give it to you."

Now it was during the reign of Amraphel, king of Shinar, that four kings captured all the possessions and all the provisions of Sodom and Gomorrah and went away; they also carried off Lot and his possessions. As soon as Abraham heard that his kinsman had been taken captive, he led forth his trained men, three hundred and eighteen of them, and went in pursuit as far as Dan, where he routed the enemy. He recovered all the possessions, and also brought back his kinsman Lot with his possessions, and the women and the people.

The king of Sodom went out to meet him, and the king of Salem brought out bread and wine, saying: "Blessed be Abraham by God Most High, Creator of heaven and earth; and blessed be God Most High who has delivered your enemies into your hand!"

The king of Sodom said to Abraham: "Let me have the prisoners, and take the goods for yourself." But Abraham answered the king of Sodom: "I swear to the Lord God Most High, Creator of heaven and earth, that I will not take a thread or string of yours! You will not have to say: 'I have made Abraham rich.' I will take nothing except what the young men have eaten; but let my comrades have their share of the spoil."

After this the Lord said to Abraham in a vision: "Fear not, Abraham, I will shield you; your reward shall be very great." But Abraham said: "Lord God, what canst thou give me when I continue childless, and Eliezer of Damascus, a slave, is my heir?" Then the Lord said to him: "This one shall not be your heir; your own son shall be your heir." He took him outside and said: "Look up to the sky and number the stars if you can; such shall be the number of your descendants."

Once Abraham sat at the door of his tent in the heat of the day and beheld three men. He ran to welcome them and, bowing to the ground, he said: "My lords, do not pass by your servant; wash you feet and rest under the tree till I fetch some food that you may refresh yourselves." They said: "Do as you say."

So Abraham hastened to Sarah's tent and said: "Quick, make some cakes." Then he ran to the herd and picked a tender calf, which he handed to the servant to prepare. He placed the food before them and they ate.

"Where is your wife Sarah?" they asked him. "She is inside the tent," he answered. Then one said: "I will come back to you next year, when your wife Sarah shall have a son." Sarah was listening behind the door. Now Abraham and Sarah were well advanced in years. So Sarah laughed

25

to herself: "After I have grown old, and my husband is old, can I regain my youth?"

The Lord said to Abraham: "Why did Sarah laugh, saying: 'Shall I indeed bear a child, although I am old?' Is anything too wonderful for the Lord? At this time next year I will return to you, and Sarah shall have a son."

The men of Sodom were wicked and sinned against the Lord. So the Lord said: "Because the outcry against Sodom and Gomorrah is great, and their sin is very grave, I will go down and see whether they have indeed acted as viciously as the outcry indicates." The men—who were angels —set out toward Sodom, and Abraham went with them to see them off.

Then Abraham stood before the Lord and said: "Wilt thou destroy the righteous along with the wicked? Suppose there are fifty good men within the city; wilt thou destroy the place and not forgive it for the sake of the fifty good people in it? Far be it from thee to act like that, to make the good perish along with the bad! Shall not the Judge of all the earth act justly?" The Lord said: "If I can find fifty good persons in Sodom, I will forgive the whole place for their sake."

Then Abraham went on: "I have taken upon myself to speak to the Lord, I who am dust and ashes. Suppose five are lacking out of the fifty good people? Will you destroy the whole city for the lack of five?" He replied: "I will not destroy it if I can find forty-five in it." Again Abraham asked him: "Suppose forty are found there?" He answered: "I will spare it for the sake of the forty."

Then he said: "Oh let not the Lord be angry if I speak again. Suppose thirty are found there?" He answered: "I will not do it if I find thirty there." And he said: "I am venturing to speak to the Lord: suppose there are twenty good people in it?" He answered: "For the sake of twenty I will not destroy it." Then he said: "Oh let not the Lord be angry and I will speak just once more: if ten good men are to be found there?" He answered: "For the sake of the ten I will not destroy it." But there were not even ten good men there.

The angels seized Lot and his wife and his two daughters

by the hand, through the mercy of the Lord toward Lot, and led them forth and set them outside the city. When they brought them forth, they said: "Flee for your life; do not look back, flee to the hills, lest you perish."

Then the Lord rained sulphur and fire on Sodom and Gomorrah; he overthrew these cities and all the inhabitants. Lot's wife looked back and she was turned into a pillar of salt. In the morning when Abraham went to the place where he had stood before the Lord, he looked in the direction of Sodom and Gomorrah, and there was smoke rising from the land like smoke from a furnace.

The Lord remembered Sarah as he had promised; the Lord did for Sarah as he had spoken. Sarah bore a son at the time of which God had spoken. Abraham named his son Isaac. When Isaac was eight days old, Abraham circumcised him as God had commanded.

Abraham was a hundred years old when his son Isaac was born, and Sarah said: "God has given me a delightful surprise; all who hear of it will be amused on my account. Who could predict to Abraham that Sarah would nurse a child?" Abraham prepared a great feast on the day that Isaac was weaned.

When Sarah saw that Ishmael, whom Hagar the Egyptian had borne to Abraham, was playing with Isaac, she told Abraham: "Send away that servant and her son." This was extremely displeasing to Abraham. But God said to Abraham: "Do not resent it: listen to whatever Sarah tells you, for it is Isaac who shall be regarded as your child. As for the son of your servant, I will make a nation out of him too, because he is your child."

Abraham rose early in the morning and gave Hagar some food and a bottle of water, and sent her away. She went off and wandered about in the desert of Beersheba. When the water in the bottle was consumed, she threw the child under a bush and sat down some distance away, saying: "Let me not see the child dying." But as she sat and wept, God heard the boy's cry; then the angel of God called from heaven to Hagar, and said to her: "What ails you, Hagar? Fear not, for God has heard the cry of the boy. Come, take hold of the boy, for I will make a great nation

27

out of him." Then God opened her eyes and she saw a well of water. She went and filled the bottle with water and gave the lad a drink. God was with the boy, who grew up and lived in the desert and became an archer.

God put Abraham to the supreme test. He said to him: "Take your son, Isaac, whom you love; go to the land of Moriah and offer him there as a burnt-offering on one of the mountains that I will tell you." So Abraham rose early in the morning, saddled his donkey and took with him his two servants and his son Isaac; he cut wood for the burnt-offering and started for the place about which God had told him.

On the third day Abraham looked up and saw the place at a distance, So he said to his servants: "You stay here with the donkey while I and the boy go yonder. We will worship and come back to you." Abraham took the wood for the burnt-offering and laid it on his son Isaac, while in his hand he held the fire and the knife; and the two of them went off together.

Isaac said to Abraham: "Here are the fire and the wood, but where is the lamb for a burnt-offering?" Abraham answered: "God will provide the lamb." They came to the place of which God had spoken, and Abraham built an altar, arranged the wood on it, bound his son Isaac, and laid him on the altar.

Then Abraham raised the knife to slay his son, but the angel of the Lord called to him from the heavens: "Abraham, Abraham, do not lay your hand on the boy, do nothing to him; now I know that you revere God, seeing that you have not refused me your son." Abraham looked up and saw behind him a ram caught in the thicket by its horns. He went and took the ram, and offered it as a burnt-offering instead of his son.

When Sarah died, at the age of a hundred and twenty-seven, Abraham buried her in the cave of Machpelah at Hebron. Now Abraham was old, well advanced in years, and the Lord had blessed him in every way. "Promise me," Abraham said to his eldest servant, "that you will not marry my son to a daughter of the Canaanites; you must go to my own country and kindred and choose a wife for my son

Isaac. The Lord God, who brought me here from the land of my birth and promised to give this land to my descendants, will send his angel ahead of you and provide you with a wife for my son back there."

The servant took ten of his master's camels and started for Mesopotamia, for the city of Nahor. Outside the city he made the camels kneel beside the well at the time of evening when women came out to draw water. "O Lord," he said, "pray grant me success today and be kind to my master, Abraham. The girl who will give me a drink and offer to water my camels as well—may she be the maiden thou hast chosen for my master's son."

Before he had done speaking, out came Rebekah, a beautiful girl, carrying a pitcher on her shoulder. She went down to the spring, filled her pitcher, and came up. Then the servant ran to her and said: "Pray let me drink a little water from your pitcher."

"Drink, sir," she said; and she quickly lowered the pitcher and gave him a drink. When she had finished giving him a drink, she said: "Let me draw water for your camels also." So she quickly emptied her pitcher into the trough and ran again to the well to draw water for all the camels. The man gazed at her in silence watching to see if the Lord would make his journey successful.

When the camels had finished drinking, he gave the girl a golden ring and two golden bracelets, and asked her: "Whose daughter are you? Is there room in your father's house for us to spend the night?" "I am the daughter of Bethuel," she said. "We have plenty of straw and fodder, and there is also room to spend the night."

The man bowed his head and said: "Blessed be the Lord, who has led me straight to the house of my master's family." Then the girl ran and told her mother's household about it. Her brother, Laban, ran out to the man at the spring, and said: "Come in; why do you stand outside? I have a house ready, and a place for the camels." So the man went into the house, while Laban brought straw and fodder for the camels.

When Abraham's servant had told them about his errand, he added: "Now, tell me whether or not you will deal kindly with my master, so that I may know what to do next." Laban and Bethuel answered: "This comes from the Lord; here is Rebekah, take her and go; let her be the wife of your master's son." When Abraham's servant heard this, he gave jewels and garments to Rebekah; he also presented costly gifts to her brother and her mother. He and his men ate and drank and stayed all night.

When they rose in the morning, he said: "Do not detain me, since the Lord has prospered my way; let me go, that I may return to my master." They said: "We will call the girl, and ask her." So they called Rebekah, and asked her: "Will you go with this man?" She replied: "I will." So they sent off their sister Rebekah with her nurse, and Abraham's servant and his men, blessing Rebekah in these words: "Our sister, may you be the mother of myriads." Then Rebekah and her maids started, riding on camels, after the man. Thus the servant took Rebekah and went off.

Now, Isaac lived in the Negev. It was evening, and he had gone out to meditate in the field; as he looked up, he saw the camels coming. When Rebekah saw Isaac, she alighted from her camel and asked the servant: "Who is the man walking in the field to meet us?" The servant said: "It is my master." Then she took her veil and covered herself. Isaac took her inside the tent, and she became his wife. He loved her, and consoled himself after his mother's death.

Abraham lived a hundred and seventy-five years; he died at a good old age, after a full life. His sons Isaac and Ishmael buried him in the cave of Machpelah.

Rebekah gave birth to twins, Esau and Jacob. When they grew up, Esau became a skillful hunter, a man of the field; while Jacob was a quiet man who stayed in tents.

One day Jacob was cooking some food, when Esau came famished from the field. He said to Jacob: "Let me eat some of that red pottage, for I am famished!" Jacob said: "First sell me your birthright." Esau replied: "Here I am dying of hunger; of what use is a birthright to me?" So he sold his birthright to Jacob for a pottage of lentils. Esau ate and drank, got up and went away—so lightly did Esau value his birthright.

Isaac charged Jacob: "You shall not marry any Canaanite woman; go to the house of your mother's father, and get a wife there." So Jacob went to Paddan Aram, to Laban the brother of Rebekah. He came to a well in the field. When he saw Rachel the daughter of Laban, he removed the heavy stone that covered the well and watered her flock. He kissed her, telling her that he was Rebekah's son. As soon as Laban heard that Jacob, his sister's son, had come, he ran to meet him and took him home.

Jacob stayed a month with Laban and worked for him. Then Laban said to Jacob: "You are my kinsman, but are you to serve me for nothing? Tell me, what shall your wages be?" Jacob loved Rachel and he answered: "I will serve you seven years for your younger daughter, Rachel."

When Jacob had served seven years for Rachel, he said to Laban: "Let me have my wife; my time is completed." So Laban took his daughter Leah and brought her to Jacob in the evening. When Jacob found in the morning that it was Leah, he said to Laban: "What is this you have done to me? Did I not serve you for Rachel? Why then have you deceived me?" Laban answered: "It is not the custom in our country to marry the younger daughter before the elder. We will let you have the other in return for serving me another seven years." So Jacob served another seven years for Rachel, and Laban gave her to him in marriage.

Jacob's family increased in number; he became exceedingly rich and had large flocks, male and female servants, camels and mules. But he heard that Laban's sons were saying: "Jacob has taken away all our father's property; he has acquired all his riches from what once belonged to our father."

Jacob also saw that Laban was no longer friendly to him. He called Rachel and Leah into the field and said to them: "I see that your father is unfriendly to me. You know that I have served him with all my strength, but he has taken advantage of me. However, God did not let him harm me." Rachel and Leah replied: "What share have we in our

31

father's house? He has treated us like strangers, for he has sold us!"

Jacob set his sons and his wives on camels, and drove off with all his cattle, which he had acquired in Paddan Aram, in order to return to his father, Isaac, in the land of Canaan. He outwitted Laban and fled with all that he had. He crossed the Euphrates and turned toward the hill country of Gilead.

Jacob had twelve sons. Those that Leah bore him were Reuben, Simeon, Levi, Judah, Issachar, and Zebulun. His sons by Rachel were Joseph and Benjamin. Bilhah, Rachel's maid, bore him Dan and Naphtali; and Leah's maid, Zilpah, was the mother of Gad and Asher.

Now Jacob loved Joseph best of all his sons because Joseph was born to him in his old age. His brothers hated Joseph and would not even speak to him. They conspired against him and sold him to a caravan of Ishmaelites, who took him down to Egypt and sold him to Potiphar, an officer of Pharaoh. But the Lord was with Joseph, and Potiphar made him his household steward and entrusted everything to him.

Years passed and Pharaoh sent for Joseph. "I have had a dream," said Pharaoh, "and there is no one to interpret it; but I have heard about you and that you can interpret dreams." Joseph replied: "God has shown to Pharaoh what he is about to do. There will come seven years of great plenty throughout the land of Egypt; after that there will arrive seven years of famine. Now therefore let Pharaoh select an intelligent man and put him in control of the land of Egypt. Let Pharaoh appoint overseers who will gather and store up the food in the good years and reserve it against the seven years of famine." Then Pharaoh said: "I hereby appoint you over all the land of Egypt. Not a man shall stir in all Egypt without your consent." Joseph was thirty years old when he entered the service of Pharaoh.

The seven years of plenty ended, and the seven years of famine began. Joseph opened all the granaries and sold grain to the Egyptians. People from other countries also came to buy grain, because the famine was severe everywhere on earth.

When Jacob learned that there was grain for sale in Egypt, he said to his sons: "I hear there is grain for sale in Egypt; go down there and buy some for us, that we may live." So ten of Joseph's brothers went down to buy grain in Egypt. Jacob did not send Benjamin for fear that harm might befall him.

When Joseph saw his brothers he recognized them but he treated them like strangers and spoke roughly to them. He asked: "Where do you come from?" They answered: "From the land of Canaan, to buy food." "You are spies," he said; "you have come to spy out the land!" "No, my lord," they replied, "your servants have come to buy food. We are honest men, we are not spies. We are twelve brothers; the youngest is with our father, and one is no more."

Joseph retorted: "You shall be tested; you shall not leave unless your youngest brother comes here also. Send one of you to bring him while the rest remain in prison. It will be a test whether you are telling the truth. Otherwise, as sure as Pharaoh lives, you are spies." So he confined them all for three days.

On the third day Joseph said to them: "Do this and you will live. If you are honest men, let one of you be held in prison, while you carry food to your starving households, but you must bring your youngest brother to me."

They said to one another: "This misfortune has befallen us because we are guilty regarding our brother, for we saw his distress and we did not heed him when he pleaded with us." They did not know that Joseph understood them, for there was an interpreter between them.

Joseph withdrew and wept. When he returned, he selected Simeon from among them and had him bound before their eyes. Then he gave orders that their baggage was to be filled with grain, that each man's money was to be replaced in his sack, and that they were to receive provisions for the journey. This was done, and they departed.

When they reached Jacob in the land of Canaan, they

told him all that had happened to them. Emptying their sacks, each one found his money. Then Jacob said: "Joseph is no more, Simeon is no more, and now you would take Benjamin." Reuben said: "Put him in my hands, and I will bring him back to you." But Jacob said: "My son shall not go with you; his brother is dead, and he is the only one left of his mother." "If you will not send our brother with us," said Judah, "we will not go. Send the lad with me, that we may live and not die. I will stand guarantee for him. If we had not delayed, we would now have returned twice."

Thereupon Jacob said: "If it must be so, then do this. Take some of the choice fruit of the land in your bags and carry it as a present to the man; take double money with you, for you must return the money that you found in your sacks; take also your brother with you."

So the men went to Egypt and presented themselves to Joseph. When Joseph saw his brother Benjamin, he said: "Is this your youngest brother of whom you spoke? God be gracious to you, my son!" He hastily retired to his chamber and wept. Having washed his face, he came out and ordered that food be served.

Joseph commanded the steward of his house: "Fill the men's sacks with food, as much as they can carry, put every man's money in his sack, and put my silver cup in the sack of the youngest man."

When the men had gone but a short distance, Joseph said to his steward: "Follow after them! Ask them: Why have you returned evil for good? Why have you stolen my lord's silver cup?" When the steward overtook them he spoke these words to them. They quickly lowered all their sacks to the ground, and the steward searched them, beginning with the eldest and going on to the youngest. The cup was found in Benjamin's sack. Rending their clothes in dismay, they went back to the city.

When Judah and his brothers came to Joseph's house, they fell before him on the ground. Judah said: "What shall we say to my lord? What shall we say? How can we clear ourselves? Now indeed we are slaves to my lord."

"Far be it from me to do that," said Joseph; "the man

in whose possession the cup was found shall be my slave, but the rest of you may go in peace to your father."

Then Judah came near to him and said: "Let your servant speak a word to my lord. You asked us, 'Have you a father or a brother?' And we told you: 'We have a father, an old man, and a young brother.' Then you said 'Bring him down that I may look at him; unless your brother comes along with you, you shall see my face no more.' Now if I go back to my father without the lad, he will surely die, for his very soul is bound up in this lad. Now therefore, let me remain instead of the lad as a slave; and let him return with his brothers. How can I return to my father without him?"

Joseph could not control himself; he called out: "Let every man leave me!" No one else was present when Joseph made himself known to his brothers. He said: "I am Joseph! Is my father still alive?" His brothers could not answer him, for they were dismayed. "Come near," he said; "I am your brother Joseph whom you sold into Egypt. Do not be distressed; it was not you but God who sent me here to preserve life. Hasten back to father and tell him that I said: God has made me lord over all Egypt; come down to me at once; you shall dwell in the land of Goshen and be near me, you, your children and grandchildren, your flocks and herds." He kissed all his brothers and wept.

Joseph gave them wagons and provisions for the journey and, as they departed, he said to them: "See that you do not quarrel on the way." So they set out from Egypt and came to their father Jacob in the land of Canaan, and told him: "Joseph is still alive, and he is ruler over all the land of Egypt!" He was stunned by the news; he did not believe them. But when they told him all that Joseph had said to them, and when he saw the wagons which Joseph had sent to convey him, his spirits revived. He said: "It is enough; Joseph my son is still alive; I will go and see him before I die."

Jacob set out with all that he had; when he arrived at Beersheba, he offered sacrifices to the God of his father Isaac. At night in a vision God said to him: "Jacob, Jacob,

I am the God of your father; do not be afraid to go down to Egypt; I will make you a great nation there. I will go down to Egypt with you, and I will also bring you back."

Jacob set out from Beersheba. The entire family of Jacob that came to Egypt numbered seventy souls. Joseph went to meet his father in Goshen. He wept as he embraced him. Jacob said: "Now that I have seen you alive I can die in peace." Joseph provided his father and the whole family with everything they needed.

Jacob lived in the land of Egypt seventeen years; his life span was a hundred and forty-seven years. When the time came for him to die, he called Joseph and said to him: "Promise me to be faithful to me; do not bury me in Egypt; let me sleep with my fathers in their burying place. Your two sons are mine; Ephraim and Manasseh are as much mine as Reuben and Simeon. I never thought I would see you, and here God has let me see even your children. May the angel who has delivered me from all evil bless the lads; may they carry on my name and the names of my fathers, Abraham and Isaac; may they grow into a multitude on earth. The people of Israel will invoke this blessing: God make you like Ephraim and like Manasseh."

Then Jacob called his sons and said: "Gather yourselves together, that I may tell you what shall befall you in days to come." He gave each a special blessing, and charged them: "Bury me beside my fathers in the cave of Machpelah. Abraham and Sarah, Isaac and Rebekah were buried there, and there I buried Leah." When Jacob finished charging his sons, he breathed his last and was gathered to his people. Joseph fell on his father's face, weeping over him and kissing him. Then he commanded the physicians to embalm his father. Forty days were required for embalming.

Joseph reported to Pharaoh, saying: "My father at the point of death made me promise on oath to bury him in the tomb which he had hewed out for himself in the land of Canaan. Now then, let me go up and bury my father, and I will return." Pharaoh replied: "Go up, and bury your father as he made you promise."

So Joseph went up to bury his father, and he was accompanied by all the courtiers of Pharaoh as well as by his brothers and his father's household. It was a very large caravan. When the Canaanites saw the mourning, they said: "This is a solemn mourning that the Egyptians are observing." Jacob's sons did for him what he had commanded them. They buried him in the cave of Machpelah, which Abraham had bought for use as a burial ground.

After burying his father, Joseph returned to Egypt along with his brothers and all who had accompanied him. Now that their father was dead, Joseph's brothers thought: "Perhaps Joseph will hate us and pay us back for all the evil we did to him." So they sent this message to Joseph: "Before he died, your father bade us to ask you to forgive the sin of your brothers and the evil they did to you." Joseph wept over their message to him.

Then his brothers came and fell down before him, saying: "We are your humble servants." But Joseph said to them: "Have no fear. Am I in the place of God? You meant to do me evil, but God meant good to come of it, so that many people should be kept alive. So do not fear; I will provide for you and your little ones." Thus he reassured them and comforted them.

Joseph remained in Egypt with all his father's family. He lived one hundred and ten years. When he was about to die, Joseph said to his brothers: "I am about to die; but God will surely remember you and bring you out of this land to the land that he promised to Abraham, Isaac and Jacob. When God will remember you, you shall carry up my bones from here." Joseph died at the age of a hundred and ten. He was embalmed and put into a coffin in Egypt.

Exodus

שְׁמוֹת

Exodus, the second book of the Torah, carries forward the history begun in Genesis and tells of the formation of Israel as a people. It contains the idyllic story of the birth of Moses, the divine revelation through the burning bush, and the detailed description of bitter contest between Moses and Pharaoh.

The second book of Moses is second to no other book of the Bible in its interest and religious significance. It describes the oppression and slavery in Egypt as well as the exodus and liberation, which came to the people of Israel in the hour of their greatest need and despair. The dramatic account of the giving of the Ten Commandments and the basic laws of the Torah are the most outstanding features of Exodus.

The plagues in the narrative portion of Exodus are miraculously intensified forms of the diseases or other natural occurrences to which Egypt is still liable. Frogs, gnats, flies and locusts are common pests in the country. Epidemics accompanied by a great mortality are frequently mentioned by historians. An unusual combination of natural calamities materially facilitated the exodus. The darkness that lasted three days in Egypt was, according to some scholars, the result of the hot wind called *Hamsin,* which often fills the air with thick clouds of dust and sand and forces people to stay indoors. During the annual inundation of the Nile, the water assumes a reddish color because of the red grass brought down from the Abyssinian mountains.

In its forty chapters, Exodus is replete with highly ethical concepts and laws. God's deep interest in human affairs is reflected in each of its narratives. He is represented as revealing himself to men and speaking with them intimately. The Ten Commandments, and the laws contained in the three chapters which are known as the Book of the Covenant (Exodus 20–23), are the quintessence of the remaining portion of the Torah.

These are the names of the Israelites who came to Egypt with Jacob: Reuben, Simeon, Levi, Judah, Issachar, Zebulun, Benjamin, Dan, Naphtali, Gad and Asher. When

Joseph and all his generation had died, a new king rose over Egypt who did not know Joseph. He said to his people: "The Israelites are too many and too mighty for us! Let us handle them shrewdly lest they multiply and fight against us." Whereupon taskmasters were set over them to crush them with heavy burdens; but the more they were oppressed the more they multiplied. Pharaoh ordered his people to throw every son born to the Hebrews into the Nile.

Now a man from the house of Levi married a daughter of Levi. She bore a son and hid him for three months. When she could hide him no longer, she put him into a basket made of bulrushes and placed it among the reeds upon the shore of the Nile. His sister stood at a distance to watch and see what might happen to him.

Now the daughter of Pharaoh came down to bathe in the river; she saw the basket among the reeds and sent her maid to fetch it. When she opened it she saw the child; it was a boy crying! She pitied him and said: "This must be a child of the Hebrews." The child's sister asked: "Shall I go and get a Hebrew woman to nurse the child?" "Go," said Pharaoh's daughter.

So the girl went for the child's mother, who took him and nursed him. When the child grew up, the mother took him to Pharaoh's daughter, who adopted him as her son. She named him Moses because she had removed him from the water.

When Moses was grown up, he went out to see his own people, and he watched them at their hard labor. He once noticed an Egyptian beating a Hebrew. Looking round, and seeing no one, he killed the Egyptian and hid him in the sand. The next day, he saw two Hebrews quarreling! Moses said to the guilty one: "Why do you strike your fellow man?" He retorted: "Who made you a prince and a judge over us? Do you mean to kill me as you killed the Egyptian?"

Fearing that Pharaoh might put him to death, Moses fled from Egypt to the land of Midian. As he was sitting beside a well, the seven daughters of Jethro came to water their flocks. Some shepherds tried to drive them from the well, so Moses went to their rescue and helped them water their flocks. When they came home, Jethro asked them: "How is it that you have returned so early today?" They answered: "An Egyptian protected us from the shepherds. He even drew water for us and watered the flock." "And where is he?" Jethro asked his daughters. "Why have you left him behind? Invite him to have bread with us."

Moses came and consented to make his home with Jethro, who gave him Zipporah, his daughter, to be his wife. She bore him a son, who was named Gershom.

One day, as Moses was tending Jethro's flock, an angel of the Lord appeared to him in a fire flaming out of a burning bush. "I will step aside," said Moses, "and behold this great sight, why the bush is in flames and yet does not burn."

God spoke out of the bush, saying: "Moses, Moses, do not come close; remove your shoes from your feet, for the place where you stand is holy ground. I am the God of your fathers Abraham, Isaac and Jacob. I have seen the affliction of my people in Egypt and heard their cry; I have come down to deliver them out of the hand of the Egyptians and bring them to a land flowing with milk and honey. I will send you to Pharaoh to bring my people out of Egypt."

Moses said: "But who am I, to go to Pharaoh and bring the people of Israel out of Egypt?" God answered: "I will be with you. Go gather the elders of Israel and tell them that the Lord has appeared to you. Then you and the elders shall go to the king and say to him: Let us go into the wilderness to worship the Lord our God."

Moses said: "My Lord, I am not a man of words, I am slow of speech."

The Lord said: "Who has made man's mouth? Who makes him speechless or deaf? Who gives him sight or makes him blind? Is it not I, the Lord? Go, then, I will teach you what to say. Aaron your brother can speak well; he shall come out to meet you. He shall speak for you to the people."

Moses then went to Jethro and said: "Pray let me return to my kinsmen in Egypt to see if they are still alive."

40

"Go in peace," said Jethro. So Moses went back to the land of Egypt. He told Aaron all that the Lord had commanded him, and Aaron told the elders of Israel what the Lord had said to Moses. And the people believed; they bowed their heads and worshiped.

Afterwards Moses and Aaron went to Pharaoh and said: "Thus says the Lord God of Israel: Let my people go." But Pharaoh said: "Who is the Lord that I should heed his voice? I do not know the Lord; I will not let Israel go!"

That very day Pharaoh commanded the taskmasters: "You shall no longer give the people straw to make bricks; let them gather straw for themselves; yet they shall make the required number of bricks." The Hebrew foremen were beaten because they could not produce the usual number of bricks. They appealed to Pharaoh: "Why do you treat us so? We are given no straw, yet we are told to make bricks." He answered: "You are lazy, lazy! That is why you say: Let us go worship the Lord."

Moses and Aaron went to Pharaoh and said: "Thus says the Lord God: How long will you refuse to humble yourself before me? Let my people go; if you refuse to let my people go, I will bring plagues upon you and your people."

Then the Lord brought ten plagues upon Egypt, namely: blood, frogs, vermin, flies, disease of cattle, boils, hail, locusts, darkness, and death of the firstborn.

It came to pass at midnight that the Lord struck down the firstborn in the land of Egypt. There was a great cry in Egypt, for there was not a house where someone was not dead.

Pharaoh sent for Moses and Aaron during the night and said: "Go, serve the Lord, as you have asked; take your flocks and your herds and be gone." The Egyptians pressed the people to hurry out of the land, crying: "We are all dead men!" So the people took their dough, unleavened as it was, and journeyed from Rameses to Sukkoth, about six hundred thousand of them on foot, besides women and children. They baked unleavened cakes of the dough which they had brought out of Egypt. They had been rushed out of Egypt and had not prepared any food for the journey.

Moses said to the people: "Remember this day in which you came out of Egypt, out of a house of slavery. You are leaving this day in the month of Aviv. And when the Lord will bring you into the land which he promised to your fathers, a land flowing with milk and honey, you shall perform this service in this month: Seven days you shall eat unleavened bread, and on the seventh day there shall be a feast in honor of the Lord. Throughout the seven days no leavened bread shall be seen in your possession. You shall tell your son on that day, saying: 'This is because of what the Lord did for me when I left Egypt.' You shall observe this precept from year to year."

When Pharaoh let the people go, God did not lead them along the shorter road through the land of the Philistines, lest the people might have regrets and return to Egypt. God led them by a roundabout road, in the direction of the wilderness and the Red Sea.

Moses took the bones of Joseph with him, for Joseph had made his people solemnly promise to do this, saying: "God will surely remember you, and you must take my bones away from here with you."

When it was reported to Pharaoh that the people of Israel had left, he and his officers changed their minds about letting them go. "What have we done!" they cried. "Why have we released the Israelites from our service?" So Pharaoh made his chariots ready and took his men with him, six hundred picked chariots and all the rest of the chariots of Egypt, manned by their captains.

The Lord hardened the heart of Pharaoh, who pursued the people of Israel. The Egyptians overtook them as they were encamped on the shore of the Red Sea. When the people of Israel looked up and saw the Egyptians marching after them, they were in great fear and cried out to the Lord.

They said to Moses: "Was it because there were no graves in Egypt that you have brought us to die in the desert? Did we not tell you in Egypt to leave us alone and let us serve the Egyptians? It would have been better for us to serve them than to die in the wilderness!"

But Moses said to them: "Have no fear, stand firm and

see the salvation of the Lord which he will perform for you today. The Egyptians you see today you shall never see again. The Lord will fight for you, and you have only to keep still."

Then Moses stretched out his hand over the sea. The waters divided, and the people of Israel went into the sea on dry ground, the waters forming a wall to right and left. The Egyptians in pursuit of them went into the sea, all of Pharaoh's horses, chariots and horsemen.

Again Moses stretched out his hand over the sea, and the sea returned to its steady flow. The Lord hurled the Egyptians right into the midst of it and not a single one of them was left.

Then Moses and the people of Israel sang this song to the Lord:

*I will sing to the Lord, for he has completely triumphed;
the horse and its rider he has hurled into the sea.*

*The Lord is my strength and song; he has come to my
aid. This is my God, and I will glorify him; my father's
God, and I will extol him.*

*Pharaoh's chariots and his army he has cast into the sea,
and his choice captains are engulfed in the Red Sea.
The depths cover them; they went down into the depths
like a stone.*

*Thy right hand, O Lord, glorious in power, thy right
hand, O Lord, crushes the enemy. Thou sendest forth
thy wrath—it consumes them like stubble. By the blast
of thy nostrils the waters piled up—the floods stood upright like a wall; the depths were congealed in the heart
of the sea.*

*The enemy said: I will pursue them, I will overtake them,
I will divide the spoil, my lust shall be glutted with
them; I will draw my sword, my hand shall destroy them.
Thou didst blow with thy wind—the sea covered them;
they sank like lead in the mighty waters.*

*Who is there like thee among the mighty, O Lord? Who is
like thee, glorious in holiness, awe-inspiring in renown,
doing marvels? Thou didst stretch out thy right hand—
the earth swallowed them.*

43

*In thy grace thou hast led the people whom thou hast re-
deemed; by thy power thou hast guided them to thy
holy habitation.*

*Peoples have heard and trembled; pangs have seized the
inhabitants of Philistia. The chieftains of Edom were in
agony; trembling seized the lords of Moab; all the inhabitants of Canaan melted away.*

*Thou wilt bring them in and plant them in the highlands
of thy own, the place which thou, O Lord, hast made for
thy dwelling, the sanctuary, O Lord, which thy hands
have established. The Lord shall reign forever and ever.*

On the third month after leaving the land of Egypt, the
people of Israel entered the desert of Sinai; there Israel
encamped in front of the mountain. On the third day, in
the morning, there was thunder and lightning, a thick
cloud on the mountain, and a very loud trumpet blast; all
the people in the camp trembled. Then Moses brought
the people out of the camp, and they took their stand at
the foot of the mountain where God was. As the trumpet
blast grew louder and louder, Moses spoke and God answered him.

God spoke all these words, saying:

I am the Lord your God, who brought you out of the
land of Egypt, out of the house of slavery.

You shall have no other gods beside me. You shall not
make for yourself any idols in the shape of anything that is
in heaven above, or that is on the earth below, or that is in
the water under the earth. You shall not bow down to them
nor worship them; for I, the Lord your God, am a jealous
God, punishing children for the sins of their fathers, down
to the third or fourth generation of those who hate me, but
showing kindness to the thousandth generation of those
who love me and keep my commandments.

You shall not utter the name of the Lord your God in
vain; for the Lord will not hold guiltless anyone who
utters his name in vain.

Remember the Sabbath day to keep it holy. Six days you
shall labor and do all your work; but on the seventh day,
which is a day of rest in honor of the Lord your God, you

shall not do any work, neither you, nor your son, nor your daughter, nor your male or female servant, nor your cattle, nor the stranger who is within your gates; for in six days the Lord made the heavens, the earth, the sea, and all that they contain, and rested on the seventh day; therefore the Lord blessed the Sabbath day and hallowed it.

Honor your father and your mother, that you may live long in the land which the Lord your God is giving you.

You shall not murder.

You shall not commit adultery.

You shall not steal.

You shall not testify falsely against your neighbor.

You shall not covet your neighbor's house; you shall not covet your neighbor's wife, nor his servant, male or female, nor his ox, nor his ass, nor anything that belongs to your neighbor.

The Lord said to Moses: These are the laws which you shall present to them:

Whoever strikes a man dead shall be put to death. But if he did not intend to do it, I will designate a place to which he may flee. If a man wilfully attacks his neighbor, to kill him, you shall take that man from my very altar and put him to death.

Whoever strikes his father or his mother shall be put to death. Whoever curses his father or his mother shall be put to death. Whoever kidnaps a man shall be put to death.

When men quarrel and one strikes the other with a stone or with his fist, not fatally but enough to confine him to bed, the one who struck the blow shall go unpunished, provided that the other can get up and walk about with his staff; still, he must pay for the man's loss of time and have him thoroughly cured.

If a man digs a pit or reopens a pit and fails to cover it, and an ox or a donkey falls into it, he shall pay for the beast, and the carcass belongs to him.

If one man's ox gores to death the ox of another man, the goring ox shall be sold and the money divided between the two men; also the dead animal shall be divided between them. If the ox is known to have been in the habit of goring, and the owner has not guarded it, he shall pay ox for ox, and the dead animal shall be his.

If a man steals an ox or a sheep and either kills it or sells it, he shall pay five oxen for the ox and four sheep for the sheep.

If a thief is caught breaking into a house and is slain, there is no one punished for his death; but if this happened after sunrise, there shall be bloodguilt for him.

If a man sets fire to a field or vineyard and lets it spread to another man's field, he shall pay for it with the very best of his own field or his own vineyard.

If a man deposits money or goods with his neighbor, and it is stolen out of the man's house, the thief shall pay double if he is found. If the thief is not found, the owner of the house shall come to the judges to prove that he has not laid hands on the other man's property.

You shall not maltreat a stranger or oppress him, for you were strangers yourselves in the land of Egypt. You shall not afflict a widow or orphan; if ever you afflict them and they cry to me, I will hear their cry, and my wrath shall blaze until I slay you; and your own wives shall become widows and your own children fatherless.

If you lend money to a poor man, you must not act as a creditor, and you shall not exact interest from him. If ever you take your neighbor's garment in pledge, you shall give it back to him before the sun goes down; for that is the only covering he has. If he cries to me, I will listen to his cry, for I am compassionate.

You shall not revile the judges, nor shall you curse any of the authorities of your people.

You shall not utter a false report; you shall not join hands with a wicked man to give malicious evidence. You shall not follow a majority to do wrong; nor shall you be partial to a poor man in his lawsuit.

You shall not violate the rights of a poor man in his lawsuit. Avoid false charges. You shall never accept a bribe, for a bribe blinds the clear-sighted and perverts a just cause.

You shall not oppress a stranger; you should know the heart of a stranger, for you, too, were strangers in the land of Egypt.

The children of Israel shall keep the Sabbath, observing the Sabbath throughout their generations as an everlasting covenant. It is a sign between me and the children of Israel forever, that in six days the Lord made the heavens and the earth, and on the seventh day he ceased from work and rested.

When the Lord had finished speaking to Moses on Mount Sinai, he gave him the two tablets of the Law, the stone tablets inscribed by the finger of God.

When the people saw that Moses delayed in coming down from the mountain, they gathered around Aaron and said to him: "Come, make us a god to go in front of us. As for the man Moses who brought us out of the land of Egypt, we do not know what has happened to him." Aaron replied: "Take off the golden rings from the ears of your wives and sons and daughters and bring them to me." So all the people took off their earrings and brought them to Aaron, who made of them a molten calf. The people cried out: "This is your god, O Israel, who brought you out of the land of Egypt!"

The Lord said to Moses: "Go down at once to your people. They have made themselves a molten calf and are worshiping it." Moses came down the mountain with the two tablets of the Law in his hand, tablets written on both sides. When Joshua, who had waited for Moses at the foot of the mountain, heard the people shouting, he said to Moses: "That sounds like a battle in the camp." But Moses answered: "What I hear is the sound of people reveling." And as soon as he came near the camp, he saw the calf and the people dancing around it. Then Moses' wrath flared up; he threw down the tablets and broke them at the foot of the mountain. He took the calf they had made and fused it in the fire and ground it into powder, which he scattered on the water and then made the Israelites drink it.

On the next day Moses said to the people: "You have committed a great sin; so I will go up to the Lord; perhaps I may be able to make atonement for your sin." Then Moses went back to the Lord and said: "Alas, this people has indeed committed a great sin in making a god of gold

47

for themselves. Yet, if thou wilt not forgive their sin, then pray strike me out of the book thou hast written." The Lord answered: "Only those who have sinned against me will I strike out of my book. Now go, lead the people where I have told you; my angel shall go before you."

The Lord said to Moses: "Cut two tablets of stone like the first, and I will write upon them the words that were on the first tablets which you broke. Be ready in the morning; come up to Mount Sinai and present yourself there to me; let no man be seen throughout all the mountain." So Moses cut two tablets of stone like the first; he rose early in the morning and went up Mount Sinai, as the Lord had commanded him, taking along the two stone tablets. Then the Lord passed before him and proclaimed: "The Lord is a merciful and gracious God, slow to anger and rich in kindness and truth. He continues his kindness to a thousand generations; he forgives iniquity, transgression and sin, though he does not allow the guilty to pass unpunished; he punishes children and grandchildren, down to the third or fourth generation, for the iniquity of their fathers."

Moses at once bowed his head to the ground in worship. Then he said: "If I have found favor with thee, O Lord, be thou in our midst; this is indeed a stiff-necked people; O pardon our iniquity and sin, and make us thy very own."

When Moses came down from Mount Sinai with the two tablets of the commandments in his hands, he did not know that the skin of his face had become radiant after speaking with the Lord. Now when Aaron and all the people of Israel saw Moses and noticed how radiant the skin of his face had become, they were afraid to come near him. But Moses called to them, and Aaron and all the leaders came back to him. Moses then spoke to them. Later on, all the people of Israel came to him, and he told them all the commands that the Lord had given him on Mount Sinai.

Leviticus

וַיִּקְרָא

Leviticus, the third book of the Torah, is primarily a book of laws, most of which concern the priests. It defines *clean* and *unclean* animals for purposes of food and contains ten chapters (17–26) commonly designated as the Holiness Code, stressing a high moral standard and containing laws of humanity and charity.

Leviticus presents a system of worship rich in symbolism and lofty in ethical standards. The desire for a visible element in worship is satisfied by numerous sacrifices, each designed to meet a particular need of the worshiper. The sacrificial system symbolized self-surrender and devotion to the will of God. The peace-offering with its communion feast conveyed the idea of fellowship. It served to keep alive the sense of dependence on God for the natural blessings of life, while it had the social value of promoting the solidarity of the nation. The daily offering symbolized Israel's pledge of unbroken service to God. The fragrant smoke of incense rising towards heaven was a natural symbol of prayer ascending to God, as in the words of the psalmist: "Let my prayer rise like incense before thee" (Psalm 141:2).

The well-known verse "You shall love your neighbor as yourself," meaning love for any human being, summarizes much of the social legislation in the book. The holiness of God requires human holiness, which includes such details as cleanliness and self-discipline. The relation between hygiene and religion is stressed in the regulations about leprosy.

Leviticus is the basis for the major part of the Jewish religion. Many Jewish virtues can be traced to the influence of this book and its ideal laws, liberating men from brutality and bestiality.

The Lord said to Moses: Speak to all the people of Israel and tell them: Be holy, for I, the Lord your God, am holy. Revere your mother and your father, every one of you, and keep my sabbaths.

You shall not steal; you shall not cheat; you shall not

speak falsely to one another. You shall not defraud or rob your neighbor; you shall not keep the wages of a hired laborer overnight. You shall not curse the deaf, or place an obstacle in front of the blind, but you shall fear your God.

You shall not act dishonestly in rendering judgment; you shall not be partial to a poor man nor favor a rich man. You shall not go about spreading slander among your people; you shall not stand by idly when your neighbor's life is at stake.

You shall not hate your brother in your heart, but you shall reason with him. Take no revenge and bear no grudge against your people; love your neighbor as yourself. Stand up in the presence of an aged man, and show respect to an old person.

When a stranger resides with you in your land, you shall not molest him. The stranger who resides with you shall be treated like a native, and you shall love him as you love yourself; for you too were once strangers in the land of Egypt. I am the Lord your God.

You shall not act dishonestly when using measures of length or weight or capacity. You shall have true scales and true weights.

Be careful to observe my commandments; I am the Lord. You shall not profane my holy name; but I must be hallowed among the people of Israel. I am the Lord who brought you out of the land of Egypt to be your God.

These are the festivals of the Lord which you shall celebrate, each in its proper season.

For six days work may be done, but the seventh day is the sabbath rest, a day for holy assembly, on which you shall do no work; it is to be kept as the Lord's Sabbath wherever you live.

The Passover falls on the fourteenth day of the first month (*Nisan*) at sunset. On the fifteenth day of this month the festival of unleavened bread begins; for seven days you shall eat unleavened bread. On the first day and on the seventh day of Passover you shall hold a holy assembly and do no hard work.

From the second day of Passover, you shall count seven

full weeks, counting fifty days to the Feast of Weeks when you shall hold a holy assembly and do no hard work.

The first day of the seventh month (*Tishri*) you shall observe as a day of rest, a day of remembrance (*Rosh Hashanah*), celebrated by trumpet blowing, when you shall do no hard work.

On the tenth day of the seventh month, the Day of Atonement, you shall hold a holy assembly; you shall fast, and do no work on that day, for it is a day on which atonement is made for you before the Lord your God. You shall observe it as a sabbath of complete rest. From the sunset of the ninth day to the sunset of the tenth day you shall keep your sabbath.

On the fifteenth day of the seventh month the seven-day feast of Tabernacles (*Sukkoth*) begins. On the first day of *Sukkoth* there shall be a holy assembly when you shall do no hard work. For seven days you shall present offerings to the Lord; on the eighth day (*Shemini Atzereth*) you shall hold a holy assembly and do no hard work. On the first day you shall take the fruit of the *Ethrog*, the branches of the palm trees and the myrtle and the water-willows (making up the *Lulav*), and rejoice before the Lord your God for seven days. These seven days you shall live in booths, that your descendants may know that I made the people of Israel to dwell in booths when I brought them out of the land of Egypt; I am the Lord your God.

The Lord said to Moses on Mount Sinai:

Tell the people of Israel: When you enter the land which I am giving you, the land shall have a sabbath in honor of the Lord. For six years you may sow your field, prune your vineyard, and gather in their produce; but during the seventh year the land shall have a complete rest, a sabbath in honor of the Lord, when you shall neither sow your field nor prune your vineyard; you shall not even reap what grows of itself after the harvest, nor shall you gather the grapes of your untrimmed vines. What grows of itself in the sabbatical year must not be enjoyed selfishly, but is to be shared with the poor and the strangers.

After counting seven times seven years, or forty-nine years, on the day of atonement, you shall sound the trumpet

51

throughout your land; you shall hallow the fiftieth year and proclaim liberty to all the inhabitants of the land; it shall be a jubilee year for you, when each of you shall return to his own property and family.

The fiftieth year shall be a jubilee year for you, when you shall neither sow nor reap what grows of itself, nor gather the grapes from the undressed vines. In this year of jubilee each of you shall return to his own property.

When you sell land to your neighbor or buy land from your neighbor, you must not defraud each other; you shall buy and sell only the number of crops till the next jubilee. If the years to the next jubilee are many, you shall increase the price; and if they are few, you shall lower the price, for it is the number of crops that is sold.

If your brother becomes poor and sells some of his property, the nearest relative shall buy it back for him. If a man has no one to buy it back for him, and afterwards becomes rich enough to buy it back himself, he shall count up the years since it was sold and refund the buyer for the rest of the years till next jubilee; in this way he will get back his own property. But if he is unable to get it back for himself, it shall remain in the hands of the purchaser only until the next jubilee; in that jubilee it shall be released, then the man can get back to his property.

If your brother becomes poor, you shall maintain him and enable him to live beside you. Take no interest from him; let your brother live beside you. You shall not ask interest on your money loans to him nor on the food which you furnish him. I am the Lord your God, who brought you out of the land of Egypt to be your God.

Numbers

בְּמִדְבַּר

Numbers, the fourth book of the Torah, contains a brief summary of the experiences of Israel in the wilderness during nearly forty years of wanderings. It records the expedition of the twelve spies into the land of Canaan, the rebellion of Korah against Moses and Aaron, the striking of the rock, and the story of Balaam. There is a clear picture of the difficulties which confronted Moses as the leader of a tired and discontented people.

Korah, the Levite, charged that the priesthood rightfully belonged to members of any Levite family, not simply the house of Aaron. Dathan and Abiram, of the tribe of Reuben, rebelled against the civil authority of Moses, charging that the leadership rightfully belonged to the descendants of Jacob's eldest son, Reuben.

Balak vainly hopes to destroy Israel by having recourse to black magic, and sends for the magician Balaam to come and curse them. But the powers of darkness could not stop the victorious march of the people of Israel. Balaam could say only what was given him to say. Therefore, he had to bless God's people.

The Lord spoke to Moses in the second year after the exodus from the land of Egypt, saying: "Take a census of all the people of Israel, family by family, all males over twenty years who are fit for active service." So Moses and Aaron, assisted by twelve men representing the twelve tribes, assembled all the people on the first day of the second month and numbered them in the wilderness of Sinai. The total number was six hundred and three thousand five hundred and fifty men able to bear arms.

The Levites were not included in the census of the Israelites. They were put in charge of the Tabernacle with all its equipment and all its belongings. Whenever the Tabernacle had to be moved, the Levites were to take it down; and whenever it had to be set up, the Levites were to set it up. The Israelites were to pitch their tents according to their companies, in military order, but the Levites were to pitch their tents around the Tabernacle.

The people of Israel complained bitterly to Moses: "Would that we had meat for food! We remember the fish we used to eat without cost in Egypt, and the cucumbers, the melons, the leeks, the onions, and the garlic. But now we are famished; we see nothing before us but this manna."

The manna was like coriander seed; the people would gather it up, grind it between millstones or pound it in a mortar, then cook it in a pot and make it into loaves which tasted like cakes made with oil. At night, when dew fell upon the camp, the manna also fell.

Moses heard the people weeping, and he said to the Lord: "Thou layest the burden of all these people upon me. I cannot carry all their burdens by myself. Where can I get meat to give to them? Pray kill me at once, and let me no longer face their distress."

Then the Lord told Moses to say to the people: "Tomorrow you shall have meat to eat; you will eat it not for one day, nor two days, nor five days, nor ten days, nor twenty days, but for a whole month, until you cannot bear the smell of it, until you loathe it. For you have spurned the Lord who is in your midst, and you have wailed: Why did we ever leave Egypt?"

So Moses went out and told the people what the Lord had said. Then there arose a wind sent by the Lord, that drove in quail from the sea and brought them down over the camp site. All that day and night, and all the next day the people gathered in the quail. As the people were devouring this food, the Lord struck them with a terrible plague. So that place was named *Graves of Greed*, because it was there that the greedy people were buried.

Miriam and Aaron spoke against Moses because he had married an Ethiopian woman. They said: "Has the Lord spoken to Moses alone? Has he not spoken to us as well?" Now the man Moses was by far the meekest man on the face of the earth. So the Lord told Moses, Aaron and Miriam to come out to the tent of meeting. The three went out, and the Lord called Aaron and Miriam to come forward. He said: "If there is a prophet among you, I shall reveal myself to him in a vision, I shall speak to him in a dream. Not so with my servant Moses, most faithful of all my household. I speak to him face to face, plainly, and not in riddles. Why then were you not afraid to speak against my servant Moses?"

The anger of the Lord was kindled against them. He departed, and behold, Miriam became leprous. Aaron cried to Moses: "My lord, let us not be punished for the sin we have foolishly committed." So Moses called to the Lord: "Heal her, O God, I beseech thee." The Lord answered: "Let her be confined for seven days outside the camp; then she can come back." So for seven days Miriam was confined outside the camp.

The Lord told Moses to send men to spy out the land of Canaan. He was to send a man from every tribe, all of them chiefs. So Moses sent spies to the land of Canaan, saying to them: "Go and see what kind of land it is; whether the people there are strong or weak, few or many; whether the cities are open or fortified; whether the land is rich or poor, and whether there is wood in it or not. Be of good courage, and bring back some fruit from there."

So they went and spied out the land. They reached the valley of Eshcol, where they cut down a branch with a single cluster of grapes on it, and two of them carried it on a pole. They also took some pomegranates and some figs. At the end of forty days they returned from spying out the land and brought back word to the people of Israel who were encamped in the wilderness at Kadesh.

Showing them the fruit, the spies said: "We came from the land to which you sent us; it flows with milk and honey, and this is its fruit. However, the people there are strong and the cities are fortified and very large; besides, we saw the Anak giants there. The Amalekites live in the Negev; the Hittites, the Jebusites and the Amorites live in the hill country; and the Canaanites dwell along the sea-coast and the banks of the Jordan. We cannot attack these people; they are too strong for us. The land that we explored is a land that consumes its inhabitants; the people

55

we saw there are huge men, a race of giants; we felt like mere grasshoppers, and so we must have seemed to them."

Upon hearing this, the people of Israel raised a loud cry. They wailed and murmured against Moses and Aaron. "Would that we had died in the land of Egypt!" they cried. "Would that we were dead here in the wilderness! Why is the Lord bringing us into this land only to have us fall by the sword? Our wives and our little ones will become prey; would it not be better for us to go back to Egypt? Let us appoint a leader and go back to Egypt!"

Joshua and Caleb, who were among those who spied out the land, said to all the people of Israel: "The land is an exceedingly good land; the Lord will bring us into this land which flows with milk and honey. Only, do not rebel against the Lord; do not fear the people of the land; the Lord is with us; do not fear them." But the people threatened to stone both Joshua and Caleb.

Then the Lord appeared to Moses and said: "How long will this people refuse to believe in me, in spite of all the signs which I have performed among them? I will strike them with pestilence and wipe them out; then I will make of you a nation greater and mightier than they." But Moses prayed: "O Lord, forgive this people, as thou hast forgiven them time after time, ever since they left Egypt."

And the Lord answered: "I pardon them, as you have asked. But, as surely as I live, not one of these who has spurned me shall see the land which I promised to their fathers. I have heard their grumblings against me. Say to them: Here in the desert shall your dead bodies fall. Of all your men of twenty years and older, who grumbled against me, not one shall enter the land, except Caleb and Joshua. But your little ones I will bring in, and they shall appreciate the land which you have despised. Your children shall be wandering shepherds in the wilderness for forty years, and shall suffer for your faithlessness until the last of your dead bodies lies in the wilderness."

The Lord spoke to Moses, saying: Speak to the children of Israel and tell them to make for themselves fringes on the corners of their garments throughout their generations, and they shall put on the fringe of each corner a blue thread. When you look upon it, you will remember to keep all the commands of the Lord, and you will not follow the desires of your heart and your eyes which lead you astray. It is for you to remember and keep all my commandments, and be holy for your God. I am the Lord your God who brought you out of the land of Egypt to be your God; I am the Lord your God.

Now Korah, Dathan and Abiram, and two hundred fifty leaders of the community, combined to oppose the authority of Moses and Aaron, saying to them: "You have gone too far! What right have you to set yourselves over the Lord's people?"

Upon hearing this, Moses said to Korah and his followers: "Listen to me, you Levites! Is it not enough that God has singled you out to do service in the sanctuary and to minister to the congregation, that you want to be priests as well? It is against the Lord that you are gathered. What has Aaron done that you should grumble against him?"

Moses sent for Dathan and Abiram, but they refused to come, saying: "We will not come up! Are you not satisfied with having brought us here from a land flowing with milk and honey to kill us in the desert? Must you also play the prince over us? You have not brought us to a land abounding in milk and honey, nor have you put us in possession of fields and vineyards. Are you trying to blind the eyes of these men? No, we will not come up!"

Moses, followed by the elders of Israel, went to Dathan and Abiram. Then he warned the people, saying: "Keep away from the tents of these wicked men and do not touch anything that is theirs; otherwise you too will be swept away because of their sins." As Dathan and Abiram came out and stood at the doorways of their tents, with their wives and sons and little ones, Moses said to the people: "This is how you shall know that the Lord has sent me to do all that I have done: If these men die an ordinary death, then the Lord has not sent me. But if the Lord creates something new, and the ground opens its mouth and swallows them up, with all that belongs to them, and they go down alive into the pit, then you will know that these men have defied the Lord."

He no sooner had finished speaking than the ground beneath them split open and swallowed them up, with their families and all the men that belonged to Korah, and all their possessions. They went down alive into the pit; the earth closed over them, and they perished from the midst of the community. All the Israelites around fled at their shrieks, fearing lest the earth might swallow them also.

The Lord said to Moses: "Speak to the people of Israel, and get twelve rods from their leaders, one rod for each tribe. Write the name of each on his rod, and Aaron's name upon the rod of Levi. Then you shall deposit them in the tent of meeting, and the rod of the man whom I choose shall blossom."

Moses spoke to the people of Israel, and all their leaders gave him rods, and the rod of Aaron was among them. Moses deposited the rods before the Lord in the tent of meeting.

The next day, when he entered the tent, he found that the rod of Aaron had sprouted, put forth buds, produced blossoms and borne ripe almonds. He brought out all the rods from the presence of the Lord to the people of Israel and they looked at them; then each leader took his own rod. But the Lord said to Moses: "Put Aaron's rod back to be kept as a sign for the rebels, that you may make an end of their grumbling against me, lest they die."

Moses did as the Lord commanded him.

The people of Israel came to the wilderness of Zin and stayed at Kadesh, where Miriam died and was buried.

There was no water, so they gathered themselves against Moses and Aaron, complaining: "Would that we had died together with our brethren! Why have you brought us into this desert to die? Why did you make us leave Egypt for this evil place? It is a place with no seed, figs, vines or pomegranates; and there is no water to drink!"

Then the Lord said to Moses: "Take the staff, assemble the people, and speak to the rock in their presence, that it may yield water for them and their cattle." So Moses and

Aaron gathered the people, and Moses said to them: "Listen, you rebels! Must we bring you water from this rock?" And raising his hand, he struck the rock with his staff twice. Water gushed out abundantly, and the people and their cattle drank of it. But the Lord said to Moses and Aaron: "Because you did not have faith in me, or vindicate me in the eyes of the people of Israel, you shall not bring this people into the land that I have given them."

The people of Israel encamped opposite Jericho, on the plains of Moab, east of the Jordan. Moab was in great dread of them because of their numbers. So Balak, who was the king of Moab at that time, sent messengers to Balaam the soothsayer, summoning him with these words:

"Here is a people that has come out of Egypt; they cover the face of the earth, and are encamped opposite me. Now then, pray come and curse this people, since they are too strong for me. Perhaps this will enable me to defeat them and drive them out of the country. For I know that he whom you bless is blessed, and he whom you curse is cursed."

God appeared to Balaam at night and asked: "Who are these men with you?" Balaam answered: "Balak has sent word to me, saying: "Please come and lay a curse upon this people, that I may be able to fight against them and drive them out." But God said to Balaam: "Do not go with them and do not curse this people, for they are blessed."

Balaam rose in the morning and said to the princes of Balak: "Go back to your country, for the Lord refused to let me go with you." So the princes of Moab went back to Balak and told him that Balaam had refused to come with them.

Balak sent a larger number of princes, who came to Balaam with this message: "Let nothing stop you from coming. I will give you great honor; whatever you tell me I will do; come, I beg you, curse this people for me." But Balaam replied: "Though Balak were to give me his very house full of silver and gold, I could not transgress the command of the Lord my God. Now then, remain here overnight, that I may find out what else the Lord may have to say to me."

In the night God came to Balaam and said to him: "As these men have come to call you, go with them; but you shall do only what I tell you." Balaam rose in the morning, saddled his donkey, and went with the princes of Moab. But God was angry because he went and the angel of the Lord stood in the road to hinder him.

Balaam was riding on the donkey, accompanied by his two servants. When the donkey saw the angel standing on the road with a drawn sword, the animal turned aside and went into the field. But Balaam struck the donkey and tried to turn her back into the road. The angel then took his stand in a narrow lane between vineyards, with a fence on either side. When the donkey saw the angel of the Lord, she pressed against the wall and crushed Balaam's foot; so he struck her again.

The angel went ahead and took his stand in a narrow place, where there was no way to turn either to the right or to the left. When the donkey saw the angel, she lay down under Balaam. Balaam's anger blazed and he struck her with his stick.

Then the Lord opened the mouth of the donkey and she said to Balaam: "What have I done to you that you have struck me these three times?"

"You have mocked me; if only I had a sword I would kill you," Balaam replied.

"Am I not your own animal on which you have always ridden? Have I ever mocked you?" the donkey complained.

The Lord opened Balaam's eyes, and he saw the angel standing on the road with a drawn sword. Balaam bowed his head and fell on his face.

The angel said to him: "Why have you struck your donkey these three times? It was I who came forth to stand in your way, because you have displeased me. The donkey saw me and swerved from me three times. Had she not swerved, I would certainly have slain you and spared her."

Balaam answered: "I have sinned; I did not know you were standing on the road to stop me. Now then, if it is displeasing to you, I will turn back."

"Go with the men," the angel said, "but you shall say

only what I tell you." So Balaam went along with the princes of Balak.

When Balak heard of Balaam's arrival, he went out to meet him. Then the Lord put a message in Balaam's mouth. Upon finding Balak together with the princes of Moab beside the burnt-offering, Balaam uttered these words:

"From Aram, Balak has brought me to lay a curse on Jacob, to denounce Israel. But how can I curse those whom God has not cursed; how can I denounce those whom the Lord has not denounced? May I die as these righteous men shall die, may my end be like theirs. God is no man to break his word, no mortal to change his mind. The Lord their God is with them! How goodly are your tents, O Jacob, your habitations, O Israel! I see them, but not as they are now; I behold them, but not as they are at present. A star has come forth from Jacob; Israel has performed valiantly."

After this, Balaam rose and went back to his place; and Balak also went his way.

The Lord told Moses and Elazar the son of Aaron to take a census of the whole Israelite community from twenty years old and upward, counting all Israelites who were fit for active service. The total number of the Israelites was six hundred and one thousand seven hundred and thirty. The total number of the Levites was twenty-three thousand, counting every male over a month old. Their number was not included in that of Israel, since they received no property in Israel. Among those numbered by Moses and Aaron in Moab, beside the Jordan opposite Jericho, there was not a man who had been in the census taken by Moses and Aaron when they counted the people of Israel in the wilderness of Sinai. Not a man of them was left, except Caleb and Joshua.

The five daughters of a man named Zelophehad appeared before Moses and the elders, pleading: "Our father died in the wilderness, though he took no part in the rising of Korah; he died for his own sin, leaving no sons. Why should our father's name be dropped from his family, just because he left no son? Give us property along with our father's kinsmen."

Moses brought their plea before the Lord, and the Lord said to Moses: "The daughters of Zelophehad are right; you shall certainly let them hold property among their kinsmen. Let a man's property always pass to his daughter, if he dies without leaving a son. If he leaves no daughter, his property shall go to his brothers; if he leaves no brothers, his property shall go to his father's brothers. If his father has left no brothers, you shall give his property to the nearest relative."

Then the Lord said to Moses: "Ascend this mountain of Abarim and see the land which I am giving to the people of Israel. When you have seen it, you shall be gathered to your people like your brother Aaron, because you disobeyed my word in the wilderness of Zin. When the people demanded water, you struck the rock instead of speaking to it in their presence."

Moses said to the Lord: "Let the Lord, God of the spirits of all flesh, appoint a leader for the community to manage all their affairs, so that the Lord's community may not be like sheep without a shepherd." So the Lord said to Moses: "Take Joshua, a man of spirit, and lay your hand upon him; have him stand before Elazar, the priest, and the whole community, and commission him in their sight. You shall invest him with some of your own authority, so that all the people of Israel may obey him."

Moses did as the Lord commanded him; he placed Joshua in front of Elazar the priest, and all the community, laid his hands upon him, and commissioned him.

Deuteronomy   דְּבָרִים

Deuteronomy, the fifth book of the Torah, carries events up to the death of Moses and prepares for the succession of Joshua. The greater part of the book is taken up with the addresses of Moses to the people of Israel as they were about to cross the Jordan to the land of Canaan. In these discourses Moses reviews the events of the forty years spent in the wilderness.

There are at least three speeches. The first is a summary of the main experiences of Israel in the desert; the second reviews the Ten Commandments and includes the declaration of God's oneness; the third stresses the duty of loyalty to God.

The final chapters comprise two poems recited by Moses in the hearing of the people, and also tell the story of his death. The moving narrative describing the death of Moses reveals the final experience of the great leader. From the peak of Mount Nebo, Moses surveys the whole extent of the promised land; he dies on Mount Nebo in solitude at the age of one hundred and twenty. Deuteronomy contains a considerable number of humane laws and is one of the most beautiful and profoundly ethical books of the Bible. The long poem *Haazinu,* in the thirty-second chapter, is one of the best productions of biblical poetry.

A number of passages from Deuteronomy have been incorporated into the daily prayers, notably the *Shema,* Israel's confession of faith, which expresses the duty of loving and serving God with our whole being.

These are the words which Moses spoke to all Israel east of the Jordan. It was in the fortieth year that Moses spoke to the people of Israel concerning all the commands which he had received for them from the Lord. He said:

O Israel, give heed to the rules and regulations which I teach you, and obey them, so that you may live and possess the land which the Lord is giving you. That will prove your wisdom and your understanding in the sight of the nations, who will say: This great nation is indeed a wise and understanding people!

What great nation has laws as just as this Torah which I am setting before you this day? Only take heed lest you forget the things which your eyes have seen. Make them known to your children and to your children's children— how on the day that you stood before the Lord your God at the foot of the mountain, while the mountain burned with fire to the heart of heaven, the Lord spoke to you out of the midst of the fire. You heard the sound of words, but saw no form; there was only a voice. He declared to you his covenant, the ten commandments, and he wrote them upon two tables of stone.

The Lord took you and brought you out of the iron furnace, out of Egypt, to be a people of his own.

The Lord was angry with me, and he forbade me to enter the fine land which he is giving you as a heritage. I must die in this land instead of crossing the Jordan; but you shall go over and take possession of that good land. Take care that you do not forget the covenant of the Lord your God which he made with you; do not make an image in the form of anything which the Lord your God has forbidden you; for the Lord your God is a consuming fire, a jealous God.

Hear, O Israel, the Lord is our God, the Lord is One.

You shall love the Lord your God with all your heart, and with all your soul, and with all your might. And these words which I command you today shall be in your heart. You shall teach them diligently to your children, and you shall speak of them when you are sitting at home and when you go on a journey, when you lie down, and when you rise up. You shall bind them for a sign on your hand, and they shall be for frontlets between your eyes. You shall inscribe them on the doorposts of your house and on your gates.

And if you will carefully obey my commands which I give you today, to love the Lord your God and to serve him with all your heart and with all your soul, I will give rain for your land at the right season, the autumn rains and the spring rains, that you may gather in your grain, your wine and your oil. And I will bring forth grass in your fields for your cattle, and you will eat and be satisfied. Beware lest your heart be deceived, and you turn and serve other gods and worship them; for then the Lord's anger will blaze against you, and he will shut up the skies so that there will be no rain, and the land will yield no produce, and you will perish quickly from the good land which the Lord gives you. So you must place these words in your heart and in your soul; you must teach them to your children, that your life and the life of your children may be prolonged in the land, which the Lord promised to your fathers, for as long as the sky remains over the earth.

You are children of the Lord your God: you must not eat any detestable food. You may eat the ox, the sheep, the goat, the deer. You may eat any animal that has the hoof parted in two and also chews the cud; but you must not eat of those that chew the cud only or have the hoof parted only. You may eat anything in the waters that has fins and scales; but you must not eat anything that has not fins and scales. You may eat any clean bird; but you must not eat the vulture, the raven, the ostrich, the hawk, the stork, and the bat. All winged insects are unclean to you. You must not eat any creature that has died a natural death. You must not boil a kid in its mother's milk.

You shall appoint judges and officers to rule the people with right justice. You shall not pervert justice; you shall not be partial to anyone; you shall not take a bribe, for a bribe blinds the eyes of the wise. You shall strive for justice, and justice only, in order that you may live and possess the land given to you by the Lord your God.

A single witness shall not testify against a man in any case; only on the evidence of two or three witnesses shall a charge be sustained.

If a malicious witness testifies against a man, accusing him of wrongdoing, the two parties in the dispute shall appear before the judges, who shall make a thorough investigation. If the witness accuses his brother falsely, you shall do to him as he planned to do to his brother.

You must not be unconcerned when you see your fellow man's ox or sheep driven astray; you must surely bring them back to your fellow man. If, however, he does not live near you, or you do not know him, you shall take it home and keep it with you until he claims it. You shall do the same with everything lost by your fellow man, which you have found; you must not be unconcerned.

If you happen to come upon a bird's nest when the mother-bird is sitting on the young ones or the eggs, you must not take away the mother-bird along with her off-spring; you must let the mother go, and you may take only the young, that you may prosper and live long.

When you make any vow to the Lord your God, you must pay it without delay. You shall be careful to perform any promise you have made with your lips.

When you go into your neighbor's vineyard, you may eat your fill of the grapes, but you must not put any in your bag.

When a man is newly married, he shall not go on active service with the army; he shall be free at home for one year, to be happy with the wife he has taken.

If a man kidnaps a fellow man in order to enslave or sell him, the kidnaper shall be put to death.

You shall not defraud a poor servant; you shall pay him each day's wages before sundown.

Fathers shall not be put to death for their children, nor shall children be put to death for their fathers; a man shall be put to death only for his own guilt.

You shall not violate the rights of the alien or of the orphan, or take the clothing of a widow in pledge.

When you reap the harvest in your field and overlook a sheaf there, you shall not go back to get it; let it be for the alien, the orphan or the widow. When you pick your grapes, you shall not go over the vineyard a second time; let what remains be for the alien, the orphan, and the widow.

You shall not muzzle an ox when it is treading out grain.

You shall not have weights of different sizes in your bag, one large and the other small; you shall have a true and just weight, a true and just measure. Everyone who is dishonest is an abomination to the Lord your God.

What I am commanding you today is not too difficult

and remote for you. It is not up in heaven that you should say: "Who will ascend to heaven to get it for us?" Nor is it across the sea, that you should say: "Who will cross the sea and bring it to us?" No, it is something very near to you, within your own hearts and minds.

If you obey the commandments of the Lord your God, you shall live and multiply in the land which you are now entering. But if your heart turns away to worship other gods and serve them, I declare to you this day that you shall not live long in the land which you are going to enter and possess.

I call heaven and earth to witness this day, that I have set before you life and death, the blessing and the curse. Choose life, then, that you and your descendants may live in the land which the Lord promised to your fathers Abraham, Isaac and Jacob.

Hearken, O heaven, and I will speak; let the earth hear the words of my mouth! May my message drop like the rain, my speech distill as the dew. When I proclaim the name of the Lord, give glory to our God!

He is the Creator, his work is perfect; all his ways are just. He is the faithful God, without iniquity, upright and just!

The corruption of his children has been their undoing; they are a twisted and crooked generation. Is this the way to treat the Lord, you foolish people? Is he not your Father who created you? Has he not made you and established you?

Remember the days of old, consider the ages that are past; ask your father and he will inform you, ask your elders and they will tell you. He found them in a desert land, in a howling waste of wilderness; he cared for them, and kept them as the apple of his eye.

This is the blessing which Moses, the man of God, pronounced upon the people of Israel before his death. He said:

"The Lord came from Sinai, and dawned on them from Seir; he shone forth from the mountain of Paran. The Torah which has been handed down to us is the heritage of the community of Jacob.

"May Reuben live and not die. Hear, O Lord, the cry of Judah; be thou a help against his adversaries. Levi shall teach Israel thy law; break the backs of his adversaries and foes, that they may not rise.

"There is none like God! The eternal God is your refuge. He drove the enemy out of your way. Happy are you, O Israel, a people saved by the Lord!"

Moses went up to Mount Nebo, opposite Jericho. There the Lord showed him all the land of Judah as far as the Mediterranean Sea, the Negev, and the Valley of Jericho, saying: "This is the land which I solemnly promised to give to the descendants of Abraham, Isaac and Jacob. I have let you look upon it, but you shall not enter it."

Moses died there in the land of Moab, but to this day no one knows the place of his burial. Moses was a hundred and twenty years old when he died, yet his eyes were un-dimmed and his vigor unabated. The people of Israel mourned over the passing of Moses for thirty days.

Joshua, the son of Nun, was filled with the spirit of wisdom; the people of Israel obeyed him, and carried out the orders given by the Lord to Moses.

Since then, no prophet has ever appeared in Israel like Moses, whom the Lord knew face to face.

Joshua

The book of Joshua continues the history of the preceding five books of Moses and narrates the conquest and settlement of the promised land, recording the completion of the great movement of which the exodus from Egypt was the beginning. It is the first of the four historical books known as Former Prophets (Joshua, Judges, Samuel, Kings) forming a continuous narrative which begins at the death of Moses and ends with the destruction of the first Temple. These writings are classed as prophetic because they were composed by divinely inspired prophets.

As successor of Moses, Joshua defeated six enemy tribes in six years and then proceeded to divide the conquered territory. The final events of his life include the distribution of the land to the tribes of Israel by lot and the appointing of the cities of refuge, which are designed to shelter anyone who might accidentally commit manslaughter. By fleeing into one of the six cities of refuge, persons pursued by avengers of blood were protected against the ancient law of life for life. Forty-two Levitical cities also served for the protection of the unintentional homicide.

Before his death at the age of one hundred and ten, Joshua delivered two addresses to the people of Israel, urging them to remain loyal to God and live according to the teachings of the Torah.

After the death of Moses, the Lord said to Joshua: "Moses my servant is dead; now arise, cross the Jordan, you and all this people, into the land which I am giving them. No man shall be able to hold his own against you all the days of your life; as I was with Moses, so I will be with you; I will never fail you nor forsake you. Be strong and brave, for you shall put this people in possession of the land which I promised to their fathers. Only observe all the law which Moses handed down to you; turn neither to the right nor to the left, that you may prosper wherever you go."

Joshua sent two spies to explore the land, especially Jericho. Upon reaching Jericho, they went into the house of a woman named Rahab. When the king of Jericho was told that some Israelites had come to spy out the land, he ordered Rahab to put them out. But the woman, who had hidden the two men on the roof, said to the king's messengers: "Yes, the men did come to me, but I do not know where they came from; at dark, they left, and I do not know where they went. You will have to pursue them immediately to overtake them."

The pursuers set out and took the road to the Jordan. Before the spies had gone to sleep, Rahab came up to them on the roof and said: "I know that the Lord has given you the land; all the inhabitants of the land are overcome with fear of you. We are disheartened; everyone is discouraged because of you. Now then, swear to me by the Lord that you will show kindness to my family and save us from death." "We pledge our lives for yours," the men answered her. "If you will not betray us, we will deal kindly and faithfully with you when the Lord gives us the land."

Then she let them down through the window with a rope, for she lived in a house built into the city wall. "Get away to the hills," she said to them, "so that the pursuers may not find you. Hide there for three days, until they have returned."

The men said to her: "When we come into the land, you shall tie this scarlet cord in the window through which you let us down; and you shall gather your father and mother, your brothers and all your family into your house. Should anyone of them pass outside the doors of your house, he will be responsible for his own death, and we shall be guiltless. But we shall be responsible if anyone in the house with you is harmed. If, however, you breathe a word about our errand, we will not be bound by the oath you have made us take."

"Let it be as you say," she replied, and she let them down by a rope through the window. When they were gone, she tied the scarlet cord in the window. They went into the hills and stayed there for three days, till the pursuers had returned. Then the two spies came down from the hills. They went to Joshua and told him all that had befallen them. They said to Joshua: "The Lord has given the entire land into our hands; the inhabitants are overcome with fear of us."

The people left their tents to cross the Jordan. They were headed by the priests, who carried the ark of the covenant. Now, as soon as the bearers of the ark reached the Jordan and their feet dipped into the water at the edge, the waters flowing down came to a stop, while the waters flowing away toward the salt sea were completely cut off. The priests carrying the ark stood still on dry ground in the middle of the Jordan, while all Israel crossed over on dry ground, opposite Jericho. When all the people had finished crossing, the priests with the ark advanced in front of the people. Then the waters of the Jordan resumed their course and overflowed their banks as before.

Twelve stones were taken out of the Jordan, and Joshua set them up at Gilgal. He said to the people of Israel: "When your children in time to come ask what these stones mean, you shall tell them that Israel crossed the Jordan here on dry ground."

The people of Israel observed the Passover when they were in camp at Gilgal. The manna ceased when they began to eat the food of the land of Canaan.

Now Jericho had shut its gates against the Israelites; no one left or entered the city. Joshua ordered the people to march around the city, with the armed men passing before the ark of the Lord and before seven priests blowing seven rams' horns. He warned the people, saying: "You must not shout, you must not say a word, until I tell you to shout; only then you shall shout."

Joshua had the ark carried around the city once; then the people returned to the camp and passed the night there. The second day they again marched around the city once and returned to the camp. This they continued to do for six days. On the seventh day, they arose at daybreak and marched around the city seven times. The seventh time, when the priests blew the horns, Joshua said to the people: "Shout, for the Lord has given you the city. Only Rahab and those who are in her house shall be spared."

The people raised a tremendous shout, and the wall collapsed; they stormed the city and captured it. Rahab and her entire family were saved and placed outside the camp of Israel because she had hidden the messengers sent by Joshua.

Joshua and all the fighting men prepared to attack Ai. He selected thirty thousand brave soldiers and sent them off by night, commanding them: "Ambush the city from the rear, at no great distance; then all of you be ready. The rest of the soldiers and I will approach the city, and when they come out against us, we will flee before them until we draw them away from it. As we run away, you shall come out of ambush and capture the city. As soon as you have captured it, you shall set it on fire."

Early the next morning, Joshua led all the people against Ai. The main army was stationed to the north of the city, with the ambush west of it. The king of Ai came out to engage Israel in battle, not knowing that there was an ambush behind the city. Joshua and all the Israelites fled, in seeming defeat, toward the desert. All the people of Ai, who pursued Joshua, were drawn away from the city which they left unprotected. Then the men in ambush rushed into the city and set it on fire, while the Israelites, who were fleeing toward the desert, turned upon their pursuers. By the time the men of Ai looked back, smoke was rising from the city! Meanwhile, the Israelites in Ai came out of the city to fight against them. They were hemmed in on either side; escape in any direction was impossible. None of them remained alive.

When the inhabitants of Gibeon heard what Joshua had done to Jericho and Ai, they acted with cunning. They went to Joshua and said: "We have come from a distant country to propose that you make a treaty with us."

"Who are you? Where do you come from?" Joshua asked. "We have come from a far off land," they replied. "Here is our bread; it was still warm the day we left home to come to you, but now it is dry and crumbled. Look at our garments and shoes; they are worn out from the very long journey."

So Joshua made a treaty with them to spare their lives.

Three days after the treaty was made, the Israelites learned that the Gibeonites were their neighbors, living in the same country. But the leaders of Israel declared: "We have sworn to them by the Lord God of Israel, and we cannot harm them; let them live!"

The five Amorite kings united all their forces and marched against Gibeon. Thereupon the Gibeonites sent an appeal to Joshua: "Do not abandon your servants; come up here quickly, save us, help us; all the Amorite kings are gathered against us."

So Joshua marched up with all the fighting men and valiant soldiers. Meanwhile, the Lord said to Joshua: "Do not fear them, for I have delivered them into your hands. Not one of them shall hold his own against you." And when Joshua made his surprise attack upon them, the Lord threw them into a panic before the Israelites, who routed them with heavy slaughter. It was on that day, when the Lord handed over the Amorites to the Israelites, that Joshua said: "O sun, stand still at Gibeon; move not, O moon, in the valley of Aijalon." The sun stood still in the middle of the sky, and did not set for about a whole day. Never before or since was there a day like this! The Lord listened to the voice of a man, for the Lord fought for Israel.

When Joshua was old and well advanced in years, the Lord said to him: "You are old, but very much of the land still remains to be conquered. However, allot the land to Israel as I commanded you."

Then the people of Judah came to Joshua, and Caleb said to him: "You know what the Lord said to Moses about you and me. I was forty years old when Moses sent me to spy out the land; I brought back to him a conscientious report. My fellow spies who went up with me discouraged the people, but I was completely loyal to the Lord my God. On that occasion Moses solemnly promised, saying: The land on which your foot has trodden shall be an inheritance for you and your descendants forever.

"And now the Lord has kept me alive for the past forty-five years, ever since the Lord spoke this word to Moses. Here I am today eighty-five years old. I am still as strong today as I was when Moses sent me off; my strength now is as it was then. Give me, then, this hill country of which the Lord spoke on that day."

Joshua blessed Caleb and gave Hebron to him for an inheritance. And the land had rest from war.

A long time afterwards, when the Lord had given rest to the people of Israel from all their enemies round about, and when Joshua was far advanced in years, Joshua summoned all Israel and said to them: "I am about to go the way of all the earth; and you know in your hearts and souls, all of you, that not one thing has failed of all the good things which the Lord promised concerning you. Thus says the Lord God of Israel:

"I took your father Abraham from the other side of the Euphrates River and led him through all the land of Canaan; I gave him Isaac, and to Isaac I gave Jacob and Esau. Jacob and his children went down to Egypt. I sent Moses and Aaron, and I brought your fathers out of Egypt. The Egyptians pursued your fathers as far as the Red Sea, and the Lord engulfed them in it. You lived many days in the wilderness, and I brought you to the eastern side of the Jordan. Then Balak, king of Moab, sent for Balaam to curse you, but he blessed you instead. You crossed the Jordan and came to Jericho, and I put the men of Jericho into your hands; it was not your sword nor bow that defeated them. I have given you a land for which you did not labor, and cities which you did not build, and you eat fruit from vineyards and oliveyards you did not plant. Now therefore revere the Lord and serve him sincerely and faithfully. But if you are unwilling to serve the Lord, then choose today whom you will serve. As for me and my house, we will serve the Lord."

The people answered: "Far be it from us to forsake the Lord and serve other gods!" Then Joshua dismissed the people; every man returned to his own home.

After this, Joshua died at the age of a hundred and ten. He was buried in his own land in the hill country of Ephraim. Israel served the Lord all the days of Joshua and all the days of the elders who outlived Joshua.

Judges   שׁוֹפְטִים

The book of Judges is a story of triumphant faith. It derives its name from the twelve heroic leaders whose deeds and prowess it describes. The Hebrew word for judges (*shoftim*) connotes champions, defenders. The judges, including Eli and Samuel who are described in the book of Samuel, were gifted and courageous persons who strengthened Israel's hold of Canaan against a variety of enemies. These champions of Israel inspired the people to fight against those who threatened their existence. The period of the judges lasted about two hundred and thirty years, during the interval between the death of Joshua and the coronation of Saul.

The book of Judges is replete with character sketches and examples of good traits and bad ones. Deborah, the prophetess who held court and settled disputes among her people, was a dynamic personality in peace and war. The song of Deborah, celebrating the victory over the army of Sisera, is an excellent example of early Hebrew poetry, even though the meaning is not clear in some of its verses. It is the outcome of a powerful imagination and reaches sublime heights of religious emotion.

Gideon was a man of peace, who succeeded in appeasing the fiery Ephraimites by minimizing his own achievements and magnifying their part in the final destruction of the enemy. His daring modesty and good temper make him a glowing personality.

Jephthah was a man of war and, unlike Gideon, fought the Ephraimites back to their Jordan boundary. He seized the fords of the river and set guards to let no Ephraimite pass over. The identity of Ephraimites was easily detected by the way they mispronounced the word "Shibboleth" (stream). They could not pronounce "sh" and said "s" instead.

Samson represents a strange combination of virtue and folly. He is the strong man who is too weak to resist feminine wiles. Delilah has become a symbol of the treacherous woman in whose clutches the strong man is helpless.

After the death of Joshua and all his generation, the people of Israel did evil in the sight of the Lord and served the

Baals. They forsook the God of their fathers, and went after the gods of the various nations around them and worshiped them. So the anger of the Lord flared up against the people of Israel, and he handed them over to their enemies. Then the Lord raised up judges, who saved them from their plunderers. But when a judge died, they would relapse and behave worse than their fathers.

The people of Israel offended the Lord by serving the Baals, so he allowed them to fall into the power of the king of Mesopotamia, whom they served for eight years. But when the people of Israel cried to the Lord, he raised up a champion for them, Othniel, who saved them. The land then was at rest for forty years, until Othniel died.

Again the people of Israel offended the Lord, so he made the king of Moab gain power over them. For eighteen years they were subject to Eglon, king of Moab. Then Israel cried to the Lord, and he raised up a champion for them, Ehud, who was left-handed. He made himself a two-edged dagger, and wore it under his clothes over his right hip.

Ehud once presented the tribute of Israel to Eglon, who was a very fat man. After the presentation, he dismissed the carriers, went back and said: "I have a private message for you, O king." "Silence!" said the king to all his attendants, and they left him. Then Ehud went in to see him, as he sat alone in his cool roof chamber. "I have a message from God for you," Ehud said, and Eglon rose from his seat.

Ehud reached with his left hand, took the dagger from his right hip, plunged it into Eglon's belly, and left it there. He then went out into the vestibule, closed the doors of the room and locked them. After he had gone, the king's servants came—and there lay their lord dead on the floor.

In the meantime, Ehud escaped and sounded the trumpet through the highlands of Ephraim. "Follow me," he said to the people of Israel, "for the Lord has delivered your enemies, the Moabites, into your hands!" So they marched after Ehud and seized the fords of the Jordan leading to Moab, permitting no one to cross. They killed about ten thousand Moabites that day. Moab was brought under the power of Israel, and the land had rest for eighty years.

After Ehud came Shamgar, who killed six hundred Philistines with an oxgoad; he too saved Israel.

After Ehud's death, the people of Israel again did evil in the sight of the Lord, so he delivered them into the power of the Canaanite king, Jabin, whose army commander was Sisera. Jabin had nine hundred iron chariots, and for twenty years he oppressed Israel severely.

At that time Israel was governed by Deborah, a prophetess, who used to sit under a palm tree, where the people came to her for judgment. She summoned Barak from Naphtali and said to him: "The Lord God of Israel commands you to gather ten thousand men. He will deliver Sisera and his chariots and his troops into your power."

Barak said to Deborah: "If you will come with me, I will go; but if you will not come with me, I will not go." She replied: "I will certainly go with you; however, the glory of the course you are undertaking will not be yours, for the Lord will give Sisera over into the hand of a woman."

Then Deborah went with Barak to Kedesh and ten thousand men marched with them.

When Sisera was told that Barak had gone up to Mount Tabor, he summoned his nine hundred chariots and all his forces.

Deborah said to Barak: "Up! This is the day when the Lord has given Sisera into your hand!" So Barak, with his men, charged down from Mount Tabor, and the Lord routed Sisera and all his chariots and all his army. Sisera alighted from his chariot and fled on foot to the tent of Jael, who went out to meet him, saying: "Come in, my lord, come in; do not be afraid." So he went into her tent, and she covered him up with a rug.

He said to her: "Pray give me a little water to drink, for I am thirsty." She opened a bottle of milk, gave him a drink and covered him up again.

He said to her: "Stand at the door of the tent; if anyone comes and asks you if there is a man here, say no." But Jael took a tent peg and a hammer in her hand and, coming quietly up to him, she drove the peg through his temple into the ground while he was sound asleep and exhausted, and he died.

Just then Barak arrived in pursuit of Sisera, and Jael went out to meet him, saying: "Come, and I will show you the man for whom you are looking!" So Barak went inside her tent, and there lay Sisera dead, with the tent peg in his temple.

On that day Deborah and Barak sang:

"Hear, O kings; give ear, O princes! I will sing to the Lord God of Israel. In the days of Jael, caravans ceased and travelers kept to the byways, Israel's hamlets were deserted until I, Deborah, arose, arose as a mother in Israel. My heart goes out to the commanders of Israel, who volunteered among the people! Bless the Lord!

"Awake, awake, Deborah! Awake, awake, utter a song! To your feet, O Barak, and lead away your captives!

"The very stars in heaven were fighting, from their spheres they fought against Sisera. The river Kishon swept them away; then the hoofs of the mighty horses struck, rushing and dashing away.

"Most blessed above women shall Jael be! He asked for water and she gave him milk; she crushed his head and pierced his temple; he sank, he fell, he lay still at her feet.

"Thus may all thy enemies perish, O Lord; may those who love thee be as the rising sun!"

The land was at rest for forty years. But the people of Israel did evil in the sight of the Lord, so the Lord handed them over to Midian for seven years.

Midian gained the upper hand over Israel. Whenever the Israelites had completed their sowing, the Midianites would come and destroy the produce of the country as far south as Gaza. They left Israel nothing to live on. They would come with their cattle and their tents, swarming like locusts; and so the people of Israel cried for help to the Lord.

Gideon, the son of Joash, was beating out some wheat in the winepress, to hide it from the Midianites. And the angel of the Lord appeared to him, saying: "The Lord is with you, mighty man of valor!" But Gideon replied: "Sir, if the Lord is with us, why then has all this befallen us?

78

Where are all his wondrous deeds of which our fathers told us? The Lord has abandoned us and has delivered us into the power of Midian."

The Lord turned to him and said: "Go, with the strength you have, and save Israel from Midian. It is I who send you."

Then Gideon said to God: "I am putting a fleece of wool on the threshing floor. If dew falls only on the fleece, while all the ground is dry, I shall know that thou wilt save Israel through me, as thou hast promised." This did happen. When he rose early next morning and squeezed the fleece, he wrung enough dew from it to fill a bowl. Gideon then said to God: "Let me make just one more test with the fleece: pray let the fleece alone be dry, and let there be dew on all the ground." That night God did so; the fleece alone was dry, and there was dew on all the ground.

So Gideon and all his men rose early and encamped beside the spring of Harod, south of the Midianite camp. But the Lord said to Gideon: "There are too many men with you. Proclaim now to the people that anyone who is fearful and trembling must return home." And so twenty-two thousand left, and ten thousand remained.

"There are still too many," the Lord said to Gideon; "take them down to the water, and I will sift them there."

When Gideon took them down to the water, the Lord said to him: "Place on one side everyone who laps up the water with his tongue like a dog, and place on the other side everyone who kneels down to drink."

The men who lapped numbered three hundred; all the rest knelt down to drink the water.

Then the Lord said to Gideon: "With the three hundred men who lapped I will save you and put Midian into your hands; let all the rest go home." So he sent all the Israelites home, and retained only the three hundred.

That same night Gideon went down with his servant to the outposts of the Midianites. They lay along the valley in swarms, like locusts. And behold, a man was telling a dream to his comrade. "I had a dream," he said, "that a cake of barley bread tumbled into the camp of Midian. It came to our tent and struck it so that it fell; it turned the tent upside down."

"This can only be the sword of the Israelite Gideon," the other replied. "God has delivered Midian into his power."

When Gideon heard the description of the dream and its interpretation, he returned to the camp of Israel and said: "Arise, for the Lord has delivered the camp of Midian into our hands."

Gideon divided the three hundred men into three companies and provided them all with trumpets, empty pitchers and torches inside the pitchers. "Watch me and do as I do," he told them; "when I and all my men blow our trumpets, you too must blow yours all around the Midianite camp and shout: For the Lord and for Gideon!"

So Gideon, and the hundred men who were with him, came to the outskirts of the camp at the beginning of the middle watch, just when the guard had been posted. They blew the trumpets and smashed the pitchers in their hands. All the three companies blew their trumpets and broke their pitchers. They held the torches in their left hands and the trumpets in their right hands, shouting: "A sword for the Lord and Gideon!"

They all remained standing in place around the camp, while the whole camp fell to running and shouting and fleeing. But the three hundred men kept blowing the horns, and throughout the camp the Lord set the sword of one against another.

The men of Israel were called to pursue Midian. Gideon sent messengers throughout the highlands of Ephraim, saying: "Come down to confront Midian and seize the water courses against them, as well as the Jordan." So all the men of Ephraim were called to arms; they seized the water courses and the Jordan, captured the two chiefs of Midian, and killed them.

The men of Ephraim then asked Gideon: "Why have you treated us like this? Why did you not call us when you started the attack on Midian?" And they quarrelled bitterly with him. But he replied: "What have I accomplished, compared to what you have? God has put the chiefs of Midian into your hands. What have I been able to do in comparison with you?" When he said this, their anger against him subsided.

Then the people of Israel said to Gideon: "Rule over us, for you have saved us from Midian." But Gideon said to them: "I will not rule over you, nor shall my son; the Lord shall rule over you."

So the Midianites were subdued by Israel and they raised their heads no more. The land had rest for forty years in the days of Gideon.

Now the Ammonites gathered for war and encamped in Gilead, while the Israelites assembled and encamped in Mizpah.

There was a chieftain, Jephthah the Gileadite, who was the son of a harlot, and Gilead was his father. The sons of Gilead's wife had driven Jephthah away, saying to him: "You shall inherit nothing in our family, for you are the son of another woman." So Jephthah fled from his brothers and stayed in the land of Tob, where worthless fellows collected round him, and went on raids with him.

When the Ammonites went to war with Israel, the elders of Gilead went to bring Jephthah. "Come, be our commander," they said to Jephthah, "that we may fight the Ammonites." But Jephthah replied: "Did you not hate me and drive me out of my father's house? Why have you come to me now when you are in trouble?"

"We have come back to you," the elders said; "if you go with us to fight the Ammonites, you shall be the leader of all of us who live in Gilead." Jephthah answered: "If you take me back to fight the Ammonites, and if the Lord delivers them into my hands, I will be your leader."

The elders of Gilead said to Jephthah: "The Lord is witness between us that we will do as you say." So Jephthah went with the elders of Gilead, and the people made him their leader and commander.

Then Jephthah sent messengers to the king of the Ammonites, saying: "What have you against me that you come to attack my country?" The king of the Ammonites answered the messengers of Jephthah: "Israel took away my land when they came up from Egypt. Now, then, restore it peaceably."

Again Jephthah sent messengers, saying: "Israel did not take the land of Moab or the land of the Ammonites. Three hundred years have passed; why have you never recaptured them during all that time? No, I have done no wrong to you; it is you who are doing me wrong by making war on me. Let the Lord decide this day between the Israelites and the Ammonites!"

Then Jephthah went to fight against the Ammonites, and the Lord delivered them into his power. Jephthah inflicted a severe defeat on them, and they were subdued by the people of Israel.

The men of Ephraim assembled to ask Jephthah: "Why did you go to fight the Ammonites without calling on us to go with you? We will burn down your house over your head." But Jephthah said to them: "My men and I were engaged in a sharp struggle, the Ammonites were pressing us hard. We summoned you, but you did not rescue us from their power. When I saw that you would not help us, I took my life in my own hand and went to the Ammonites, and the Lord gave them over to me. Why, then, have you come up this day to fight against me?"

Then Jephthah gathered all the men of Gilead and fought with the men of Ephraim, whom they defeated. The Gileadites seized the fords of the Jordan toward Ephraim. When any of the fleeing Ephraimites said, "Let me cross," the men of Gilead would ask him whether he was of the tribe of Ephraim. If he said "No," they asked him to say "Shibboleth." If he said "Sibboleth," not being able to pronounce the word correctly, they knew that he belonged to Ephraim and killed him at the fords of the Jordan.

Jephthah governed Israel for six years. Then Jephthah died and was buried in his town in Gilead.

Again the people of Israel did what was evil in the sight of the Lord, so the Lord handed them over to the Philistines for forty years.

There was a certain man named Manoah whose wife had borne no children. An angel of the Lord appeared to the woman and said to her: "Be careful to drink no wine or strong drink and to eat no unclean food, for you shall bear a son. No razor shall touch his head, for this boy shall be a

Nazirite, consecrated to God from birth; he shall begin the deliverance of Israel from the Philistines." The woman did bear a son, and she called him Samson. The boy grew up, and the Lord blessed him.

Once Samson told his father and mother: "I saw a Philistine woman at Timnah; get her to be my wife." So they said to him: "Can you find no wife among all our people that you must go and take a wife from the Philistines?" But Samson insisted: "Get her for me; I like her!"

Samson went down to Timnah, and a young lion came roaring toward him. He tore the lion in two, although he had no weapon in his hand. After a while he stepped aside to look at the remains of the lion, and there was a swarm of bees and honey in the body of the lion. He scraped the honey into his hands and ate as he went along. He gave some of it to his father and mother, but he did not tell them that he had taken it from the lion's body.

When Samson married the woman in Timnah, he held a feast. He said to the thirty companions who had been sent from Timnah to be with him: "Let me ask you a riddle. If you can solve it within the seven days of the feast, I will give you thirty suits of clothes; but if you cannot guess it, you shall give me thirty suits of clothes." They said to him: "Tell your riddle. Let us hear it." So he said to them: "Out of the eater came something to eat. Out of the strong came something sweet."

For three days they could not guess the riddle. On the fourth day they said to Samson's wife: "Entice your husband to tell us what the riddle means, or we will burn you and your family. Have you invited us here to make us poor?"

She wept and said to Samson: "You hate me. You do not love me. You have proposed a riddle to my countrymen, and you have never told me the answer." She pressed him so hard that, at last, on the seventh day of their feast, he told her. Then she explained the riddle to her countrymen.

That day, before sunset, the men of the town said to Samson: "What is sweeter than honey? What is stronger than a lion?" And he said to them: "If you had not plowed with my heifer, you would not have solved my riddle."

Samson went down to Ashkelon and killed thirty men of the town; he gave their clothes to those who had answered the riddle. Then he went off to his own family in anger. And Samson's wife was given to one of his companions, he who had been his best man.

After some time, Samson went to visit his wife with a present. But her father would not let him enter the house, saying: "I thought that you hated her, so I gave her to your companion. Her younger sister is more beautiful; take her instead."

Samson went and caught three hundred foxes. Turning them tail to tail, he tied between each pair of tails one of the torches he had at hand. He then set fire to the torches, and let the foxes loose in the standing grain of the Philistines. The shocks, the standing grain and the olive orchards were burned to ashes.

When the Philistines were told that Samson, the son-in-law of the Timnite, had done this because his wife had been taken away from him and given to another man, they came up and destroyed her and her family by fire.

"If this is what you do," Samson said to the Philistines, "I will have my revenge on you before I am done." He inflicted a heavy slaughter on them; then he went down and stayed in a cavern.

The Philistines came up and camped in Judah. "Why have you come up against us?" the men of Judah asked. "To seize Samson," the Philistines replied; "to do to him what he has done to us."

So three thousand men of Judah went to the cliff and said to Samson: "Do you not know that the Philistines are our overlords? Why have you done this to us?" He answered: "As they have done to me, so have I done to them."

But the men of Judah declared: "We have come to take you prisoner and hand you over to the Philistines." Samson said to them: "Swear to me that you will not kill me yourselves." They replied: "No, we will not kill you; we will only bind you and hand you over to them." So they bound him with two new ropes and brought him up from the cliff.

When the Philistines came to meet him shouting, the ropes around his arms became like flax that has caught fire, and his bonds melted from his hands. He seized a fresh jawbone of a mule, and with it he slew a thousand men.

After that he fell in love with a woman whose name was Delilah. The Philistine tyrants came to her and said: "Find out the secret of his great strength, and how we may overpower him. If you do this, we will each give you eleven hundred pieces of silver." So Delilah said to Samson: "Tell me the secret of your great strength and how you may be tied up and made helpless." Samson replied: "If I am tied with seven fresh bowstrings that have not been dried, my strength will fail, and I shall be like any other man."

The Philistine tyrants brought her seven fresh bowstrings which had not been dried, and with these she tied up Samson. Then she shouted: "The Philistines are upon you, Samson!" He snapped the bowstrings like a piece of yarn at the touch of fire, and the secret of his strength still remained unknown.

Delilah said to Samson: "You have deceived me! You have told me a lie! Now, do tell me how you may be bound." He said to her: "If they bind me tight with new ropes that have not been used, my strength will fail, and I shall be like any other man." So Delilah took new ropes and bound him. She shouted: "The Philistines are upon you, Samson!" He broke the ropes from his arms like thread.

Delilah said to Samson: "You have been deceiving me all the time; you have told me lies. Tell me why you are so strong." He said to her: "If you weave my seven locks of hair into a web, I shall be as weak as any other man." So while he was asleep, Delilah wove his seven locks of hair into the web, and shouted: "The Philistines are upon you, Samson!" He woke up and pulled out both loom and web.

Then she said to him: "How can you say that you love me when you do not confide in me. Three times you have trifled with me, and you have not told me wherein your great strength lies." At last, when she had pressed and urged him day after day, he became tired to death of it and told her the truth: "A razor has never been used on my head, for I have been a Nazirite to God from birth. If I were to be shaved, my strength would leave me and I should become like any other man."

She made Samson sleep on her lap, and called for a man who shaved off the seven locks of his head. His strength left him, and she shouted: "The Philistines are upon you, Samson!" He woke up and thought he might again shake himself free, not realizing that the Lord had left him. The Philistines seized him and gouged out his eyes; they brought him down to Gaza and bound him with bronze chains. He spent his time in prison grinding at the mill.

Now the Philistine tyrants had gathered for a great sacrifice to their god Dagon, and for merrymaking. "Our god," they said, "has put Samson, our enemy, into our hands." They were in high spirits, and shouted: "Call for Samson that he may amuse us!"

So Samson was called from prison. He was made to stand between the pillars, and he said to the attendant who held him by the hand: "Let me feel the pillars on which the house rests, that I may lean against them." Now the house was full of men and women; all the Philistine lords were there, and on the roof there were about three thousand men and women, looking down in amusement at Samson.

Samson called to the Lord and said: "Lord God, remember me; give me strength, I pray thee, only this once, O God, to wreak vengeance upon the Philistines for one of my two eyes."

Samson grasped the two middle pillars on which the house rested, one with his right hand and the other with his left, and leaned his weight upon them.

"Let me die with the Philistines!" Samson cried. He pulled with all his might, and the temple fell on the tyrants and on all the people that were inside. So those he killed in death were more than he had killed in life.

His kinsmen and all his family came and took him away to be buried in the tomb of his father Manoah. He had championed Israel for twenty years.

Samuel   שְׁמוּאֵל

The two books of Samuel are considered as one book in the Hebrew Bible, and continue the history of Israel from the tribal stage to the development of a united nation. They cover a period of about one hundred years (1070–970). It was one of the most important centuries in the life of Israel. In the long struggle against its surrounding enemies, Israel learned its own strength and prepared to play its part in the history of mankind. Events during this period are centered about three great personalities: Samuel, Saul and David.

The books of Samuel, containing the first records of prophecy, are among the most important sources for the history of religion. The first book records the life of Samuel and the events that occurred during his administration and that of King Saul. It also describes David's good character and his triumphs, spiritual and temporal.

The second book describes the career of David and the expansion of his kingdom. It contains a vivid portrayal of the demoralization in David's family, traceable to David's own moral collapse. The story of Absalom's rebellion against David, and of David's mourning over the death of Absalom is considered to be one of the greatest narratives that has come down to us from ancient times.

There was a man by the name of Elkanah who had two wives, one named Hannah and the other Peninnah. Peninnah had children, but Hannah had none. Year after year this man would go from his town to worship and sacrifice to the Lord at Shiloh.

Upon a certain day, when Elkanah offered a sacrifice, he gave portions to his wife Peninnah and all her sons and daughters; but to Hannah he gave a double portion because he loved her, though the Lord had made her childless. This was done year after year—whenever they went up to the house of the Lord, and Peninnah provoked Hannah, who wept and could not eat. Elkanah said to her:

87

"Hannah why are you weeping? Why are you not eating? Why is your heart sad? Am I not more to you than ten sons?"

After the eating and drinking at Shiloh, Hannah rose to pray, while Eli, the priest, was sitting near the doorpost of the temple of the Lord. With a sad heart she prayed to the Lord and wept bitterly. She vowed, saying: "Lord of hosts, if thou wilt remember me and grant me a son, I will give him to thee for all his life."

As she prayed, Eli watched her. Now Hannah was speaking inwardly; only her lips moved, her voice could not be heard; Eli thought she was drunk. So Eli said to her: "How long will you be drunk? Remove yourself from wine and sober up!"

Hannah replied: "I am a distressed woman; I have drunk neither wine nor any other intoxicating drink. Do not take your servant for a worthless woman; it is because of my great distress that I have spoken so far."

Then Eli answered: "Go in peace; may the God of Israel grant you what you have asked of him." And she said: "May your servant find favor in your eyes." Then the woman went away; she ate, and was sad no more.

Early in the morning they arose, worshiped before the Lord, and returned home. The Lord remembered Hannah, and at the turn of the year she bore a son, whom she named Samuel, meaning: *I asked the Lord for him.*

Elkanah and all his household went up to offer the Lord the annual sacrifice; but Hannah did not go up, for she told her husband: "When the child is weaned I will take him to stay there forever." Elkanah said to her: "Do what seems best to you; and may the Lord carry out his purpose."

So the woman remained, and nursed her son until she weaned him. Then she brought the boy to the house of the Lord at Shiloh and to Eli. She said to him: "As sure as you live, I am the woman who stood beside you praying for this boy, and the Lord has granted my petition. I lend him to the Lord for as long as he shall live." Then Hannah sang this prayer:

"My heart exults in the Lord, my glory is raised by the Lord. There is none holy like the Lord!

"Do not speak boastfully, let no arrogance come from your mouth. The Lord is a God of knowledge, and by him actions are weighed.

"The strong men's bows are broken, while the feeble are girded with strength. Those who had plenty have hired themselves out for bread, while those who were hungry toil no more. The barren woman has seven children, while the mother of many is bereaved.

"The Lord causes death and bestows life; he lowers to the grave and brings up. The Lord makes poor and makes rich. He brings low, he also raises up. He lifts the poor out of the dust, and he raises the needy from the rubbish. He guards the steps of godly men, but the wicked perish in darkness; not by might shall man prevail.

"The foes of the Lord shall be crushed. He will thunder in heaven against them. The Lord will judge all parts of the world!"

The child Samuel ministered in the temple under Eli. And once, when Samuel lay down to sleep beside the ark, the Lord called him. He ran to Eli, saying: "Here I am." But Eli said: "I did not call you; go back and lie down." Again the Lord called him. Samuel got up and went to Eli. "Here I am," he said. But Eli answered: "I did not call you, my son; go back and lie down."

When the Lord called Samuel a third time, Eli understood that the Lord was calling. So he said to Samuel: "Go lie down. If you are called again, say: Speak, O Lord, thy servant is listening."

Then Samuel went and lay down, and when the Lord called, he answered: "Speak, thy servant is listening." And the Lord said to Samuel: "Behold, I am about to do a thing in Israel that will make the ears of everyone who hears it tingle. Eli has known for some time that his sons blasphemed God and he did not stop them, therefore the iniquity of his house shall never be expiated by sacrifice or offering."

Samuel was afraid to reveal the vision to Eli; but Eli

89

asked: "Samuel, my son, what was it that the Lord said to you? Do not hide it from me." So Samuel told him everything, and Eli said: "He is the Lord; let him do what seems good to him."

Samuel grew up, and the Lord was with him. All Israel from Dan to Beersheba knew that Samuel was a prophet of the Lord.

When Samuel grew old, he made his sons judges over Israel. But his sons did not follow in his footsteps. They took bribes and perverted justice. So the elders of Israel came to Samuel at Ramah and said to him: "You are old, and your sons are not following in your footsteps. Now appoint a king to govern us that we may be like all other nations."

It displeased Samuel to hear them asking for a king, but the Lord said to him: "Listen to the voice of the people; but give them warning and explain to them the ways of the king who shall reign over them."

Samuel then said to the people: "Here are the ways of the king who shall reign over you. He will take your sons and make them his horsemen; some will plow his ground and reap his harvest; some will make his arms and his chariots. He will take your daughters to be cooks and bakers; he will take the best of your fields and vineyards and present them to his officers. He will take a tenth of your grain and give it to his servants; he will use your servants and your cattle for his own work. And you yourselves shall be slaves to him." However, the people refused to listen to the voice of Samuel, and said: "No, we must have a king over us!"

Now, there was a man by the name of Kish, who had a son, Saul, a handsome young man. There was not a man among the people of Israel more handsome than he. Saul was a head taller than any of the people.

When Samuel saw Saul, the Lord said to him: "Here is the man of whom I told you; this man shall rule over my people." So Samuel said to Saul: "Tell your servant to go on ahead; but stop here yourself, that I may reveal to you God's message." Then Samuel poured oil on Saul's head and kissed him, saying: "The Lord has anointed you to be prince over his people Israel. You shall reign over them and save them from the power of their enemies."

God gave Saul another heart, and he prophesied along with the young prophets. On seeing him prophesy, the people who knew him said to one another: "What has happened to the son of Kish? Is Saul also among the prophets?"

When he returned home, his uncle asked him and his servant: "Where have you been?" "In search of the lost donkeys," Saul replied. "When we saw that they were not to be found, we went to Samuel the seer."

Saul's uncle asked: "Pray tell me what Samuel said to you." And Saul replied: "He told us that the donkeys had been found." But concerning the kingdom Saul said nothing.

Samuel called the people together to the Lord at Mizpah, and he said to them: "Do you see whom the Lord has chosen? There is not a man like him among all the people!" And all the people shouted: "Long live the king!"

Then Samuel said to all Israel: "I have listened to your plea and have appointed a king over you. As for me, I have led you from my youth until this day. Here I am! Testify against me in the presence of the Lord and his anointed king. Whose ox have I seized? Whose donkey have I taken? Whom have I defrauded? Whom have I oppressed? From whom have I taken a bribe? Testify against me, and I will restore it to you."

They replied: "You have not defrauded us, nor oppressed us, nor taken anything from anybody."

Then Samuel said to the people: "Stand here, that I may recount all the saving deeds performed by the Lord for you and for your fathers.

"When the Egyptians oppressed your fathers, they cried to the Lord. He sent Moses and Aaron to bring your fathers out of Egypt, and he settled them in this place. But they forgot the Lord their God, so he delivered them into the hands of Sisera and the Philistines and the king of Moab. They cried to the Lord, saying: 'We have sinned, we have worshiped the Baals; but deliver us from our enemies, and we will serve thee.' So the Lord sent Gideon and Barak and Jephthah and Samuel, and rescued you from your enemies.

Yet, when you saw the king of Ammon coming to attack you, you demanded a king, whereas the Lord your God is your King. And now, here is the king you have chosen! If you will revere the Lord and listen to his voice, well and good. But if you persist in doing wrong, both you and your king will be swept away." Then Samuel dismissed all the people, and each one returned home.

Saul had chosen three thousand men for active service. Two thousand were with him, and a thousand were with Jonathan, his son. The rest of the people he had sent home. When all Israel heard that Saul had defeated the garrison of the Philistines, the people were summoned to join Saul at Gilgal.

The Philistines gathered to fight against Israel with troops as numerous as the sands of the seashore, and the people hid in caves and holes and rocks and tombs and pits. Saul waited seven days, the time fixed by Samuel; but Samuel did not come to Gilgal, and the people were trembling and deserting. Saul then offered a burnt-offering himself, without waiting for Samuel. No sooner had he finished offering the burnt-offering than Samuel arrived.

Saul went out to greet him, but Samuel asked: "What have you done?" Saul answered: "I saw that the people were scattering, and you did not come within the appointed time. While the Philistines were massing for an attack, I forced myself to offer the burnt-offering and entreat the favor of the Lord before they pounced on us."

Samuel said to Saul: "You have done foolishly. If you had obeyed the command of the Lord your God, he would have established your kingdom over Israel forever. But now your kingdom shall not continue. The Lord has sought out a man after his own liking, and he has appointed him to be prince over his people."

The Lord said to Samuel: "I have rejected Saul from reigning over Israel; I will send you to Jesse of Bethlehem, for I have chosen me a king among his sons; you shall anoint the man whom I point out to you."

Samuel went to Bethlehem and invited Jesse and his sons to the banquet. When they came, the Lord said to Samuel: "Do not look at his appearance nor at his stature, for the Lord does not see as man sees. Man looks at the outward appearance, but the Lord looks at the heart."

Jesse made seven of his sons pass before Samuel, but Samuel said to Jesse: "The Lord has not chosen these. Are all your sons here?" Jesse answered: "There is still the youngest, and just now he is tending the flock."

"Send and fetch him," Samuel ordered; "we will not sit down to the banquet till he comes." Jesse sent for his youngest son. He was a youth with beautiful eyes and of a handsome appearance.

And the Lord said: "Arise, anoint him. This is the man!" Samuel took the horn of oil and anointed David in the midst of his brothers. From that day onward David was divinely inspired.

Now the spirit of the Lord departed from Saul, and an evil spirit troubled him. Saul's servants said to him: "An evil spirit is tormenting you. Let your servants find a skillful harpist, who will play music whenever the gloomy spirit overpowers you, and you will get well." Saul replied: "Find me a man who plays well, and bring him to me." One of them said: "I have noticed a son of Jesse, who is a skillful player and a brave man, intelligent and with a good presence."

Saul sent messengers to Jesse, requesting: "Send me your son David, who is with the sheep." When David came to Saul and presented himself, Saul loved him greatly and made him his armor-bearer. Whenever the evil spirit overpowered Saul, David took the harp and played until Saul was refreshed and his depression left him.

The Philistines again gathered their armed forces for war, so Saul and the men of Israel drew up in line of battle against them. The Philistines stood on a mountain on one side, and the Israelites stood on a mountain on the other side, with the valley between them. A champion by the name of Goliath came forward from the ranks of the Philistines. He was about ten feet tall. He wore a bronze helmet, and was armed with a coat of mail. The shaft of his spear was like a weaver's beam.

Goliath shouted to the ranks of Israel: "Choose a man from among you, and let him come down to me; if he can kill me, we will be your servants; but if I kill him, you shall be our servants. I defy the forces of Israel this day! Give me a man, and let us have a fight!" When Saul and all Israel heard the words of the Philistine, they were exceedingly dismayed and very much afraid. For forty days the Philistine came forward and took his stand, morning and evening.

David said to Saul: "I will go and fight the Philistine." Saul replied: "You are not able to fight this Philistine; you are only a youth, and he has been a warrior from his boyhood!" But David said: "I used to keep sheep for my father, and when a lion came, or a bear, and seized a lamb from the flock, I went after him and struck him down and rescued the lamb. If the lion or bear turned against me, I caught it by the chin and killed it with a blow. I have killed both lions and bears. This Philistine shall fare like them! The Lord who rescued me from the paw of the lion and the paw of the bear, will rescue me from the hand of this Philistine." "Go," Saul said to David, "and may the Lord be with you!"

Then Saul clothed David with his armor. He put a helmet of bronze on his head and clad him in a coat of mail. David girded on his sword over his armor, and he tried to walk but he could not, for he was not used to wearing armor. "I cannot move with these," he said, "I am not used to them." So he removed them, took his staff, picked five smooth stones from the brook and put them in his shepherd's bag. He then took his sling and went to meet the Philistine.

When the Philistine saw David, he said disdainfully: "Am I a dog that you come to me with sticks? Come to me, and I will give your flesh to the birds of the air and the beasts of the field."

David said to the Philistine: "You come to me with a sword and a spear and javelin, but I come to you in the name of the God of Israel whom you have defied. This day the Lord will deliver you into my hands, that all may learn that the Lord does not save by sword and spear."

When the Philistine drew near to attack David, David hurried forward to meet him. Putting his hand into his bag, David took out a stone and slung it, striking the Philistine on the forehead. The stone sank into his forehead, and he dropped on his face to the ground. David ran over to the Philistine, drew his sword from its sheath and killed him. When the Philistines saw that their champion was dead, they fled. Then the armies of Saul raised their battle-cry and pursued the Philistines as far as Gath and Ekron.

David returned from killing Goliath the Philistine, and the women came out dancing and singing: "Saul has slain his thousands, David his tens of thousands!" And Saul was very angry. "They give David tens of thousands," he said, "and I get only thousands! What more can he have but the kingdom itself?" From that day on Saul kept his eye on David.

Samuel died, and all Israel mourned for him. Shortly afterwards, the Philistines gathered their forces for war, and Saul gathered together all Israel, and they camped at Gilboa. When Saul saw the Philistine army, his heart trembled greatly. He disguised himself and went to the witch of Endor by night and said to her: "Bring me up the ghost of someone whom I shall name to you."

The woman said to him: "You know what Saul has done, how he has cast the mediums and the wizards from the land. Why, then, are you laying a trap for me? To have me put to death?" But Saul swore to her by the Lord, saying: "As the Lord lives, no punishment shall come upon you for this guilt." So the woman asked: "Whom shall I bring up for you?" And he said: "Bring me up Samuel."

When the woman saw Samuel, she gave a great shriek and said to Saul: "Why have you deceived me? You are Saul!" The king said to her: "Have no fear; what do you see?" The woman replied: "I see a divine being rising out of the earth." And he said to her: "What is he like?"

She said: "It is an old man coming up; he is wrapped in a cloak." Saul realized it was Samuel. He bowed with his face to the ground and prostrated himself.

Then Samuel said to Saul: "Why have you disturbed me by bringing me up?" Saul answered: "I am in great distress, for the Philistines are waging war against me. I have called you to ask what I should do, for the Lord has departed from me and answers me no more." And Samuel said: "Tomorrow you and your sons shall be with me; the Lord will give the army of Israel into the hand of the Philistines."

Saul fell full length upon the ground. He was exceedingly alarmed by what Samuel said. There was no strength in him, for he had eaten nothing all day and all night. When the woman went up to Saul and saw that he was panic-stricken, she said to him: "I have taken my life in my hands by doing what you ordered me to do; now let me put a bite of food before you; eat that you may have strength for your journey." But he refused, saying: "I will not eat." His attendants as well as the woman urged him, and he listened to them. He got up from the ground and sat on the couch. The woman put food before Saul and his attendants, and they ate. Then they went away that very.night.

When the Philistines made their attack on Israel, they slew Jonathan and two of his brothers. The men of Israel fled before the Philistines; and Saul, hard pressed in the battle and badly wounded by the archers, said to his armor-bearer: "Draw your sword and run me through with it. I will not be taken prisoner." But his armor-bearer refused. He was terrified! Therefore, Saul took his own sword and fell on it. When his armor-bearer saw that Saul was dead, he also fell on his sword and died with him. Thus Saul and his three sons and his armor-bearer and all his men died together on the same day.

David meanwhile had fought and defeated the Amalekites. Three days after this victory, a man with torn clothes came and threw himself on the ground before David, saying: "I have escaped from the camp of Israel. The people have fled from the field of battle, and Saul and Jonathan are dead!"

Then David tore his garments, as did all the men with him. They lamented and wept and fasted till evening for Saul, his son Jonathan and for the house of Israel, because they had fallen by the sword. Then David uttered this lamentation over Saul and his son Jonathan:

"Your glory, O Israel, is slain! How are the mighty

fallen! Tell it not in Gath, announce it not in the streets of Ashkelon, lest the daughters of the Philistines rejoice.

"Mountains of Gilboa, let there be no dew, no rain upon you! For there the shield of the mighty was defiled, the shield of Saul. Saul and Jonathan, beloved and lovely, never parted in life or in death. They were swifter than eagles, stronger than lions.

"Daughters of Israel, weep over Saul who clothed you in scarlet and jewels. How are the mighty fallen in the midst of battle!

"Jonathan lies slain upon your hills, O Israel! I am distressed for you, my brother Jonathan. You were very dear to me; your love to me was wonderful, far beyond the love of women. How are the mighty fallen!"

After this, David defeated and subdued the Philistines as well as Edom, Moab, Ammon and Amalek. He won a name for himself, reigning over all Israel and administering justice and equity to all his people. Joab was in command of his army. Now Joab and his troops ravaged the Ammonites and besieged Rabbah. David, however, remained at Jerusalem.

One afternoon David walked on the roof of the royal palace and saw a beautiful woman bathing. He sent to make inquiries about her, and someone told him that she was Bathsheba, the wife of Uriah the Hittite. He sent for her, and she came to him. Then she returned to her house.

David sent word to Joab: "Put Uriah in the front line to be struck down and killed." When Uriah's wife heard that her husband was dead, she mourned for him. When the mourning was over, David brought her to his house. She became his wife and bore him a son.

Now what David had done displeased the Lord, and the Lord sent Nathan the prophet to David. Nathan went to him and said: "There were two men in one town, a rich man and a poor man. The rich man had many sheep and cattle; the poor man had nothing but a single lamb. He fed her, and she grew up with him and his children. She ate his bread, drank from his cup, and lay on his bosom; she was like a daughter to him. Now a traveler came to visit the rich man. The rich man refused to take from his own flock or his own herd to prepare for the guest. He took the poor man's lamb and prepared it for the visitor." David's anger blazed against the man, and he said to Nathan: "As the Lord lives, the man who has done this deserves to die!"

Nathan said to David: "You are the man! Thus says the Lord God of Israel: Why have you done what is evil in my sight? You have taken Uriah's wife to be your wife, having slain him by the sword of the Ammonites. Therefore, the sword shall never depart from your house. I will stir up evil against you in your own household. You have acted in secret, but I will act before all Israel, and in the sight of the sun." Then David said to Nathan: "I have sinned against the Lord." And Nathan replied: "The Lord has taken away your sin; you shall not die; but because you have utterly spurned the Lord, the child that is born to you shall surely die."

Then Nathan went home. The Lord struck the child that Uriah's wife bore to David, and it became sick. David prayed to God for the child, fasting and lying on the ground all night. On the seventh day, the child died.

David's servants were afraid to tell him that the child was dead, for fear that he would do something desperate to himself. But when David saw that his servants were whispering to one another, he understood that the child was dead. "Is the child dead?" he asked them; and they answered: "He is dead."

Then David got up from the ground; he washed himself and changed his clothes; he went to the house of the Lord and worshiped; after that he went home, asked for food and ate. "What is the meaning of this?" his servants asked him; "you fasted and wept for the child when it was still alive, but when the child died you got up and ate!" He replied: "When the child was still alive I fasted and wept because I thought that—who knows?—the Lord might have been gracious to me and allowed the child to live. But now he is dead; why should I fast? Can I bring him back again? I am going to him, but he will never come back to me."

Then David consoled his wife Bathsheba, and she later bore him a son whom he named Solomon.

Absalom, one of David's sons, used to rise early and

stand at the entrance of the city, and whenever any man came with a case for the king to judge, Absalom would call to him and say: "From what town are you? Your claims are good and right, but no one has been deputed by the king to hear you. O that I were appointed judge in the land, so that any one with a case or plea might come to me! I would give him justice!" Whenever a man approached to bow to him, he would put out his hand and take hold of him and kiss him. In this way Absalom stole the hearts of the men of Israel.

Absalom sent secret messengers throughout all the tribes of Israel, saying: "As soon as you hear the sound of the trumpet, shout: 'Absalom is king at Hebron!'" The conspiracy was strong; the number of people who joined Absalom increased.

A messenger came to David, saying: "The hearts of the men of Israel are with Absalom." David said to all his officers in Jerusalem: "Let us flee, or else we shall never escape from Absalom!" So the king went forth, and all his household after him. David went up the ascent of the Mount of Olives, weeping as he went, barefoot, with his head covered; and all the people who were with him wept as they went.

David mustered the men who were with him, and set over them commanders of thousands and commanders of hundreds. He divided the troops into three columns, one commanded by Joab, one by Joab's brother, and one, by Ittai the Gittite. The king said to the men: "I will go with you myself." But the men replied: "You shall not. If we run away, or if half of us die, it will not matter to anyone; but you, you are equal to ten thousand of us!" So the king said to them: "I will do whatever you think best." He ordered all his commanders, saying: "Deal gently, for my sake, with young Absalom."

The troops went out into the field against Israel, and the battle was fought in the forest of Ephraim. The men of Israel were defeated there by the soldiers of David. The slaughter that day was heavy—twenty thousand fell. Absalom rode his mule and, as the mule passed below the thick branches of a great oak, his head caught fast in the oak and he was left hanging in the air, while the mule went on without its rider. A certain man saw this and told Joab, who took three spears and thrust them into the heart of Absalom while he was still alive. Then Joab blew the trumpet, and the troops withdrew from pursuing after Israel. Now, Absalom in his lifetime had set up for himself a pillar known as Absalom's Monument, because he had no son to honor the memory of his name.

David was sitting between the gates and, behold, the Cushite came and said: "Good tidings for my lord the king! The Lord has delivered you this day from all who rose against you." The king said to the Cushite: "Is it well with the young man, Absalom?" And the Cushite answered: "May the enemies of my lord the king fare like that young man." The king was deeply moved; he went up to the chamber over the gate and wept. He cried: "O my son Absalom! My son, my son Absalom! O that I had died instead of you, Absalom, my son, my son!"

Joab was told that the king wept and mourned for Absalom. The victory that day turned into mourning for all the people who heard of the king's grief for his son. They stole into the city like people ashamed of having run away in a battle, while the king kept his face covered and cried aloud: "O my son Absalom, O Absalom, my son, my son!"

Then Joab came into the house of the king and said: "Today you have disgraced all your servants who have saved your life and the lives of your sons and daughters, because you love those who hate you, and hate those who love you. You have made it clear today that commanders and troops are nothing to you. If Absalom were alive, and all of us were dead today, you would be pleased. Go out and speak to your servants. If you do not, you will not have a man left on your side tonight; and that will be worse for you than all the evil that has befallen you from your youth until now." So the king got up and sat in the gateway, and all the people came before him.

David sang this song when the Lord had saved him from all his enemies:

"The Lord is my rock, my fortress, my deliverer, in

whom I seek refuge. I call to him, and I am rescued from my foes.

"Waves of death encompassed me, floods of ruin terrified me, deadly nets entangled me. I called the Lord in my plight, and my cry came to his ears.

"He reached from on high, he took me, he drew me out of many waters. He delivered me from my enemies, who were too mighty for me. The Lord rewarded me according to my uprightness, he requited me according to the cleanness of my hands. I was blameless in his sight, and I kept clear of guilt.

"To the kind thou art kind, and true to the true. Thou dost help the humble, and bringest down the haughty. Thou art my lamp, O Lord, lightening my darkness. By thy help I can crush a troop, by God's help I can leap a wall. For this I will extol thee, O Lord, among the nations, and sing praises to thy name."

These are the last words of David, the sweet psalmist of Israel.

"By me the spirit of the Lord speaks; his word is upon my tongue. When a man rules men justly, he dawns on them like the morning light, like the sun shining forth upon a cloudless morning; he is like rain upon the tender grass. But godless men are like thorns that are thrown away; they are utterly consumed with fire."

Once, when David was in the cave of Adullam while the garrison of the Philistines was in Bethlehem, David said longingly: "O that someone would give me a drink of water from the well of Bethlehem." Then three courageous men broke through the camp of the Philistines and drew water out of the well of Bethlehem. But David refused to drink it, saying: "Far be it from me, O Lord, that I should do this. Shall I drink the blood of the men who went at the risk of their lives?"

Kings מְלָכִים

The two books of Kings, which tell the history of the king-doms of Judah and Israel, are treated as one book in the Hebrew Bible. They cover a period of about four hundred years, extending from the last days of David to the destruction of the first Temple. It is the period of Israel's glory, division, decline, disintegration, and fall. The prophets who appeared in the course of history contained in the books of Kings were statesmen as well as ethical teachers.

According to a statement in the Talmud, the books of Kings were written by the prophet Jeremiah, author of the books of Jeremiah and Lamentations. Aiming to set forth the lessons which the history of his people affords, the writer of Kings traces the dire results of disobedience, and the happy conse-quences of loyalty to the precepts of the Torah. He charac-terizes the kings of Judah and Israel according to their faith-fulness or faithlessness to the divine teachings.

Judah survived by nearly one hundred and fifty years the rival kingdom of Israel, which was the larger and more power-ful of the two. The accumulation of large estates in the hands of a few holders, oppression of the poor, perversion of justice, luxury and over-indulgence undermined the kingdom of Israel and hastened its end. In the story of Naboth's vineyard we have the beginnings of the transition from small peasant ownership to that of large estates in the kingdom of Israel, from the privileges of freemen to the ills of a serfdom under large landowners.

When King David was well advanced in years, and his time to die drew near, he charged Solomon his son, saying: "I am about to go the way of all the earth. Be strong and be a man. Keep the commandments of the Lord, so that you may succeed in whatever you do." David reigned over Israel for forty years. When he died, he was buried in the city of David. Solomon sat upon the throne of his father, and his kingdom was firmly established.

One night, the Lord appeared to Solomon in a dream,

102

and said: "Ask, what shall I give you?" Solomon answered: "Lord my God, I am a mere child; I do not know how to manage. O grant me an understanding heart to govern thy people, that I may discern between good and evil."

God said to him: "Because you have asked neither long life, nor wealth nor the death of your enemies, I shall give you a wise and understanding heart, so that none shall ever be like you. I am giving you, moreover, what you have not asked—both wealth and honor—so that no king shall ever be your equal. Walk in my ways and keep my commandments and I will also give you a long life."

Shortly afterwards, two women came to the king and argued before him. One woman said: "My lord, this woman and I live in the same house. I gave birth to a child, and three days later she bore one; we were together and there was no one else in the house. During the night her child died, so she got up and took mine while I was asleep and put her dead child beside me. When I rose in the morning to nurse my child, behold it was dead; but as I looked at it closely I saw that it was not mine." But the other woman retorted: "No, the living child is mine, the dead one is yours!"

Then the king said: "Fetch me a sword." And the king ordered: "Divide the living child in two and give half to the one and half to the other.".At this, the mother of the living child cried out: "My lord, give her the child, do not kill it!" "No!" exclaimed the second woman; "it shall be neither mine nor yours! Divide it!" "Give the child to the first woman; *she* is its mother," the king commanded.

All Israel heard of this decision, and stood in awe of the king, for they saw that the wisdom of God was in him.

Solomon's wisdom surpassed the wisdom of all the people of the east. His fame reached all the nations round about. He composed three thousand proverbs, and his songs numbered one thousand and five. He could talk about all kinds of plants, animals, birds, reptiles and fish. Men came from every nation to hear his wisdom.

Solomon sent word to Hiram, king of Tyre, saying: "You know that my father David could not build a temple for the Lord because of the hostile forces that surrounded him.

But now the Lord has given me peace, and I propose to build a temple. Now order, I pray you, that cedars of Lebanon be felled for me. My servants will join your servants, and I will pay any wage you fix for your servants. There is no one among us who knows how to cut timber like the Sidonians."

Hiram supplied Solomon with all the timber that he needed, while Solomon sent him wheat and oil. Solomon raised a labor force from all Israel, a contingent of thirty thousand men, which he sent to Lebanon in relays of ten thousand a month; one month they were at Lebanon and two months they stayed at home. Solomon also employed seventy thousand carriers, eighty thousand stonemasons and three thousand three hundred foremen who supervised the work. They quarried huge blocks of stone for the foundation of the temple.

In the four hundred and eightieth year after the people of Israel had gone out of Egypt, in the fourth year of Solomon's reign, he began to build the temple of the Lord, and in the eleventh year of his reign it was completed. Solomon also built a palace for himself. It took thirteen years to build it.

When the temple was completed, all the men of Israel gathered before Solomon. The priests brought the ark of the Lord and all the holy vessels. They placed the ark inside the inner sanctuary, the most holy place, underneath the wings of the cherubim. There was nothing in the ark except the two stone tablets which Moses had put there.

Then the king spread forth his hands toward heaven and said: "Lord God of Israel, all the heavens cannot contain thee, how much less this house which I have built! May thy eyes ever be opened toward this house; hearken to the supplication of thy people when they turn in prayer to this place. As for the stranger who does not belong to Israel, when he prays in this house, accept thou his prayer, so that all the nations of the world may know thy name and revere thee."

So Solomon and all Israel held the feast for seven days. On the eighth day he sent the people away; they went home rejoicing, glad with the goodness that the Lord had shown to David, his servant, and to Israel his people.

When the queen of Sheba heard about the fame of Solomon, she came to test him with puzzling questions. She arrived in Jerusalem with a great retinue and with camels bearing spices and gold and precious stones. Solomon answered all her questions. She said to him: "Your wisdom and wealth surpass all that I had heard in my own land. Happy are they who continually stand before you and hear your wisdom!" She gave him a hundred and twenty talents of gold and a huge quantity of spices and precious stones. King Solomon, too, gave the queen of Sheba whatever she desired. Then she went back to her own land.

King Solomon excelled all kings on earth in wealth and wisdom. Men from all parts of the world came to hear his wisdom; everyone brought presents of silver and gold, garments, spices, horses and mules.

King Solomon had seven hundred wives and three hundred concubines. They came from nations against whom the Lord had warned the people of Israel: "You shall not enter into marriage with them, for they will turn your heart after their gods." His wives seduced him to follow their foreign gods. He put up shrines for the idols of the Phoenicians, the Ammonites and the Moabites. He did the same for all his foreign wives, burning incense and offering sacrifice to their gods.

The Lord was angry with Solomon for allowing himself to be seduced, so he said to him: "I will tear the kingdom from you and give it to your servant. Yet for the sake of David your father I will not do it in your days. I will tear it out of the hands of your son. Still, I will not tear away all the kingdom. I will let your son have one tribe, for the sake of David, my servant, and for the sake of Jerusalem which I have chosen."

The Lord raised up an adversary against Solomon, and Jeroboam turned traitor against the king. Jeroboam was a capable man, and Solomon had put him in charge of the entire labor force of the house of Joseph. One day as Jeroboam was leaving Jerusalem, the prophet Ahijah met him and took him aside. The two of them were alone in the open country. Ahijah took the new garment which he was wearing and tore it into twelve pieces, saying to Jeroboam: "Take ten for yourself, for the Lord is about to tear the kingdom of Solomon apart and give you ten tribes." Solomon, therefore, sought to kill Jeroboam, so he fled to Egypt, and remained there till the death of Solomon.

Solomon reigned in Jerusalem over all Israel for forty years. He slept with his fathers and was buried in the city of David. Rehoboam, who succeeded him, went to Shechem where he was to be made king by all Israel. The people said to Rehoboam: "Your father made our yoke heavy; lighten the heavy yoke he imposed upon us and we will serve you." "Go now and come back in three days," he replied.

When the people went away, King Rehoboam consulted the old councillors who had served his father Solomon. And they said to him: "If you will speak kindly to them, they will be your servants forever." But he rejected their advice and took the counsel of the young men, who said: "Tell them: My little finger is thicker than my father's loins. My father lashed you with whips, but I will lash you with scorpions."

On the third day, when Jeroboam and all the people came to Rehoboam, he answered them harshly, speaking to them according to the counsel of the young men. When the people of Israel saw that the king refused to heed them, they exclaimed: "We have no part in David, no share in the son of Jesse. To your tents, O Israel! Look after your own house, David!"

On reaching Jerusalem, Rehoboam assembled all the men of Judah and Benjamin, a hundred and eighty thousand picked troops, to fight against Israel and recover the kingdom. But the word of God came to Shemaiah, the prophet: "Say to Rehoboam: 'You shall not fight against your kinsmen. Return home, every man of you! This thing has come about directly from me.'" So they returned home, as the Lord had told them.

Then Jeroboam thought to himself: "If these people go up to offer sacrifices at the temple in Jerusalem, their heart

106

will again turn toward Rehoboam." So he made two golden calves and said to the people: "You need no longer go up to Jerusalem; here are your gods, O Israel, the gods that brought you out of the land of Egypt!" He placed one of them at Bethel, and the other at Dan. He chose the priests for the shrines from among all the people.

Jeroboam reigned for twenty-two years, and was succeeded by Nadab his son. There was constant war between Rehoboam and Jeroboam. Rehoboam was succeeded by his son Abijam, who reigned for three years in Jerusalem. When Abijam died, Asa his son succeeded him as king.

Asa reigned forty-two years in Jerusalem, and did what was right in the eyes of the Lord. He expelled the sodomites from the land and removed all the idols that his fathers had made. He deposed his mother, Maakah, from the position of queen-mother, because she had made an obscene image of Asherah; he demolished this image and burned it in the Kidron valley. War raged between Asa and Baasha, king of Israel, all their days.

Nadab the son of Jeroboam began his two-year reign over Israel in the second year of Asa king of Judah. Baasha conspired against him, killed him, and reigned in his stead. No sooner did he ascend the throne than he killed all the household of Jeroboam. Baasha reigned twenty-four years, and was succeeded by his son Elah who reigned two years. Zimri, one of his officers, conspired against Elah and struck him down. It was in the twenty-seventh year of Asa king of Judah that Zimri reigned seven days in Tirzah. When it became known that Zimri had conspired and killed the king, the entire Israelite camp at once elected Omri, the commander of the army, to be king. Omri marched with all Israel and besieged Tirzah. When Zimri saw that the town was captured, he set the palace on fire and perished in its flames.

Omri began to reign over Israel in the thirty-first year of Asa king of Judah. Omri died and was buried in Samaria. He was succeeded by his son Ahab. It was in the thirty-eighth year of Asa, king of Judah, that Ahab, the son of Omri, began his twenty-two-year reign over Israel. Ahab did evil in the sight of the Lord, more so than all the kings of Israel before him.

Elijah, the Tishbite, said to Ahab: "As the Lord God of Israel lives, there shall be neither dew nor rain these years except by my word." Now the famine was severe in Samaria, and Ahab summoned Obadiah the overseer of the palace. Ahab said to Obadiah: "Go through the land in search of springs and brooks; perhaps we may find grass and save the lives of the horses and mules." So they divided the country between them; Ahab went in one direction and Obadiah went in another.

As Obadiah went his way, he was met by Elijah who said to him: "Go! Tell your master that Elijah is here." So Obadiah went to Ahab with the news, and Ahab went to meet Elijah. When Ahab saw Elijah, he exclaimed: "Is that you, troubler of Israel?" Elijah answered: "I have not troubled Israel, but you and your family, by forsaking the commands of the Lord and following the Baals. Send now and gather all Israel at Mount Carmel, together with the four hundred and fifty prophets of Baal, who are maintained by Jezebel."

So Ahab sent to all Israel and gathered the prophets at Mount Carmel. Elijah drew near to all the people and said: "How long will you jump from one belief to another? If the Lord is God, follow him; if Baal, then follow him." The people gave no answer. Then Elijah said to them: "I alone am left as a prophet of the Lord, while Baal has four hundred and fifty prophets. Let us have two bullocks. They can choose one bullock for themselves and chop it up, laying the pieces on the wood but putting no fire underneath it. I will prepare the other bullock and lay it on the wood, putting no fire under it. You call to your god, and I will call to the Lord; and the God who answers by fire—he is the real God."

"Well spoken," said the people. So the prophets of Baal took their bullock, prepared it, and called to Baal from morning until noon, crying: "O Baal, answer us!" But not a sound came, there was no answer as they danced about the altar they had made. When it came to midday, Elijah mocked them, saying: "Cry aloud, for he is a god! Perhaps he is asleep and must be wakened!" So they shouted, cutting themselves with knives and lances, as was their custom, until the blood gushed from their bodies. And as midday passed, they raved on until evening; but there was no sound; no one answered, no one heeded.

Then Elijah said to the people: "Come close to me." All the people came close to him, and he repaired the altar of the Lord which had been broken down. He then arranged the wood and laid the pieces of his bullock on the wood. Elijah the prophet came forward and said: "O Lord, God of Abraham and Isaac and Israel, answer me, answer me, that this people may know that thou art God, and that thou hast made their hearts turn to thee again." Then the fire of the Lord fell and consumed the offering, the wood, the stones, and the dust, and licked up the water that was in the trench. On seeing this, all the people fell on their faces, crying: "The Lord is God, the Lord is God!" They seized the prophets and killed them. In a very short time the sky grew black with clouds and wind, and there was a heavy rain.

When Ahab told Jezebel all that Elijah had done, she sent this message to Elijah: "May the gods punish me again and again, if by this time tomorrow I do not make your life as the life of any one of the slain prophets."

Elijah was afraid and ran for his life. When he reached Beersheba, he left his servant there and went into the desert, where he sat down under a broom bush, praying for death. "I have had enough of it," he cried; "O Lord, take away my life now." Then he lay down under the bush and fell asleep; and behold, an angel touched him, saying: "Arise and eat." He opened his eyes, and there was a cake baked on hot stones and a jar of water. He ate and drank, and lay down again. The angel of the Lord came a second time and touched him, saying: "Arise and eat, else the journey will be too much for you." So he rose, ate and drank, and strengthened by the food he went for forty days and forty nights to Horeb, the mountain of God, where he took shelter in a cave. And behold, the Lord passed by. A strong, fierce wind tore the mountain, crashing the rocks, but the Lord was not in the wind. After the wind came an earthquake, but the Lord was not in the earthquake; after the earthquake a fire, but the Lord was not in the fire; after the fire a still small voice. As soon as Elijah heard that, he wrapped his face in his mantle and went out and stood at the entrance of the cave. Then a voice came to him, saying: "What are you doing here, Elijah?" He replied: "I have been very zealous for the Lord. The people of Israel have forsaken thy covenant, thrown down thy altars, and killed thy prophets; I am the only one left, and they are after me, to take my life."

"Go back," the Lord said, "take the desert road of Damascus; when you arrive, you shall anoint Hazael to be king over Syria; you shall anoint Jehu to be king over Israel; and you shall anoint Elisha to succeed you as prophet. Jehu shall slay him who escapes the sword of Hazael, and Elisha shall slay him who escapes the sword of Jehu. But I will spare seven thousand men in Israel—all who have not knelt to Baal or kissed him."

When Elijah had departed from there, he came upon Elisha who was plowing behind twelve yoke of oxen. Elijah passed by and cast his mantle upon Elisha, who left the oxen and ran after Elijah and said: "Let me kiss my father and my mother, and then I will follow you." Elijah replied: "Go back; what have I done to you?" He went back, slaughtered a pair of oxen, used their harness to boil the meat, and gave to the people to eat. Then he started to follow Elijah, acting as his attendant.

Now Naboth of Jezreel had a vineyard close to the palace of Ahab, king of Samaria. Ahab said to Naboth: "Give me your vineyard that I may have it for a vegetable garden, since it is near my house. I will give you a better vineyard for it or I will give you its value in money."

But Naboth said to Ahab: "The Lord forbid that I should part with the inheritance of my fathers." Ahab went home angry and sullen. He lay down on his bed, turned his face to the wall and refused to eat.

His wife, Jezebel, came and asked him: "Why are you so depressed that you cannot eat?" He said to her: "I asked Naboth of Jezreel to sell me his vineyard, or let me give him another vineyard for it, and he refused." Then Jezebel

110

said to him: "Are you not in command of Israel's kingdom? Get up, take some food and cheer up. I will get you the vineyard of Naboth the Jezreelite."

So she wrote letters in Ahab's name and sealed them with his seal. She sent the letters to the elders and the nobles who lived with Naboth in his city. She had written in the letters: "Proclaim a fast, choose two men to bring charges against Naboth, saying that he has cursed God and the king. Then take him out, and stone him to death."

The fellow citizens of Naboth, the elders and nobles who dwelt in his city did as Jezebel had requested. They proclaimed a fast, and two evil men came and brought charges against Naboth in the presence of the people, saying: "Naboth cursed God and the king." So they took him outside the city, and stoned him to death. They sent word to Jezebel: "Naboth has been stoned and is dead."

As soon as Jezebel heard that Naboth had been stoned to death, she said to Ahab: "Arise, take possession of Naboth's vineyard for he is no longer alive." Ahab then went to take possession of Naboth's vineyard.

But the word of the Lord came to Elijah, saying: "Arise, go down to meet Ahab, king of Israel, who is in the vineyard of Naboth. Say to him: You have murdered and now you inherit? Thus says the Lord: Where dogs licked up the blood of Naboth, there shall dogs lick up your blood also."

Ahab said to Elijah: "Have you found me, O enemy of mine?" Elijah answered: "I have found you because you have given yourself over to what is evil in the sight of the Lord.

"Behold, I will bring evil upon you; I will utterly sweep you away and I will make your house like the house of Jeroboam, because you have made Israel to sin." And of Jezebel the Lord said: "The dogs shall eat Jezebel within the bounds of Jezreel."

When Ahab heard these words, he tore his garments and put on sackcloth. He fasted and went about quietly. Then the word of the Lord came to Elijah, saying: "Have you seen how Ahab has humbled himself before me? Because he has humbled himself before me, I will not bring the evil in his day. I will bring evil on his house during the reign of his son."

Now for three years there had been no war between Syria and Israel. But in the third year, Jehoshaphat the king of Judah agreed to join the king of Israel in attacking Ramoth-gilead. The king of Israel disguised himself before he entered the battle. The king of Syria had ordered his thirty-two chariot captains to fight with no one except the king of Israel. When the captains of the chariots saw Jehoshaphat in royal robes, they thought this must be the king of Israel and they surrounded him. Finding that he was not the king of Israel, they turned back from pursuing him. Then a certain man drew his bow and struck Ahab, the king of Israel, between the joints of his armor.

"Turn around," cried the king to the driver of his chariot, "get me out of the battle, for I am wounded." However, the king remained propped up in his chariot facing the Syrians until evening and the blood from his wound flowed into the bottom of the chariot. At about sunset a cry passed through the army: "Back to your towns, back to your country, every man of you, for the king is dead!"

They buried Ahab in Samaria. They washed the chariot at the pool and dogs licked up his blood. His son Ahaziah succeeded him.

In the fourth year of Ahab king of Israel, Jehoshaphat the son of Asa had begun to reign over Judah. He was then thirty-five years of age. He reigned in Jerusalem for twenty-five years, following the ways of his father, Asa, and doing what was right in the eyes of the Lord. He also made peace with the king of Israel. When he died, he was buried with his fathers in the city of David. Jehoram his son succeeded him.

Ahaziah fell through the lattice of his upper chamber in Samaria and lay ill, so he sent messengers to ask the god of Ekron whether he would recover from his illness. The messengers soon returned, and Ahaziah asked why they had come back. They told him that a man had come to meet them and said: "Go back to the king who sent you and tell him this from the Lord: Is it because there is no

God in Israel that you send to consult the god of Ekron? For this you shall never leave your bed; you shall surely die." The king asked: "What kind of a man was he who told you this?" They answered: "He wore a garment of haircloth, with a belt of leather round his waist."

"It is Elijah the Tishbite," the king said, and he sent a captain with fifty men to seize him. Elijah was sitting on the top of a hill, when the captain went up to him and said: "O man of God, the king orders you to come down." Elijah answered: "If I am a man of God, let fire come down from heaven and destroy you and your fifty men." Fire then came down from heaven and destroyed the captain and his fifty men.

Again the king sent another captain with fifty men. He went up to Elijah and said: "O man of God, this is the king's order: Come down at once." But Elijah answered: "If I am a man of God, let fire come down from heaven and consume you and your fifty men." Again the fire of God came down from heaven and consumed him also and his fifty men.

The king sent a third captain with fifty men. The third captain went up and fell on his knees before Elijah, entreating him: "O man of God, pray spare my life and the lives of these fifty men, your servants." Then the angel of the Lord said to Elijah: "Go down with him; do not be afraid of him." He rose and went with him to the king, and said to him: "Thus says the Lord: Because you have sent messengers to consult the god of Ekron, you shall never leave your bed, but you shall surely die." So Ahaziah died and, since he had no son, Jehoram his brother succeeded him.

Now when the Lord was about to take Elijah up to heaven by a whirlwind, Elijah and Elisha went to Bethel and then to Jericho. When they had crossed the Jordan, Elijah said to Elisha: "Before I am taken from you, ask what I shall do for you." Elisha answered: "Let me have a double share of your spirit." Elijah answered: "You have asked a hard thing; if you see me when I am being taken from you, it shall be yours, but not if you fail to see me." Suddenly, as they walked and talked, a fiery chariot with fiery horses drove between them, and Elijah went up by a whirlwind into heaven.

When Elisha saw this, he cried: "My father, my father, the chariot and horsemen of Israel!" And he saw him no more. Then he took up the mantle of Elijah that had fallen from him and went back and stood on the bank of the Jordan. He struck the water, crying: "Where is the Lord God of Elijah?" The water parted right and left, and Elisha crossed over.

When the disciples of the prophets in Jericho saw him at a distance, they said: "The spirit of Elijah rests on Elisha." They came forward and bowed to the ground, saying: "We have fifty strong men; pray let them go in search of your master; perhaps he is upon some mountain or in some valley." Elisha refused their request at first, but when they persisted, he yielded. So fifty men searched for three days but failed to find Elijah. When they returned, Elisha said: "Did I not tell you not to go?"

The wife of one of the disciples of the prophets appealed to Elisha, saying: "My husband is dead, and now a creditor has come to seize my two sons as his slaves." "What shall I do for you?" said Elisha. "Tell me what you have in your house." She replied: "I have nothing in the house except a jar of oil." Then he said: "Go borrow vessels from all your neighbors; shut yourself in the house, you and your sons; pour the oil into all the vessels; and whenever one is full set it aside."

The woman shut herself and her sons in the house. They brought the vessels while she poured the oil. When the vessels were full, she said to her son: "Bring me another vessel," and he said: "There is not another vessel." Then the oil stopped flowing. She told it to the man of God, who said: "Go sell the oil and pay your debts. You and your sons can live on what is left."

One day Elisha went to Shunem. A rich woman, who lived there, persuaded him to partake of her food. After this, he had a meal at her house whenever he went to Shunem. The woman said to her husband: "This is a holy man of God, who continually passes our way. Let us build a small roof-chamber for him, with a bed and a table,

114

a seat and a lamp, so that whenever he comes to us he can go in there."

One day when he came and stayed in the chamber, he said to his servant Gehazi: "Tell the Shunammite: You have taken all this trouble for us; what can we do for you? Would you have a word spoken in your behalf to the king or to the commander of the army?" She answered: "I live safely among my own people." So he asked Gehazi what should be done for her, and Gehazi replied: "She has no son, and her husband is old." Elisha said: "Call her." And as she stood in the doorway, he said: "At this time next year you will be embracing a son." The following year she bore a son, as Elisha had told her.

When the boy grew up, he went out one day to his father among the reapers. He called to his father: "My head, my head!" The father told a servant to carry the boy to his mother. He was taken to his mother, and died sitting on her lap. She carried the boy to the bed of the man of God, laid him on it and closed the door.

She went to Elisha at Mount Carmel. When the man of God saw her coming, he said to Gehazi: "Look, there is the Shunammite; run at once to ask her if she is well and if the child is well." When she came to the man of God, she grasped his feet. Gehazi would have pushed her away, but the man of God said: "Let her alone; she is in bitter distress." Then she said: "Did I ask my lord for a son? As the Lord lives, I will not leave you." So he rose and went with her.

Gehazi went ahead and laid Elisha's staff upon the face of the child, but there was no sound or sign of life. When Elisha went into the house, he saw the child lying dead on his bed. He shut the door and prayed to the Lord. Then he lay down upon the child, put his mouth to the child's mouth, his eyes upon the child's eyes, and his hands upon the child's hands, until the flesh of the child became warm. Then he got up, walked to and fro, and went again and stretched himself over the child. The child sneezed seven times and opened his eyes. Elisha told Gehazi to call the Shunammite, and he said to her: "Take up your son." She fell at his feet; then she took up her son and went out.

Once Elisha went to Gilgal when there was a famine in the land. As the disciples of the prophets were sitting before him, he told his servant to put a large pot on the fire and boil some pottage for the disciples. One of them went out into the field to gather herbs; he cut them up and put them in the pot of pottage, not knowing what they were. The pottage was then poured out for the men to eat. But as they were eating they cried out: "Man of God, there is death in the pot!" They could not eat the pottage. He said: "Bring some flour." He threw it into the pot and said: "Pour out for the men that they may eat." And now there was nothing wrong with the pottage.

Now Naaman, commander of the Syrian army, was highly regarded by the king; he was a valiant man, but he was afflicted with leprosy. The Syrians had carried off from the land of Israel a little girl who waited on Naaman's wife. She said to her mistress: "The prophet who lives at Samaria would cure my lord of his leprosy." Whereupon the king of Syria sent a letter to the king of Israel, which read: "I am sending you my servant Naaman, that you may cure him of his leprosy." When the king of Israel read the letter, he rent his garments and cried out: "Am I God to bring about life and death, that he wants me to cure a man of his leprosy? He is seeking a pretext to start a quarrel with me."

When Elisha heard of the king's despair, he sent word to him: "Let the man come to me, and he shall find there is a prophet in Israel." So Naaman drove his chariot and horses to Elisha's house. Elisha sent out word to him: "Go wash seven times in the Jordan; and your body shall become clean again."

Naaman was enraged and said: "Surely, the rivers of Damascus are better than all the waters in Israel! Could I not wash in them and be clean?" So he drove away in anger. But his servants went up to him and said: "If the prophet had commanded you to do something difficult, would you not have done it? How much rather, then, when he tells you only to wash and be clean?" So Naaman went down and dipped seven times in the Jordan; and his body became clean once more, like the body of a child.

Then he returned to the man of God and said: "Now I know there is no God in all the earth except in Israel! Pray accept a present from your humble servant." But Elisha said: "As the Lord lives, I will not take a single thing." When Naaman had gone a short distance, Gehazi followed him and said: "My master has sent me to say that two young disciples of the prophets have just come to him from the hill country of Ephraim. Give them a talent of silver and two festal garments." "Accept two talents," Naaman said. He tied up the silver and the two festal garments and handed them to Gehazi's two servants.

"Where have you been, Gehazi?" Elisha asked. "Your servant has not been anywhere," he answered. But Elisha said to him: "Was it a time to accept money and garments? Therefore the leprosy of Naaman shall cleave to you forever." He left Elisha's presence stricken with leprosy, white as snow.

Now the disciples of the prophets said to Elisha: "This dwelling of ours is too small for us. Let us go to the Jordan and get each of us a log to build a dwelling-place for ourselves there." Elisha told them to go, and agreed to go along. On reaching the Jordan, they cut down trees. But as one was felling a tree, the head of the axe fell into the water. "Alas, my master," cried the man, "it was borrowed." Then the man of God said: "Where did it fall?" He showed him the place, whereupon Elisha cut off a stick, threw it there, and made the iron float. "Take it," he said. The man put out his hand and took it.

Now Elisha said to the woman whose son he had restored to life: "Move away with your household and stay wherever you can, for the Lord is bringing on the land a famine that will last seven years." So she left and stayed in the land of the Philistines for seven years. When she returned, she appealed to the king for her house and land. Gehazi said to the king: "My lord, here is the woman whose son Elisha restored to life!" The king appointed an official to see that she got back all her property.

Elisha sent a young disciple of the prophets to anoint Jehu king over Israel. The young man poured oil on Jehu's head, saying: "Thus says the Lord God of Israel: I anoint

you king over the people of Israel. You shall strike down
the house of your master Ahab, that I may avenge the
blood of my prophets and my servants. The whole house of
Ahab shall perish, like the house of Jeroboam and the
house of Baasha. Dogs shall eat Jezebel in Jezreel, and
none shall bury her."

Jehu conspired against Jehoram, who had come to
Jezreel to be cured of the wounds he had received in fighting against the king of Syria. He drove off in a chariot to
Jezreel where Jehoram was lying. In the meantime, Ahaziah
king of Judah had come down to visit the ailing king. A
sentinel posted on the tower caught sight of the company
of Jehu. A man on horseback was sent to ask: "Is all well?"
And Jehu said: "Fall in behind me!" The sentinel reported: "The man is not coming back, and the driving is
like the driving of Jehu; he drives like a madman."

Then Jehoram and Ahaziah set out, each in his chariot,
and went to meet Jehu in the field of Naboth the
Jezreelite.

Jehoram asked: "Is it peace, Jehu?" He answered: "What
peace can there be so long as your mother Jezebel goes on
with all her seductions and sorceries?" Jehoram turned
around and fled, calling to Ahaziah: "Treachery, Ahaziah!"
Jehu drew his bow and struck Jehoram. The arrow pierced
his heart, and he sank in his chariot. "Fling him out on the
field of Naboth the Jezreelite!" Jehu commanded.

When Ahaziah king of Judah saw this, he fled. He was
pursued by Jehu, who shouted: "Kill him too! Kill him in
the chariot!" They struck him, but he got away to Megiddo,
where he died. His servants carried him in a chariot to
Jerusalem, and buried him in the city of David.

When Jezebel heard that Jehu had come to Jezreel, she
painted her eyes, adorned her head and looked out of the
window. As Jehu entered the gateway, she cried: "How
are you, murderer of your master?" Jehu looked up to the
window. "Who is on my side?" he inquired. Then he said:
"Throw her down!" They threw Jezebel down and
trampled on her.

When Athaliah saw that her son, Ahaziah, was dead, she
destroyed the entire royal family except Joash, the son of

Ahaziah, who was hidden for six years in the house of the Lord while Athaliah reigned over the land. But in the seventh year, Jehoiada, the priest, armed the guards with the spears and shields belonging to King David, which had been kept in the temple. He brought out Joash the king's son, put the crown upon his head, proclaimed him king and anointed him, while they were clapping their hands and shouting: "Long live the king!"

When Athaliah heard the noise of the guard, she went into the house of the Lord and saw the king standing on the platform with the captains and trumpeters beside him, while all the people were rejoicing and blowing trumpets. She rent her garments and cried: "Treason! Treason!" But Jehoiada, the priest, ordered the captains: "Bring her out, and slay anyone who follows her. Let her not be slain in the house of the Lord." So they seized her, and she was put to death.

Joash was seven years old when he began to reign; he reigned forty years in Jerusalem. When his servants made a conspiracy and slew him, Amaziah his son reigned in his stead.

Jehoahaz the son of Jehu reigned over Israel in Samaria for seventeen years. He had an army of no more than fifty horsemen, ten chariots and ten thousand footmen, for the king of Syria had destroyed the rest. When he died, Joash his son reigned in his stead.

Joash reigned over Israel in Samaria for sixteen years. He recovered from the king of Syria the towns which had been captured from his father Jehoahaz. When Amaziah king of Judah challenged him to an encounter, Joash sent this answer to the king of Judah: "You are proud of having defeated Edom. Stay at home with your pride. Why should you provoke trouble and bring ruin to yourself and to Judah?" But Amaziah would not listen to him, so they had an encounter and Judah was overthrown by Israel. Joash captured Amaziah and took him to Jerusalem, where he seized the gold and silver and all the vessels that were found in the temple, as well as the treasures of the royal palace. When Joash died, Jeroboam his son succeeded him.

Amaziah king of Judah lived fifteen years after the death

of Joash king of Israel. A conspiracy was formed against him in Jerusalem, so he fled to Lachish; but men were sent after him, and they killed him. Then the people of Judah took his sixteen-year-old son, Azariah, and made him king. Azariah rebuilt Elath and restored it to Judah. He reigned forty-two years, but he became a leper. His son Jotham managed the royal household and ruled the nation. When Azariah died, Jotham succeeded him.

Zechariah the son of Jeroboam reigned over Israel in Samaria for six months. Shallum conspired against him, killed him, and reigned in his stead for one month. He in turn was struck down by Menahem, who reigned in his stead for ten years. During Menahem's reign, the Assyrian king, Pul, invaded the country. They had to give him a thousand talents of silver before he turned back and left the country. Pekah conspired against Menahem, killed him, and succeeded him as king.

Pekah reigned over Israel for twenty years. In his days, Tiglath-pileser king of Assyria captured Gilead and Galilee, all the land of Naphtali, and carried off the people into exile. Then Hoshea made a conspiracy against Pekah, killed him, and reigned in his stead.

Jotham was twenty-five years old when he began to reign over Judah. When he died, his son Ahaz reigned sixteen years in Jerusalem. He sent messengers to Tiglath-pileser king of Assyria, saying: "I am your servant and your son; come and rescue me from the king of Syria and from the king of Israel, who are attacking me." He sent all the silver and gold, that was in the house of the Lord and in the treasures of the royal palace, as tribute to the king of Assyria. The king of Assyria then marched against Damascus, captured it, and carried off its inhabitants as prisoners.

Hoshea reigned over Israel in Samaria for nine years. He submitted to Shalmaneser king of Assyria who marched against him, and offered tribute. But when the king of Assyria discovered that Hoshea was conspiring against him, he besieged Samaria for three years, and carried Israel off to Assyria; and people from Babylon were placed in the cities of Samaria.

Hezekiah the son of Ahaz reigned twenty-nine years in Jerusalem. He did what was right in the eyes of the Lord. There was none like him among the kings of Judah after him, nor among those who were before him. The Lord was with him; he succeeded wherever he went. He defeated the Philistines as far as Gaza and its surrounding territory.

Sennacherib, king of Assyria, marched against all the fortified towns of Judah and captured them. Then Isaiah sent Hezekiah this message from the Lord God of Israel: "The king of Assyria shall not come to the city of Jerusalem or shoot an arrow there." That night the angel of the Lord slew a hundred and eighty-five thousand in the camp of the Assyrians. Sennacherib departed and went home to Nineveh. When Hezekiah died, Manasseh his son reigned in his stead.

Manasseh was twelve years old when he began to reign, and he reigned fifty-five years in Jerusalem. He did evil in the sight of the Lord, for he rebuilt the shrines which his father Hezekiah had destroyed, and erected altars for Baal. He burned his son as an offering, and practised augury and sorcery. He filled Jerusalem with murders from end to end. When he died, his son Amon reigned two years in Jerusalem. Amon was killed in his house by his servants, who conspired against him. The people then made his son Josiah their king.

Josiah, who was eight years old when he became king, reigned thirty-one years in Jerusalem. In the eighteenth year of King Josiah, Hilkiah the high priest found the book of the Torah in the house of the Lord and handed it to Shaphan, who read it to the king. When the king heard the words of the book of the Torah, he rent his garments and commanded that inquiry be made of the Lord concerning the words of this book.

So Hilkiah and Shaphan went to Huldah the prophetess and talked with her. She said: "Thus says the Lord God of Israel: I will bring evil upon this place and upon its inhabitants, all the words of the book which the king of Judah has read, because they have forsaken me." Then the king went to the temple of the Lord, accompanied by all the men of Judah and all the inhabitants of Jerusalem, young and old. He read aloud to them all the words of the book of the covenant which had been found in the house of the Lord.

The king ordered Hilkiah, the high priest, and the wardens to bring out of the temple all the vessels made for Baal and for star-worship; these he burned outside Jerusalem at the brook Kidron. He commanded all the people: "Keep the Passover in honor of the Lord your God, as it is written in the book of the covenant." Passover had not been kept since the days when the judges had ruled over Israel. Josiah put away the mediums and the wizards, the household idols and all the abominations that were seen in the land of Judah and in Jerusalem.

There had never been a king like him who turned to the Lord with all his heart and with all his soul and with all his might; nor was there a king like him afterwards.

When Pharaoh-nechoh, king of Egypt, marched to fight the king of Assyria, Josiah marched against him and was slain at Megiddo. His servants carried their dead king in a chariot to Jerusalem, where he was buried in his own tomb. Then the people of the land anointed Jehoahaz the son of Josiah and made him king.

Jehoahaz, who was twenty-three years old when he became king, had reigned only three months in Jerusalem when Pharaoh-nechoh imprisoned him and made his brother, Jehoiakim, king. Jehoiakim was twenty-five years old when he became king, and he reigned eleven years in Jerusalem. Nebuchadnezzar, king of Babylon, made Jehoiakim his vassal for three years. The king of Egypt no longer stirred from his country, for the king of Babylon had conquered all that belonged to Egypt.

When Jehoiakim died, his son Jehoiachin became king at the age of eighteen, and reigned three months in Jerusalem. Nebuchadnezzar attacked Jerusalem at that time, and besieged the city. Jehoiachin surrendered to the king of Babylon, who took him prisoner and carried off all the treasures of the temple and the royal palace, cutting to pieces all the golden vessels made by Solomon for the house of the Lord. Nebuchadnezzar exiled all the nobles, all the brave soldiers, ten thousand of them, with all the craftsmen and locksmiths. None remained, except the poorest people of the land.

The king of Babylon made Jehoiachin's uncle, Zedekiah, king over Jerusalem. He reigned eleven years. In the ninth year of his reign, Zedekiah rebelled against the king of Babylon, so Nebuchadnezzar came with all his army against Jerusalem and laid siege to it till the eleventh year of king Zedekiah. By the ninth day of the fourth month, Tammuz, a breach was made in the walls of the city. The king and all the soldiers fled from the city by night, though the Chaldeans surrounded it. They pursued the king and overtook him in the plains of Jericho. He was captured and carried off to the king of Babylon, who passed sentence upon him. The sons of Zedekiah were killed before his eyes. Then they put out Zedekiah's eyes and carried him in chains to Babylon.

On the seventh day of the fifth month (Av), Nebuzaradan, who was chief in command of Nebuchadnezzar's troops, burned the house of the Lord, the royal palace and all the houses of Jerusalem. The Chaldean army demolished the walls around the city, and Nebuzaradan carried off into exile most of the people left in the city as well as those who had already surrendered to the king of Babylon. He left a small number of the poorest people to be vintners and plowmen.

Gedaliah, who was appointed governor over them, said to them: "Do not be afraid; live in the land, serve the king of Babylon, and it shall be well with you." But in the seventh month (Tishri), one of the royal family, Ishmael, came with ten men and killed Gedaliah and those who were with him at Mizpah. Then all the people, young and old, went to Egypt, for they were afraid of the Chaldeans.

In the thirty-seventh year of the exile of Jehoiachin king of Judah, Evil-Merodach king of Babylon freed him from prison. He spoke kindly to him and gave him a seat among the kings who were in Babylon. Jehoiachin changed his prison-dress, and dined with the king every day. A daily allowance was made for him, to maintain him as long as he lived.

Isaiah

יְשַׁעְיָה

Isaiah is considered the greatest of the prophets because of the grandeur of his style and the great power of his personality. Isaiah began his prophetic career toward the end of the eighth century before the common era, at a time when there was abundant prosperity in Judea, vast stores of silver and gold, and a tremendous variety of treasure. He witnessed the growth of large estates, the oppression of the poor, the pursuit of wanton pleasure and the spread of idolatrous practices. Isaiah was convinced that all this could not continue with impunity. If it persists, he warned, God will destroy both the kingdom of Israel and the kingdom of Judah.

According to tradition, Isaiah was of royal blood. He suffered martyrdom by being torn asunder when King Manasseh persecuted the loyal worshipers of the God of their forefathers.

The book of Isaiah contains sixty-six chapters and is the first of the three Major Prophets, the other two being the books of Jeremiah and Ezekiel. The term Major refers to the fact that these prophetic books are longer than the other prophetic books in the Bible.

The fortieth chapter of Isaiah introduces the great theme of deliverance and restoration and has been credited by scholars to another or second Isaiah. This second Isaiah is referred to as the great unknown prophet of the exile, because chapters forty through sixty-six are addressed to the Jews in the Babylonian exile, which occurred more than a century after the first Isaiah.

The eloquence of the entire book of Isaiah is without parallel in the literature of the ancient world. In the vision of Isaiah, the black night of exile is at its end; the period of Zion's affliction is over; the morning of deliverance dawns before his eyes.

The vision of Isaiah concerning Judah and Jerusalem.

Wash yourselves; make yourselves clean; remove your evil doings from my sight; cease to do wrong, learn to do

124

right; seek justice, restrain oppression; defend the father-less, plead for the widow.

Let me sing for my Friend a song concerning his vine-yard. My Friend had a vineyard on a fertile hill. He trenched it, cleared it of stones, and planted it with choice vines. He built a watchtower in the midst of it, and had a winepress hewn in it; then he looked for good grapes, but it yielded wild grapes.

Now, O citizens of Jerusalem and men of Judah, pray judge between me and my vineyard. What more could have been done for my vineyard? What have I left un-done? When I looked for good grapes, why did it yield wild grapes?

Let me tell you now what I will do to my vineyard. I will break down its fence, and it shall be trampled. I will make it a waste; it shall be unpruned, unweeded; it shall be overgrown with thorns and thistles. I will also com-mand the clouds that they drop no rain on it.

The Lord's vineyard is the house of Israel, the men of Judah are his plant of delight; he looked for justice, and behold, violence; for uprightness, and behold, a cry from the oppressed!

In the year that King Uzziah died, I saw the Lord sitting on a high and lofty throne; seraphim hovered round him, each with six wings. They kept calling one to another: "Holy, holy, holy is the Lord of hosts; the whole earth is full of his glory." Then I heard the voice of the Lord say-ing: "Whom shall I send? Who will go for us?" And I said: "Here I am! Send me."

Woe to those who call evil good and good evil, who re-gard darkness as light, and light as darkness; who regard bitter as sweet, and sweet as bitter!

Woe to those who are wise in their own eyes, and shrewd in their own sight. Woe to those who are heroes at drink-ing wine, brave men in mixing strong drink; who clear the guilty for a bribe, and deprive the innocent man of his right!

Thus says the Lord God, the Holy One of Israel: By sitting still and resting shall you be saved; in quietness and confidence your strength shall be.

Woe to those who go down to Egypt for help and rely on horses, who trust in her many chariots and very strong horsemen, but do not heed the Holy One of Israel, and do not seek the Lord. The Egyptians are only men, their horses are flesh; when the Lord strikes, both the helper and the one who is helped shall stumble and collapse.

Strengthen the feeble-handed, make firm the weak-kneed; say to those with fluttering hearts: "Have courage, fear not! Behold, your God comes to save you!"

Then the blind shall see, and the deaf shall hear. Waters shall break forth in the wilderness, and streams in the desert; the burning sand shall become a pool, and the thirsty ground—springs of water. A highway shall be there, and it shall be called the Holy way. No unclean one shall pass over it; no lions shall be there, no wild beasts shall haunt it. On it the redeemed shall walk; those whom the Lord has set free shall return to Zion singing. They shall be crowned with unending joy; sorrow and sighing shall flee away.

Sennacherib, king of Assyria, marched against all the fortified cities of Judah and captured them. He sent his commander with a large army against King Hezekiah at Jerusalem. And the commander shouted in Hebrew: "Hear the words of the great king of Assyria! He warns you not to let Hezekiah deceive you. Do not listen to Hezekiah! Make your peace with me, surrender to me! Then every one of you will eat the fruit of his own vine and his own fig tree, every one of you will drink from his own water supply, until I come and take you away to a land like your own land, a land of grain and wine, a land of bread and vineyards. Beware of letting Hezekiah mislead you by saying that the Lord will save you. Has any god of any nation saved his land from the hands of the king of Assyria, that the Lord should now save Jerusalem from me?"

Upon hearing this, King Hezekiah tore his clothes, put on sackcloth, and went into the house of the Lord. He sent this message to Isaiah: "This is a day of distress and of disgrace. Pray for this remnant of the people." Isaiah replied: "Thus says the Lord: Do not be afraid of the

126

Assyrian king. Behold, he shall hear a rumor; he shall go back to his own land and fall by the sword of his own country. He shall never come into this city, nor shoot an arrow here; by the way he came shall he return, for I will defend this city for my own sake and for the sake of my servant David."

The angel of the Lord went forth and slew one hundred and eighty-five thousand in the camp of the Assyrians. Then Sennacherib, king of Assyria, returned home to Nineveh. And one day, as he was worshiping in the temple of his god, two of his sons struck him down with the sword and escaped.

At that time, the king of Babylon sent envoys with a present to Hezekiah, for he heard that Hezekiah had just recovered from an illness. Hezekiah welcomed them and showed them his treasures, the silver, the gold, the spices, the precious oil, and his whole armory. There was nothing in his palace or in all his realm that he did not show them. Then Isaiah came and asked Hezekiah: "What did these men say? Whence have they come to you?" Hezekiah replied: "They have come to me from a far country, from Babylon."

"And what have they seen in your palace?" Isaiah asked. "They have seen everything in my palace," Hezekiah answered; "there is nothing in my storehouses that I did not show them."

Then Isaiah said to Hezekiah: "Behold, the days are coming, when all that is in your house, with all that your fathers have stored up, shall be carried to Babylon; nothing shall be left, says the Lord. Some of your sons shall be taken away to serve in the palace of the king of Babylon." And Hezekiah said to Isaiah: "The word of the Lord which you have spoken is good," thinking to himself: "At least there will be peace and security in my time."

"Comfort, O comfort my people," says your God; "speak tenderly to Jerusalem, proclaim to her that her guilt is pardoned, that she has received from the Lord's hand double for all her sins . . ."

Get up on a high mountain, O herald of good news to

Zion! Raise your voice strongly, fear not, and tell the towns of Judah: Here is your God! Like a shepherd he tends his flock, gathering the lambs in his arm and carrying them in his bosom.

Do you not know? Do you not hear? Has this not been told you from the first? It is he who sits above the globe of the earth; its inhabitants look like grasshoppers. He brings nobles to nothing, and makes the rulers of the world a thing of nought. Look up and see! Who created these stars? He brings out their host in order, calling them all by name, not one fails to appear.

Why should you say, O Jacob, "My way is hidden from the Lord"? Do you not know? Have you not heard? The Lord is the everlasting God, the Creator of the world from end to end. Young men may faint and grow weary, strong youths may fall exhausted, but those who hope in the Lord shall renew their strength, they shall put forth wings like eagles, they shall run and never weary, they shall walk and never faint.

Israel my servant, you whom I fetched from the ends of the earth, fear not, for I am with you; be not dismayed, for I am your God. I will strengthen you, I will help you, I will uphold you with my victorious right hand.

All who are angry with you shall be put to shame, those who quarrel with you shall perish and vanish. You will not find them when you look for them. I, the Lord your God, will say to you: "Fear not, I will help you."

Fear not, Jacob my servant. For I will pour water on the thirsty land, and streams on the dry ground, I will pour my spirit upon your children, my blessing upon your offspring. They shall grow up like grass amid waters, like willows by flowing streams.

Look around you, look! They all gather together, they come to you, your sons from far away, your little daughters carried in arms! See and be radiant, let your heart thrill and rejoice; for the abundance of the sea shall be turned to you, the wealth of nations shall come to you.

Whoever is thirsty, come to the waters! Whoever has no money, come for food and eat! Why spend your money on what is not food, your earnings on what does not satisfy?

128

If you but listen to me, you shall eat what is good and be delighted with rich nourishment.

Incline your ear, come to me; listen and you shall live. Seek the Lord while he may be found, call to him while he is near. Let the wicked man give up his way, and the evil man his designs; let him turn back to the Lord who will have mercy on him, to our God who forgives abundantly.

My thoughts are not like your thoughts, nor are your ways like my ways, says the Lord. As the heavens are higher than the earth, so are my ways higher than your ways and my thoughts than your thoughts. As the rain and the snow come down from heaven and return not thither, but water the earth and make it yield seed for the sower and bread for the eater, so is the word that comes forth from my mouth: it does not return to me fruitless, but carries out the plan for which I sent it.

You shall depart with joy, and be led forth in peace; the mountains and the hills shall burst into song before you, and all the trees of the field shall applaud. Instead of the thorn shall come up the cypress; instead of the brier shall come up the myrtle; this shall be a memorial to the Lord, an everlasting monument.

Cry out, spare not, raise your voice like a trumpet; tell my people their guilt, tell Jacob's house their sins. Daily, indeed, they seek me, desiring to know my ways; they keep asking me about righteous ordinances; they seemingly delight to draw near to God. "Why seest thou not when we fast?" they ask. "Why heedest thou not when we afflict ourselves?"

Is that what you call fasting, a day acceptable to the Lord? Behold, this is what I consider precious: Loosen the chains of wickedness, undo the bonds of oppression, let the crushed go free, break all yokes of tyranny! Share your food with the hungry, take the poor to your home, clothe the naked when you see them, and never turn from your fellow.

The Lord will answer you when you call, if you remove from your midst oppression, scorn and malice. If you share your food with the hungry, and clothe the naked, then shall your light rise in darkness and be bright as noon; the Lord will always guide you and nourish you; you shall be like a watered garden, a never-failing spring.

Arise, shine, your light has come! The Lord's splendor has risen upon you. Though darkness covers all the earth, and a black cloud shrouds the nations, yet the Lord shines out upon you. Nations shall walk by your light, and kings by your rising brightness.

For Zion's sake I will not keep silent, for Jerusalem's sake I will not rest until her triumph comes forth clear as light and her deliverance like a blazing torch. The nations shall see your triumph, all the kings shall behold your glory; you shall be called by a new name, a name given by the Lord. You shall be a crown of beauty in the hand of the Lord. No more shall you be named "Forsaken," your land shall no longer be called "Desolate"; you shall be called "My Delight."

I will exult over Jerusalem, and rejoice in my people; no more shall be heard in it the sound of weeping and the cry of distress. No more shall there be in it an infant that lives but a few days, or an old man who has not completed the span of his life.

They shall build houses and inhabit them; they shall plant vineyards and eat their fruit. They shall not labor in vain, nor bring forth children for disaster. Before they call, I shall answer. The wolf and the lamb shall feed together, and the lion shall eat straw like the ox; dust shall be the serpent's food. None shall injure, none shall kill, says the Lord.

Jeremiah

יִרְמְיָה

Jeremiah began to prophesy in Jerusalem about seventy years after the death of Isaiah. More is known about his life and teachings than about any other prophet, since the book of Jeremiah contains a mass of historical and biographical material. He was gentle and sensitive. He yearned for the comforts of a normal life; yet he felt impelled to speak the truth and be "a man of strife and contention," delivering messages of doom and foretelling the fall of Jerusalem. He was often imprisoned and in danger of his life, yet he did not flinch. He was cruelly insulted and accused of treason by the people he loved tenderly—those whom he sought to save. After the fall of Jerusalem in 586 before the common era, he was forcibly taken into Egypt by those who fled the wrath of the Babylonian conqueror.

Tradition has it that Nebuchadnezzar, king of Babylon, had instructed his general to treat Jeremiah with consideration and kindness. But the prophet insisted on sharing the hardships and tortures that were inflicted on his people. Afterwards Jeremiah was killed in Egypt, where he had continued his fiery speeches for some time.

Jeremiah also foretold the restoration of Israel, and those who survived the agonies of captivity were promised a safe journey home to Judea. He looked forward to a reunion of deported Israel with the people of Judah, to an ingathering of all the exiles.

The book of Jeremiah is the longest of the prophetic books, even though it has fourteen chapters less than Isaiah. Jeremiah's dictations to his faithful secretary Baruch were written down upon a scroll of leather which the king of Judah slashed with a knife and burned. But the prophet was not easily discouraged. He ordered his scribe to take another scroll and write therein all the words of the book which the king had burned.

The Greek version of the Bible, which was prepared by a group of scholars in the third century before the common era, contains about two thousand and seven hundred words (or about one-eighth of Jeremiah) less than the Hebrew text. This has led to the conjecture that either the translators abbreviated at certain points, or that they had another text from which they made their translation.

The word of the Lord came to me, saying: "Before you were born I set you apart for my service; I appointed you a prophet to the nations." So I said: "Lord God, I cannot speak, I am too young!" But the Lord said to me: "Do not say that you are too young; you shall go to whomever I send you, and you shall speak whatever I command you. Be not afraid of them, for I am with you to help you."

Then the Lord stretched forth his hand and touched my mouth, saying: "Behold, I have put my words in your mouth. See, I have set you this day over nations and over kingdoms to tear up and to break down, to destroy and to overthrow, to build and to plant."

The word of the Lord came to me, saying: "Go and proclaim in the hearing of Jerusalem: I remember the devotion of your youth, the love of your early days, how you followed me in the wilderness. Israel is holy to the Lord, the first-fruits of his harvest; all who ravage him shall be punished, evil shall come upon them.

"Is Israel a slave? Why then has he become a prey? The lions have roared at him, growling loudly. They have made his land a waste; his cities are in ruins, empty of inhabitants.

"You have brought this upon yourself by forsaking the Lord your God! Why do you go to Egypt to drink from the Nile? Why do you go to Assyria to drink from the Euphrates? You shall be put to shame by Egypt as you were put to shame by Assyria, for the Lord has rejected those in whom you trust, and you will gain nothing from them.

"Return, O Israel, for I am merciful; I will not be angry forever. Only acknowledge your guilt in not hearkening to my voice. I will take you, one from a city and two from a family, and I will bring you to Zion. I will give you shepherds after my own heart, who shall feed you with knowledge and understanding. At that time Jerusalem shall be called the throne of the Lord, and all nations shall gather to it, walking no longer in the stubbornness of their evil hearts. In those days the house of Judah shall join the house of Israel and together they shall come from the land of the north to the land that I gave your fathers for a heritage."

Behold, a people is coming out of the north-land, a great nation is stirring from the far ends of the earth! They are cruel and have no mercy; the sound of them is like the roaring sea; they ride upon horses to attack you, O Zion! We have heard the news, and our hands fall helpless; panic has taken hold of us, and pain, as of a woman in travail. Venture not into the field, walk not on the road; for the enemy has a sword, terror is on every side.

Thus says the Lord God of Israel: "Mend your ways and your doings, and I will let you dwell in this place. If you truly mend your ways and your doings, if you really practise justice between man and man, if you do not oppress strangers, orphans or widows, I will allow you to remain in this place, in the land that I gave to your fathers forever."

I went down to the potter's house; there he was at work with his wheel. Whenever the vessel he was making out of clay became spoiled, he remolded it into another vessel. Then the word of the Lord came to me:

"O house of Israel, can I not do with you as this potter has done? Behold, like the clay in the potter's hand, you are in my hand. At one time I may speak of tearing up a nation; but if that nation turns from its evil, I will repent of the evil which I planned to inflict upon it. Again, I may speak of building up a nation; but if that nation does evil in my sight, I will repent of the good which I intended to do for it. Turn, therefore, every one from his evil paths; mend your ways and your doings."

Hear the word of the Lord, O kings of Judah and inhabitants of Jerusalem: "Behold, I am bringing a disaster upon this place, because the people have forsaken me and have filled this place with innocent blood. I will make them fall by the sword before their enemies; I will make this city a desolation; I will break this people and this city just as one breaks a potter's vessel so that it cannot be repaired."

Now when Pashhur, the priest, heard Jeremiah prophesying these things, he beat the prophet and put him in the stocks. The next morning, when Pashhur released Jeremiah from the stocks, Jeremiah said to him: "Thus says the Lord: I will hand over all Judah to the king of Babylon; I will hand over all the wealth of this city and all the treasures of the kings of Judah to their enemies, who shall carry them to Babylon. And you, Pashhur, and all your household, shall go into exile; you shall go to Babylon and die there and be buried there, you and all your friends to whom you have prophesied falsely."

These are the words of the letter which Jeremiah the prophet sent to the people whom Nebuchadnezzar had exiled to Babylon.

"Build houses and live in them; plant gardens and eat their fruit; take wives and beget sons and daughters; get wives for your sons and husbands for your daughters, and multiply where you are. Seek the welfare of the country where you have been exiled; pray to the Lord for it, since your welfare rests on its welfare."

"Days are coming," says the Lord, "when I will restore the fortunes of my people, and I will bring them back to the land which I gave to their fathers, and they shall possess it.

"Sing merrily for Jacob, shout on the hilltops of the nations, ring out your praises and say: Save thy people, O Lord, the remnant of Israel. I am bringing them from the north-land, and will gather them from the uttermost parts of the world; the blind and the lame, women with child and women in travail, a great company shall come back here. They shall come weeping, and I will lead them with grace; I will guide them to streams of water, by a smooth road where they shall not stumble; for I am a father to Israel; Ephraim is my firstborn."

Hear the word of the Lord, you nations, and announce it in far-off islands, saying: "He who has scattered Israel gathers them, and tends them as a shepherd tends his flock." They shall come singing on the heights of Zion, and shall stream to the goodness of the Lord—to the corn, the wine, the oil, the sheep and cattle; they shall be like a watered garden, and they shall languish no more. Then shall maidens delight in dancing, young men and old shall rejoice alike.

A voice is heard in Ramah—lamentation and bitter weeping; it is Rachel crying for her children. She refuses to be comforted, for they are gone. Thus says the Lord: "Restrain your voice from weeping, your eyes from tears; your work shall have its reward; they shall return from the land of the enemy. There is hope for your future: your children shall return to their own land.

"I will gather them from all the countries where I drove them; I will bring them back to this place, where I will make them dwell in safety; they shall be my people, and I will be their God. I will rejoice over them and plant them in this land securely. In this land that you call desolate, fields shall again be bought. Men shall buy fields for money in the places round about Jerusalem and in the Negev, for I will restore their fortunes," says the Lord.

The word came from the Lord to Jeremiah, when Nebuchadnezzar and all his army were attacking Jerusalem. "Go to Zedekiah, king of Judah, and say to him that I am giving this city over to the king of Babylon, who shall burn it with fire. You cannot escape from him; you shall be captured and delivered into his hand; you shall face the king of Babylon and speak to him in person, and to Babylon you must go. You shall not die by the sword; you shall die in peace." So Jeremiah spoke these words to Zedekiah when the army of the king of Babylon was fighting against Jerusalem, Lachish and Azekah, the only fortified cities of Judah that remained.

King Zedekiah had made a covenant with all the people in Jerusalem that every one should set free his Hebrew slaves, male or female, so that no one should hold his fellow-Jew in slavery. But afterwards the people turned around and forced back into slavery those they had liberated. Then the word of the Lord came to Jeremiah that he should say to the people: "Since you have not obeyed me by proclaiming freedom, each to his brother and neighbor, I now proclaim you free to fall under the sword, the pestilence, and the famine!"

Pharaoh's army had set out from Egypt, and news of this led the Chaldeans to abandon their siege of Jerusalem. Then the word of the Lord came to Jeremiah: "Thus shall you say to the king of Judah: Behold, Pharaoh's army which came to help you is about to retreat to Egypt, and the Chaldeans shall come back and fight against this city; they shall capture it and burn it in flames. Do not deceive yourselves with the notion that the Chaldeans will leave you alone; they will not stay away."

When the Chaldean forces had abandoned the siege of Jerusalem, in fear of Pharaoh's army, Jeremiah set out from Jerusalem to go to the land of Benjamin. But a sentry, who was posted at the Benjamin Gate, arrested him, saying: "You are deserting to the Chaldeans." Jeremiah replied: "That is not true; I am not deserting to the Chaldeans." However, the sentry would not listen to him. He arrested Jeremiah and brought him to the princes, who in anger had Jeremiah flogged and confined in prison, where he remained for a number of days.

Then King Zedekiah sent for him privately and asked him: "Is there any word from the Lord?" Jeremiah answered: "There is. You shall be handed over to the king of Babylon. What wrong have I done to you or your servants or this nation, that you have put me in prison? I pray you, my lord king, be gracious to my plea; do not send me back to prison, or I shall die there." So King Zedekiah gave orders for Jeremiah to be placed in the guardhouse, where he was given a loaf of bread daily, until all the bread of the city was gone.

Now the princes had heard Jeremiah declaring in public: "Anyone who remains in the city shall die by the sword or by famine or by plague, but anyone who surrenders to the Chaldeans shall live." So they said to the king: "Let this man be put to death, for he is discouraging the people and the soldiers within the city by talking like this! This man is not seeking the welfare of the people, but their harm!" King Zedekiah said: "Behold, he is in your hands," for the king was powerless against them. So they took Jeremiah and cast him into an underground cistern, below the guardhouse, lowering him down with ropes. There was no water in the cistern, only mud, and Jeremiah sank in the mud.

However, an Ethiopian servant, belonging to the royal

house, left the palace to find the king. "Your majesty," he said, "these men have done evil to the prophet by casting him into the cistern; he will die there of hunger, for there is no bread left in the city."

Then the king commanded the Ethiopian to take three men and pull Jeremiah out of the cistern. So he took the men with him and went to the palace, where he got some old rags and worn-out clothes; these he lowered by ropes to Jeremiah in the cistern, saying: "Put the rags and clothes between your armpits and the ropes." Jeremiah did so. And they pulled him up by the ropes out of the cistern.

King Zedekiah sent for Jeremiah and said to him: "I am going to ask you a question; do not hide anything from me." Jeremiah replied: "But if I tell you the truth, you certainly will put me to death. Besides, you will not listen to any advice from me." So King Zedekiah took an oath in secret, saying: "As the Lord lives, I will neither put you to death, nor hand you over to those men who seek your life."

Then Jeremiah said to Zedekiah: "If you surrender to the officers of the king of Babylon, your life shall be spared, and this city shall not be burned in flames; you and your household shall live. But if you do not surrender, this city shall be given over to the Chaldeans to be burned, and you shall not escape from their hands."

King Zedekiah said to Jeremiah: "But I am afraid of the Jews who have deserted to the Chaldeans; they may subject me to indignity and abuse." "You shall not be handed over to the Jews," Jeremiah said; "just listen to what I say, and all will go well with you; you shall live."

Then Zedekiah said to Jeremiah: "Let no one know of this conversation, and your life is safe. If the princes hear that I have been talking with you, and if they come and ask you to tell them what you said to the king and what the king said to you, you shall say to them that you presented a humble plea to the king not to be sent back to die in prison."

All the princes did come to question Jeremiah, and he answered them just as the king had told him; so they said no more. Jeremiah then remained in the guardhouse until the day that Jerusalem was taken.

Nebuchadnezzar with all his army attacked Jerusalem and besieged it. When Zedekiah and the garrison saw that a breach had been made in the walls of the city, they took to flight and left the city during the night. But the Chaldean army pursued them. Zedekiah was caught and brought to Nebuchadnezzar, who slew his sons before his very eyes. The king of Babylon also slew all the nobles of Judea. He then put out the eyes of Zedekiah and bound him with chains to carry him to Babylon.

The Chaldeans burned down the royal palace and the houses of the common people, and demolished the walls of Jerusalem. Then Nebuzaradan, the commander, carried captive to Babylon the rest of the people that were left in the city and the deserters who had surrendered to him. However, he did leave in the land of Judah some poor people who had nothing; he allotted them vineyards and fields.

Nebuchadnezzar had ordered Nebuzaradan to take good care of Jeremiah, so the commander-in-chief took Jeremiah and said to him: "The Lord your God pronounced evil against this place, and has done as he decreed. Well now, I release you today from the chains on your hands. If you like to come with me to Babylon, come, and I will take good care of you. If not, think no more of it; the whole land is before you, go wherever you please. Go back, if you wish, to Gedaliah, whom the king of Babylon has appointed governor over the cities of Judah; stay with him, or go wherever else you choose." Then the commander sent him off with some food and a present. Jeremiah went to Gedaliah and stayed with him among the people who were left in the land.

But Ishmael, the son of Nethaniah, a member of the royal family, came with ten men to Gedaliah at Mizpah. They drew their swords and murdered Gedaliah and all the Jews who were with him at Mizpah, as well as the Chaldean soldiers who happened to be there.

Jeremiah summoned all the people and said to them: "Thus says the Lord God of Israel: If you will remain in this land, I will build you up and not pull you down. Do not fear the king of Babylon, for I am with you. But if

138

you say: 'We will not remain in this country; no, we will go to Egypt where we shall not see war nor hear the sound of the trumpet nor be hungry for bread.' If you really are bent on going to Egypt to live, the sword you dread shall overtake you, the famine you fear shall follow you, and you shall die there. All who are bent on settling in Egypt shall die by the sword, by famine, or by plague. O remnant of Judah, do not go to Egypt!"

When Jeremiah had finished speaking, a group of insolent men said to him: "You are telling a lie; the Lord our God did not send you to forbid us to settle in Egypt—it is Baruch the son of Neriah who has set you against us to deliver us into the hand of the Chaldeans that they may put us to death, or carry us captive to Babylon." So they did not listen to the voice of the Lord, telling them to stay in the land of Judah; but they took the remnant of Judah, the men, women and children, including Jeremiah and Baruch, and went to the land of Egypt.

Then the word of the Lord came to Jeremiah: "Take some large stones in your hands; let some of the men of Judah see you hiding them in the pavement which is at the entrance to Pharaoh's palace, and say to them: Thus says the Lord God of Israel: I am sending for my servant Nebuchadnezzar, king of Babylon, who will set his throne above these stones that you have buried. He shall come to ravage the land of Egypt, inflicting death upon those who are doomed to die, capturing those who are doomed to captivity, and putting to the sword those who are doomed to the sword. He shall set fire to the temples of the gods in Egypt, burning them and carrying off the idols. He shall clean the land of Egypt, and then leave unmolested."

Ezekiel

Ezekiel lived during the last days of Jerusalem and received inspiration from the utterances of Jeremiah, his elder contemporary. Ezekiel prophesied in Babylon for a period of twenty-two years, having been taken into captivity eleven years before the fall of Jerusalem.

Prior to the destruction of the Temple by Nebuchadnezzar in 586, Ezekiel's prophecies were messages of doom; after it, they were messages of hope and assurances of restoration. Ezekiel dwells on a prophet's responsibility for the fate of his people. He maintains that a prophet is a watchman, responsible for warning his people of the consequences of misdoings. He tells us that each man possesses the power to be good or evil regardless of heredity and predisposition, and that the individual is master of his own destiny and responsible for his own deeds. Ezekiel stresses the idea that everybody can turn over a new leaf and look hopefully toward the future. His vision of the dry bones vividly illustrates the hope of restoration and revival of a nation that was given up as dead.

The book of Ezekiel is the third in the division of the Bible known as Latter Prophets, the first two books being those of Isaiah and Jeremiah. Its forty-eight chapters are divided into two equal parts. The first twenty-four chapters contain speeches uttered by Ezekiel prior to the national disaster of 586. The last twenty-four chapters consist of visions that occurred after the destruction of Jerusalem. The final chapters of Ezekiel concerning the glorious future of Israel have provided the Jewish people with a beacon of light through the lonely years of exile.

The word of the Lord came to me, saying: "Son of man, I set you up as a watchman for the people of Israel. If you say nothing to warn the wicked man from his evil course, that his life may be saved, the wicked man shall die for his iniquity, but I will hold you responsible for his death. If, however, you warn him and he does not turn from his

140

evil course, he shall die for his iniquity, but you have saved yourself.

"Son of man, speak to your people and say to them: If I bring down the sword upon a land, and if the watchman blows the trumpet to warn the people, then whoever does not heed the warning, and is swept off by the sword, is to blame for his own death. But if the watchman does not blow the trumpet when he sees the sword coming, and the sword comes and strikes down any one of the people, I will hold the watchman responsible.

"Tell the people of Israel: As I live, says the Lord God, I have no pleasure in the death of the wicked; let the wicked man turn from his way and live. Turn back, turn back from your evil ways! Why should you die, O Israel?"

The word of the Lord came to me, saying: "What do you mean by quoting this proverb in the land of Israel: 'The fathers eat sour grapes, and the children's teeth are set on edge'? By my life, you shall no more use this proverb in Israel. All souls are mine, the soul of the father as well as the soul of the son; he who sins shall die. If a man oppresses no one and robs no one, if he feeds the hungry and clothes the naked, if he abstains from crime and observes strict justice between man and man—he is upright and shall surely live. If he has a son who is a violent man, given to bloodshed, who oppresses the poor and commits robbery, that son shall not live. He has done abominable things, he shall surely die; he is responsible for his own death.

"But if this son, in turn, has a son who, seeing all the sins committed by his father, does not act likewise but lives by my laws, he shall not die for the iniquity of his father, he shall live. His father died for his own iniquity because he practised oppression and outrage and wrongdoing among his fellow men.

"You ask: 'Why should not the son suffer for the iniquity of his father?' If the son does what is right and honest, if he observes and obeys all my laws, he shall live. The person who sins shall die. A son shall not suffer for the iniquity of his father, nor a father for the iniquity of his son.

"But if a wicked man turns away from all the sins which he has committed and keeps all my laws, he shall surely

141

live; he shall not die. None of the transgressions which he has committed shall be remembered against him.

"Again, when a good man turns away from his uprightness and practises iniquity, none of his good deeds shall be remembered; for the sin he has committed he shall die.

"O Israel, repent and turn from all your transgressions, or iniquity will be your ruin; get yourselves a new heart and a new spirit! I have no pleasure in the death of anyone. So repent and live."

"Son of man, prophesy to the mountains of Israel and say: Mountains of Israel, hear the word of the Lord! Because you have been left desolate and crushed on every side, and because you have become the possession of the rest of the nations and the subject of popular evil gossip, I speak in fiery indignation against the surrounding nations who siezed my land for themselves.

"Prophesy concerning the land of Israel, and say to the mountains and hills, watercourses and valleys: Thus says the Lord God: Behold, I speak in my indignation and fury, because you have suffered the reproach of the nations. I swear that the nations that are round about you shall themselves suffer reproach.

"But you, mountains of Israel, shall bear fruit for Israel my people; for they will soon return. I am for you, I will care for you, and you shall be tilled and sown; I will put many people on you—the whole house of Israel; the cities shall be inhabited and the waste places rebuilt. I will multiply both man and beast; they shall increase and be fruitful; I will do more good to you than ever before. Then you will know that I am the Lord. I will let men walk upon you again, the men of my people Israel; they shall possess you, and you shall be their heritage.

"Say to the house of Israel: Thus says the Lord your God: I will take you from the nations and gather you from all countries and bring you back to your own land. A new heart I will give you and a new spirit I will put within you. I will make you live by my laws, and you shall obey and observe my ordinances. You shall dwell in the land which I gave to your fathers; you shall be my people, and I will be your God; I will keep you clear of all your impurities. I will summon the grain and make it abundant, that you may never again suffer the disgrace of famine among the nations. And it will be said that this land which was desolate has become like the garden of Eden. The surrounding nations shall know that I the Lord have rebuilt the ruined places and replanted the desolate land. I the Lord have spoken, and I will do it."

The word of the Lord came to me: "Son of man, set your face toward Gog in the land of Magog; prophesy against him and say: Thus says the Lord God: Behold, I am against you, O Gog! Be ready, you and all the hosts that are assembled about you; hold yourself in reserve for me. In the latter days you will go against the land that has been restored, the land where people have been gathered from many nations. You will advance, coming on like a storm, you will be like a cloud covering the land, you and all your hordes. On that day you will devise an evil plan to invade this land of villages, to attack the quiet people who live in security. You will come from the far north, you and many a nation with you—a huge army, sweeping up against my people Israel like a storm cloud covering the country.

"On that day, when Gog invades the land of Israel, my wrath will be roused. There shall be a mighty earthquake in the land of Israel; mountains shall be torn apart, and cliffs shall topple over, and every wall shall tumble to the ground. I will overwhelm him with utter panic, I will punish him with pestilence and bloodshed.

"Son of man, prophesy against Gog and say: Thus says the Lord God: Behold, I am against you, O Gog! I will strike your bow from your left hand and will make your arrows drop out of your right hand. You shall fall upon the mountains of Israel, you and all your hordes.

"I will restore the fortunes of Jacob and have mercy on the whole house of Israel. They shall forget their shame and all their faithlessness toward me, when they live undisturbed in their own land with none to make them afraid. Then they shall know that I am the Lord their God. I sent them into exile among the nations but now I have gathered them back into their own land."

143

The hand of the Lord was upon me and carried me off in the spirit, and set me down in the midst of a valley which was full of bones. He made me go all round them, and I saw that they were very many and very dry.

He said to me: "Son of man, can these bones live?" and I answered: "Lord God, thou knowest." Again he said to me: "Prophesy over these bones, say to them: O dry bones, listen to the word of the Lord. Thus says the Lord God: Behold, I will cause breath to enter into you, and you shall live. I will put sinews upon you and cover you with flesh; I will spread skin over you, then I will put breath into you, and you shall live; and you shall know that I am the Lord."

So I prophesied as I was commanded. While I was prophesying, there was a rattling sound—the bones came together, bone to bone. And as I looked, there were sinews upon them! Flesh and skin spread over them, but there was no breath in them. Then he said to me: "Prophesy to the breath, son of man, and say to the breath: Thus says the Lord God: Come from the four ends of the earth, O breath, and breathe into these lifeless bodies that they may live." So I prophesied as he commanded me, and the breath came into them and they lived and stood upon their feet, an exceedingly great host.

Then he said to me: "Son of man, these bones are the people of Israel. Behold, they keep saying: Our bones are dry, our hope is lost, we are undone! Prophesy therefore to them and tell them: Thus says the Lord God: O my people, I will open your graves and bring you back to the land of Israel. You shall know that I am the Lord when I have raised you from your graves, O my people. I will put my spirit into you, and you shall live. I will place you in your own land; then you shall know that I, the Lord, have spoken and performed it."

Hosea　　　　　　　　　　　　　　הוֹשֵׁעַ

Hosea lived after Amos during the eighth century before the common era, and prophesied in the kingdom of Israel before Isaiah did in the kingdom of Judah. His prophetic work began before the death of Jeroboam II, and he was still living when the kingdom of Israel was destroyed by the Assyrians in 721 before the common era.

The book of Hosea appears as the first among the twelve Minor Prophets, commonly known as "The Twelve." The name Minor Prophets, as compared with Major Prophets, does not refer to value but to volume, that is, the length of the individual books. Since these twelve books were so short, they were gathered into a single collection to safeguard their preservation; hence they count as one book in the Hebrew Bible.

Chronologically, the book of Hosea should come after the book of Amos, but it is placed first because of its length. The length of the Major Prophets likewise determined that they should be placed before the Minor Prophets.

The style of Hosea is highly poetic and difficult to follow. Many passages in Hosea are not clearly understood particularly because we are no longer fully acquainted with certain events to which they allude.

The word of the Lord that came to Hosea during the reign of Jeroboam the son of Joash, king of Israel:

The number of the people of Israel shall be like the sand of the sea that cannot be measured or counted. The people of Judah and the people of Israel shall be gathered together; they shall appoint one leader for themselves, and spread out beyond their land.

"On that day," says the Lord, "I will abolish bow, sword and war from the land, and I will let them lie down in safety. On that day I will answer the heavens, and they shall answer the earth; the earth shall answer the grain, the wine and the oil, and they shall answer Jezreel."

Hear the word of the Lord, O people of Israel, for the Lord has a quarrel with the inhabitants of the land. There is no faithfulness, no kindness, no knowledge of God in the land; there is swearing, lying, killing, stealing, and adultery; one crime follows hard upon another. Hence the land mourns, and its inhabitants languish; even the beasts and birds and the very fish within the sea are perishing. My people are destroyed for lack of knowledge.

I will go back to my place, until they realize their guilt and seek my face, searching me out in their distress and crying: "Come, let us return to the Lord; he has torn, and he will heal us; he has wounded, and he will bind us up; in a day or two he will revive us, to live under his care. Let us know the Lord; he will come to us like spring rain that waters the land."

Ephraim is like a dove, silly and without sense, calling to Egypt, going to Assyria. Woe to them, for they have strayed from me! Ruin to them, for they have rebelled against me! Woe to them when I depart from them!

Like grapes in the wilderness I found Israel. Like the first ripe fig on the fig tree I welcomed your fathers. But when they devoted themselves to Baal, they became as detestable as the thing they loved. Sow justice for yourselves, and reap a harvest of love!

How can I give you up, O Ephraim! How can I hand you over, O Israel! I will not carry out my fierce anger, for I am God and not man; I will not destroy. Come back to the Lord your God, O Israel, for you have stumbled because of your iniquity.

I will heal their faithlessness; I will love them truly, for my anger has turned from them. I will be like the dew to Israel; he shall blossom like a lily, and strike roots like a poplar. Once again they shall dwell beneath my shadow; they shall blossom like a vine.

Whoever is wise, let him understand this: The ways of the Lord are right; good men walk in them, while sinners stumble in them.

Joel   יוֹאֵל

Nothing is known about the personality of the prophet Joel, the author of the second book of the Minor Prophets. Even the date of his book is subject to speculation and is greatly disputed among Bible scholars. Authorities place Joel either in a very early period or in post-exilic times.

The book of Joel consists of three chapters; its style is fluent, clear and of a high order. The general subject of Joel is divine judgment. A plague of locusts, accompanied by a drought of unusual severity, sweeps in successive swarms over Judea and destroys the produce of the fields and vineyards. Remarkably vivid is the description of the locust swarms filling the entire air; their destructiveness is compared with that of a mighty army. Joel summons the people to a penitential fast, and promises that God will bring back prosperity and abundance. The third and last chapter of Joel describes the future glory of Judea.

The word of the Lord that came to Joel:

Hear this, you who are old; listen, all inhabitants of the land! Has such a thing ever happened in your days, or in the days of your fathers? Tell it to your children, and let your children tell their children, and their children to the coming generation.

What the cutting locust left, the swarming locust ate; what the swarming locust left, the hopping locust ate; and what the hopping locust left, the devouring locust ate.

Wake up, you drunkards, and weep for the wine that is snatched from your mouth! An army has invaded our land, powerful and numberless; their teeth are the teeth of a lion, with fangs of a lioness. They have ruined our vines, and splintered our fig trees; they have stripped them clean, till their branches are made white.

Blow the trumpet in Zion; sound the alarm in my holy mountain! Let all the inhabitants of the land tremble, for the day of the Lord is coming, it is near, a day of darkness

147

and gloom. Like blackness spread over the mountains is the huge and powerful army, the like of which has never been before. Before them the land is a paradise, behind them it is a desolate wilderness. Nothing escapes them. They rush on the city, run over the walls, climb into the houses, and enter through the windows like thieves.

"Yet even now," says the Lord, "return to me with all your heart, fasting, weeping, mourning; rend your hearts and not your garments." Turn to the Lord your God, for he is gracious and merciful, slow to anger, rich in kindness, and ready to relent. Blow the trumpet in Zion; gather the people; assemble the old men; collect the children; let the priests, the ministers of the Lord, weep and say: "Spare thy people, O Lord; why should they say among the nations: Where is their God?"

Then the Lord had pity on his people and said to them: "I will now send you grain and wine and oil; I will drive out the northern foe into a parched and desolate land. Fear not, O land, rejoice and be glad. I will make it up to you for the years that the swarming locusts have eaten, that huge army which I sent among you. So you shall eat and eat and be satisfied. My people shall never again be put to shame.

"And it shall come to pass afterward, that I will pour out my spirit on all flesh; your sons and your daughters shall prophesy; your old men shall dream dreams, your young men shall see visions; even upon your servants, both men and women, I will pour out my spirit in those days.

"For in those days and at that time, when I restore the fortunes of Judah and Jerusalem, I will gather all the nations and bring them down into the Judgment Valley, where I shall enter into judgment with them, because they scattered my people Israel among pagans and divided up my land. Then the mountains shall drip wine, the hills shall flow with milk, and all the stream beds of Judah shall flow with water. Judah shall be inhabited forever, and Jerusalem to all generations."

Amos   עָמוֹס

Amos, the earliest known literary prophet, lived in the village
of Tekoa, about twelve miles south of Jerusalem, during the
middle of the eighth century before the common era. He left
the kingdom of Judah and proceeded to make known the
divine warnings in the kingdom of Israel, which had then
reached the zenith of its power and prosperity. Though a
native of Judah, he addresses himself primarily to the citizens
of Israel.

Amos denounces the brutalities and cruel wrongs perpe-
trated by various nations. He strongly insists upon social justice, respect for the lowly, and the defense of the weak against
the powerful. He condemns self-indulgence which breeds
cruelty, and compares the pampered women of Samaria to
cows grown fat through feeding in the rich pastures of Bashan,
east of the Jordan. Their chief delight being luxurious living,
they keep saying to their husbands: "Bring, and let us drink!"
When the priest of Bethel tells Amos to go back home and
prophesy there, he replies that he is not a professional prophet
who tries to please people, but simply a shepherd who has been
charged to prophesy to the people of Israel.

Though classed as the third of the Minor Prophets, the
book of Amos should come first from a chronological point of
view. The word "minor" refers to the small size of each of the
twelve books of the Minor Prophets in comparison with the so-
called Major Prophets, Isaiah, Jeremiah, and Ezekiel.

The words of Amos, a shepherd of Tekoa, who prophesied
concerning Israel during the reign of Jeroboam son of
Joash, King of Israel, two years before the earthquake:

Do two men walk together, unless they have made an
appointment? Does a lion roar in the jungle, unless he has
some prey? Does a young lion growl in his lair, unless he has
made a capture? Does a bird fall into a snare, unless a trap
is set for it? Does the trap spring up, unless there is something to catch? Do not the people tremble when a trumpet

149

is sounded? If there is a disaster in a city, has not the Lord caused it? When the lion roars, who does not shudder? When the Lord God speaks, who can but prophesy?

Hear this, you cows of Bashan, you women in Samaria, who cheat the poor and crush the needy, who tell your husbands: Bring, and let us drink! The time is coming, when you will be dragged out of the city with hooks; out you shall go headlong through breaches in the walls.

Seek good and not evil, that you may live. Hate evil and love good, and establish justice in the gate. Let justice roll down like waters, and righteousness like an ever-flowing stream.

Woe to those who are at ease in Zion, and to those who feel secure in Samaria; woe to those who lie upon beds of ivory and sprawl upon their couches, eating fresh lamb and fatted veal, crooning to the music of the lute, composing songs like David himself, lapping up wine by the bowlful and anointing themselves with the best of oil, but never grieving over the ruin of the nation. So now they shall be the first to be exiled; the dissolute revellers shall disappear.

Amaziah, the priest at Bethel, sent word to Jeroboam, king of Israel: "Amos is conspiring against you in the very midst of Israel, saying that Jeroboam shall die by the sword, and Israel shall go into exile." Amaziah also said to Amos: "You seer, be off to Judah and prophesy there, but never again at Bethel, for it is the royal sanctuary, the national temple."

Then Amos answered Amaziah: "I am no prophet, nor the son of a prophet; I am only a shepherd and a dresser of sycamore trees. But the Lord took me from the flock and said to me: 'Go, prophesy to my people Israel.' Now then, hear the word of the Lord. You say that I am not to prophesy against Israel. The Lord says: Your wife shall be a harlot in the city, your sons and daughters shall fall by the sword, your land shall be divided up, you yourself shall die in a foreign land, and Israel shall go into exile, far from its own country."

Hear this, you who would destroy the poor of the land, saying: "When will the new-moon festival be over, that we may sell our grain? When will the sabbath be done, that we may offer wheat for sale?" You deal deceitfully with false balances; you sell the very refuse of your grain.

"On that day," says the Lord, "I will make the sun go down at noon, and darken the earth in broad daylight. I will turn your feasts into mourning, and all your songs into lamentation."

"The days are coming," says the Lord, "when I will send a famine on the land; not a famine of bread, not a thirst for water, but of hearing the word of the Lord. Men shall wander from sea to sea, and run from north to east; they shall run to and fro, in quest of the Lord's word, but they shall not find it.

"On that day I will raise again the fallen booth of David, repair its breaches and rebuild it as in the days of old.

"Behold, the days are coming, when the plowman shall overtake the reaper, when he who treads the grapes shall overtake the sower; the mountains shall drip sweet wine, and all the hills shall be aflow with milk. I will restore the fortunes of my people Israel, and they shall rebuild the ruined cities and inhabit them; they shall plant vineyards and drink their wine, and they shall make gardens and eat their fruit. I will plant them upon their land, and they shall never again be uprooted from the land which I have given them," says the Lord.

Obadiah   עֹבַדְיָה

The shortest of all prophetical books, Obadiah contains only
one chapter of twenty-one verses. The unknown author predicts the destruction of Edomites, who will be treated measure
for measure as they treated Israel when they helped the Baby-
lonians to bring about the downfall of Jerusalem. From their
mountainous strongholds, south of the Dead Sea, the warlike
and cruel Edomites, the archenemies of Israel, looked down
upon their neighbors. Obadiah's prophecy brings to mind
Psalm 137, where we read: "Remember, O Lord, Jerusalem's
fall against the Edomites, who said: Raze it, raze it, to its very
foundation!"

Thus says the Lord God concerning Edom: "I will make
you least among the nations, you shall be utterly despised.
Your pride of heart has deceived you, thinking none could
pull you down. Though you soar aloft like an eagle, though
you set your nest among the stars, I will pull you down.

"All your allies shall betray you; your trusted friends
shall set a trap under you. On that day I will destroy the
wise men from Edom; your heroes shall be dismayed. For
the outrage to your brother Jacob, shame shall cover you,
and you shall be cut off forever. On that day you stood
aloof, when strangers carried off his wealth and cast lots
for Jerusalem; you were like one of them.

"You should not have gloated over your brother's fate on
the day of his misfortune; you should not have rejoiced
over the people of Judah on the day of their disaster; you
should not have laughed aloud on the day of distress; you
should not have entered the gates of my people on the
day of their calamity; you should not have looted their
goods on the day of their calamity; you should not have
stood at the passes to cut off their fugitives; you should
not have delivered up their survivors on the day of distress. As you have done, it shall be done to you; your deeds
shall return upon your own head."

Jonah יוֹנָה

The book of Jonah contains the noblest expression of the universality of religion. It is designed to show that kindness of heart and readiness to repent may be found everywhere amongst men.

The episode of the great fish swallowing Jonah has been interpreted figuratively as the captivity which swallowed up Israel. The deliverance from exile has been likened to being disgorged alive from the mouth of the devouring beast. Jonah's reluctance to denounce the heathen city of Nineveh was prompted perhaps by fear of exposing himself to the wrath of the king and the people.

The book of Jonah is recited as the prophetic lesson (Haftarah) in the afternoon service of Yom Kippur to show that the compassion of God extends to all his creatures, even those who are as sinful as the people of Nineveh.

Jonah is included among the Minor Prophets, even though it is not actually a prophecy but a short story about a prophet. Jonah, son of Amittai, is mentioned in II Kings 14:25 as having lived during the reign of Jeroboam II, about the middle of the eighth century before the common era.

The Lord spoke to Jonah, saying: "Arise, go to the great city of Nineveh and proclaim against it; their wickedness has come up before me." But Jonah went down to Jaffa and found a ship bound for Tarshish. He paid his fare and went aboard in an attempt to get away from the presence of the Lord.

The Lord then hurled a furious wind upon the sea; the ship was about to be smashed to pieces. The sailors were frightened, each cried to his own god, and they threw overboard the cargo that was in the ship in order to lighten it. But Jonah was fast asleep on the lower deck. The captain came and said to him: "Why are you sleeping? Get up and call upon your God! Perhaps God will think of us and we shall not perish."

They said to one another: "Come, let us cast lots to find out on whose account this evil has come upon us." They cast lots, and the lot fell on Jonah. Then they said to him: "Tell us now, you who are the cause of our present distress, what is your occupation? Where do you come from? What is your country? To what people do you belong?" He told them: "I am a Hebrew; I revere the Lord God in heaven who made the sea and the dry land." The men were terrified, and said to him: "What have you done?"; for they knew that he was running away from the Lord's presence. Jonah had told them that. They asked him: "What shall we do with you, so that the sea may again be calm for us? It is growing more and more stormy." He told them :"Take me and throw me overboard so that the sea may calm down for you, for I know that on my account this great tempest is upon you." Nevertheless, the men rowed hard to get back to land; they could not, however, for the seas ran higher and higher against them.

They cried to the Lord: "O Lord, let us not perish for this man's life, let us not be guilty of shedding innocent blood; for thou, O Lord, hast done as it pleased thee." Then they lifted Jonah and threw him overboard, and the sea ceased from its raging. The men feared the Lord exceedingly. They offered a sacrifice to the Lord and made vows.

Now the Lord ordered a great fish to swallow Jonah, and for three days and three nights Jonah lay inside the fish. He prayed to the Lord his God. Then the Lord spoke to the fish, and it threw Jonah out upon the dry land.

The Lord spoke to Jonah for the second time, saying: "Arise, go to the great city of Nineveh and proclaim what I tell you." Jonah started for Nineveh, as the Lord had commanded. He entered the city proclaiming: "Forty days more and Nineveh shall be overthrown!"

The people of Nineveh, great and small alike, believed God, so they proclaimed a fast and put on sackcloth. When the news reached the king of Nineveh, he rose from his throne, threw off his robe, covered himself with sackcloth, and sat in ashes. He published this proclamation: "By order of the king and his nobles! Let neither man nor beast, neither cattle nor sheep, taste any food or drink water: they shall put on sackcloth and cry earnestly to God. All must turn from their evil ways and from their acts of violence. Who knows but that God may relent and turn from his fierce anger and we shall not perish?"

When God saw what they were doing and how they turned from their evil ways, he relented and did not inflict upon them the evil he had threatened.

Jonah was painfully distressed and prayed to the Lord: "O Lord, this is what I foresaw when I was still in my own land; I therefore hastened to run away to Tarshish, for I knew that thou art a gracious and merciful God, patient and abundant in kindness. Now, O Lord, take my life away! It is better for me to die than to live."

Jonah made a tent for himself and sat in its shade, waiting to see what would happen to the city. The Lord God made a gourd grow up over Jonah to shade his head and alleviate his discomfort, and Jonah was exceedingly pleased with it. But next morning, at dawn, God caused a worm to attack the gourd and it withered. At sunrise, God sent a hot east wind and the sun beat on Jonah's head until he fainted. He longed for death, saying: "It is better for me to die than to live." Thereupon God said to Jonah: "Are you sorely grieved about the gourd?" He replied: "I am grieved enough to die."

Then the Lord said: "You would spare the gourd though you spent no work upon it. You did not make it grow—it sprang up in a night and perished in a night. Should I not then spare the great city of Nineveh with more than a hundred and twenty thousand human beings, who do not know their right hand from their left?"

Micah   מִיכָה

Micah was a younger contemporary of Isaiah. Both envisioned
the messianic future when war among nations would be no
more. The fact that the prophecy concerning universal peace
is phrased alike in both Isaiah and Micah has raised the question whether Micah quotes from Isaiah, or Isaiah from Micah,
or both quote the same prophecy from an earlier unknown
prophet. It was Micah who set forth the perfect ideal of religion when he said: "The Lord requires of you only to do
justice, to love mercy and to walk humbly with your God."

Woe to those who devise iniquity and work evil. They covet
fields and seize them; they covet houses and snatch them.

"I will surely assemble all of you, O Jacob, I will gather the
remnant of Israel, all together like sheep in a fold, a noisy multitude of men, led by their King, by the Lord at their head."

It shall come to pass in the latter days that the mountain
of the Lord's house shall be established as the highest mountain, towering over every hill, and peoples shall stream
to it.

Many nations shall say: "Come, let us go up to the
mountain of the Lord, to the house of the God of Jacob;
he will teach us his ways, and we will walk in his paths."

Out of Zion shall go forth Torah, and the word of the
Lord from Jerusalem.

They shall beat their swords into plowshares, and their
spears into pruning hooks; nation shall not lift up sword
against nation, neither shall they learn war any more.

They shall sit each under his vine and under his fig tree,
and none shall make them afraid.

"On that day," says the Lord, "I will assemble the
lame; I will gather those who have been cast off and those
whom I have afflicted. I will make the lame and the sick
into a mighty nation."

Now what does the Lord ask of you? Only to do justice,
to love mercy, and to walk humbly with your God.

156

Nahum נַחוּם

The prophet Nahum, whose name signifies consolation, limits himself to the graphic description of the downfall of the Assyrian empire. His book, containing only three chapters, is one of the best productions of biblical literature in terms of style and sublimity of thought. Nahum's message is a permanent expression of the cry for justice. He speaks in the name of outraged humanity, trampled by the ruthless armies of tyrannical Assyria. Nahum's breathless account of the destruction of Nineveh, the Assyrian capital, in the year 612, must have been written during or immediately after this historic event. Unlike other prophets, Nahum does not allude to the sins of his own people.

An oracle concerning Nineveh; the vision of Nahum.

The Lord is an avenging God, he takes vengeance upon his enemies. The Lord is slow to anger and of great might; he will by no means clear the guilty. The Lord is good to those who wait for him, a stronghold in the day of trouble; he cares for those who trust in him.

Behold, upon the hills, the feet of the messenger who brings good news, who proclaims peace! Keep your feasts, O Judah, for never again shall the villain invade you; he is utterly destroyed.

The shatterer has come up against you! The shields of his mighty men are crimson, his soldiers are clad in scarlet, his armored chariots gleam like fire. The chariots rage in the streets, flashing like torches, darting like lightning.

The palace is in panic, the queen is stripped and carried off, her ladies lamenting, moaning like doves, beating their breasts. And Nineveh is like a pool of water, desolate, dreary, drained; hearts are fainting, knees are shaking, all faces grow pale.

What has become of the lion's den, the lion who tore enough for his whelps and strangled prey for his lionesses? He filled his caves with prey, his dens with torn flesh.

"Behold, I am against you, Nineveh," says the Lord of hosts. "I will burn your chariots, and the sword shall devour your young lions; I will wipe your prey from the earth, and the voice of your envoys shall be heard no more."

O city, bloody throughout, full of lies and plunder! "Behold, I am against you," says the Lord of hosts. "I will expose you to nations; I will show kingdoms your shame. I will throw filth at you and treat you with contempt. Everyone who sees you will flee from you and say: Nineveh is ruined; there is none to lament her; where can I find comforters for her?"

Will you fare better than Thebes that sat by the Nile, with water around her? Yet she was exiled, she went away captive, at every street corner her infants were dashed to the ground; all her great men were bound in chains. You too shall reel and swoon, you too shall seek refuge from the foe; all your fortresses are like fig trees with ripe figs —if they are shaken they drop into the hungry mouth. The people inside you are but women! The gates of your land are wide open to your foes; your bars are burned by fire.

Draw water for the siege, strengthen your forts, plunge into the mud, trample the clay, take hold of the brick mold! But there fire shall devour you, the sword shall cut you down. Multiply yourselves like locusts, multiply like grasshoppers! Locusts spread their wings and fly away. Your officers are like grasshoppers, settling on the fences in a cold day—when the sun rises they fly away; no one knows where they are.

King of Assyria, your shepherds are asleep, your heroes slumber! Your people are scattered all over the hills, with none to rally them. There is no healing for your disaster, fatal is your wound. All who hear the news about you shall clap their hands over you; for upon whom has not your malice passed unceasingly?

Habakkuk חֲבַקּוּק

Nothing is known of the personal life of Habakkuk, the great prophet who, like Job, asked searching questions and received answers from God. Some scholars maintain that Habakkuk was a younger contemporary of Isaiah; others place him later, as a younger contemporary of Jeremiah. The three chapters of Habakkuk are well worth repeated readings, for they contain some of the noblest utterances in the history of religious experience. The book is full of force, thought, and poetic expression.

Habakkuk complains against the cruelties and inhumanities of the oppressors. Their continued victories and successes seem to him inconsistent with divine justice. He stations himself on a watchtower and looks hopefully for a divine answer. The tower is not a literal tower, but the inner light of revelation whereby he ponders the problem. The answer is that evil shall ultimately perish from the earth, and the upright shall live by their faithfulness.

How long, O Lord, shall I cry for help and thou wilt not hear? I complain to thee of wrongs, and thou dost not help. Why dost thou show me evil and make me look upon misery? Oppression and outrage confront me; strife and contention arise. The law is slack, and justice never appears; the wicked beset the righteous, so justice goes forth twisted.

Thou art eternal, Lord my God, my Holy One; we shall not die. Thy eyes are too pure to behold evil; thou canst not gaze upon wrongdoing. Why then dost thou look on faithless men and keep silent when the wicked swallow up the innocent? Thou hast made men like the fish in the sea, like crawling things without a ruler. The foe hooks all of them, drags them out with his net, and joyfully gathers them up. Through them he lives in luxury, and his food is plentiful. Shall he keep on emptying his net, murdering people without pity? I will station myself on the tower, and look forth to see what God will say to me!

The Lord answered me and said: Write down this vision on your tablets plainly, that one may read it swiftly: If it seems slow, wait for it; it will surely come without delay. The good man lives by reason of his faithfulness; the arrogant man shall not abide. His greed is as wide as the netherworld; like death he never has enough. Woe to him who heaps up what is not his own—for how long? Woe to him who acquires unjust gain, seeking to set his nest on high, safe from the reach of calamity. You have brought disgrace upon your house, you have forfeited your life. The stone shall cry from the wall, and the beam in the woodwork shall echo the call.

Woe to him who builds a city by bloodshed and founds a town on crime! The toil of nations ends in smoke, and peoples wear themselves out for naught. The knowledge of the Lord's glory shall fill the earth, as waters cover the sea.

O Lord, I have heard of thee; thy work, O Lord, I fear. In wrath, remember to be merciful. I have heard, and my body trembles; my lips quiver at the sound. Decay enters my bones; my steps totter beneath me. I will calmly await the day of trouble that comes upon people who assail us.

Though the fig tree may not blossom, and no fruit is on the vines; though the olive crop has failed, and the fields yield no food; though the flock is cut off from the fold, and there are no cattle in the stalls—yet I will exult in the Lord, I will rejoice in the God who saves me. The Lord God is my strength.

Zephaniah

צְפַנְיָה

Zephaniah, an older contemporary of Jeremiah, was of royal blood, and lived in Jerusalem during the reign of Josiah. He aimed to arouse the moral sense of his people, who had adopted the religion and customs of their Assyrian conquerors. Zephaniah was one of the first to break the long silence of more than fifty years which followed the death of the great prophet Isaiah.

The brief book of Zephaniah, consisting only of three chapters, stresses the demand for purity of heart and conduct. It contains also the idea that suffering has a disciplinary value. Zephaniah's prophecy was occasioned by the Scythian invasion of western Asia, which marked the beginning of the end to the Assyrian empire. Zephaniah pictures the approaching calamity and predicts the future glory of Jerusalem.

The word of the Lord which came to Zephaniah during the reign of Joshiah, king of Judah:

"I will utterly sweep away everything from the face of the earth. I will sweep away man and beast, birds of the air and fish of the sea. I will strike at Judah and all the inhabitants of Jerusalem. I will punish those who enrich the palace by violence and fraud. I will punish those who are at ease, who say to themselves that the Lord will do neither good nor ill. Their goods shall be plundered, and their houses laid waste. They shall not live in the houses they build, nor drink wine from the vineyards they plant."

The great day of the Lord is near, a day of distress and anguish, a day of ruin and devastation, a day of trumpet blast and battle cry against the fortified cities. No silver and no gold shall avail to protect them on the day of the Lord's wrath.

Seek the Lord, seek righteousness, seek humility; perhaps you may be hidden on the day of the Lord's wrath.

Gaza shall be deserted, and Ashkelon shall become a

desolation; Ashdod shall be exiled, and Ekron shall be uprooted. The seacoast shall belong to those left of the house of Judah; in the houses of Ashkelon they shall lie down at evening. For the Lord their God will remember them and restore their fortunes.

Moab shall become like Sodom, and Ammon like Gomorrah, lands overrun by weeds and salt pits, desolate forever. Those left of my people shall possess them. They shall be paid back for their pride, for taunting the people of the Lord.

And this was the exultant city that sat so secure, that thought herself supreme, saying: "I am and there is none else." What a desolation she has become! All who pass by her hiss and shake their fist. Woe to her, the defiled and oppressing city! Her officials are roaring lions; her prophets are faithless men; her priests do violence to the law. The unjust are shameless.

Sing, O Zion! Shout, O Israel! Rejoice with all your heart, O Jerusalem! The Lord is in your midst; you shall fear evil no more. "I will deal with all your oppressors. I will save the lame, and gather the outcast; I will lift them out of their shame to world-wide praise and fame. At that time I will bring you home; I will grant you praise and renown among all the peoples of the earth," says the Lord.

Haggai

חַגַּי

Haggai, one of the last three literary prophets, was a contemporary of Zechariah and Malachi. His prophetic activity centered around four months of the year 520, eighteen years after Cyrus had permitted the exiles to return to Judea. The work of rebuilding the Temple had been at a standstill for seventeen years, because of the hostile Samaritans who interfered with the work of restoration. Haggai sent four messages urging the returning exiles to rebuild the Temple in Jerusalem. They had lost courage, and needed renewed enthusiasm and hopefulness. Haggai roused the energies and aspirations of the people who started a new life in Judea.

In the second year of King Darius, the word of the Lord came to Haggai the prophet.

The people say that the time has not yet come to rebuild the house of the Lord. Is it a time for you to live in panelled houses of your own, while this house lies in ruins? Consider how you have fared. You have sown much and harvested little; you eat and yet you never have enough; you drink, but you never have your fill; you clothe yourselves but cannot keep warm; and he who earns wages puts them into a bag with holes.

"Now then, go up to the hills and bring wood to build the house. You expected a rich harvest, and it came to little; and when you brought it home, I blew it away. Why? Because of my house that lies in ruins, while each of you runs to his own house. Therefore the sky withholds its dew and the earth withholds its produce."

The people obeyed and went to work on the temple. And the Lord told Haggai the prophet to say to Zerubbabel, governor of Judah, and to the high priest Joshua, and to the rest of the people: "You who saw the temple in its former splendor, what do you think of it now? You think nothing of it? Yet, take courage, all you people of the land; work, for I am with you. Once again the treasures of all nations shall come in, and I will fill this house with splendor. The silver is mine, the gold is mine; the future splendor of this house shall be greater than the former; and upon this place I will bestow prosperity."

The word of the Lord came again to Haggai: "Speak to Zerubbabel, governor of Judah, tell him that I am about to shake the heavens and the earth; I will overthrow royal thrones, and shatter the power of empires; I will overthrow chariots and their riders; horses and their riders shall be struck down, each falling by the sword of his fellow. But on that day I will take you, O Zerubbabel my servant, and make you like a signet ring that is highly cherished, for I have chosen you as mine, says the Lord of hosts."

Zechariah   זְכַרְיָה

The book of Zechariah consists of fourteen chapters. The first eight chapters, generally referred to as part one, contain a series of eight visions, by means of which the prophet expresses his assurance that the Lord will restore Israel's former glory. The last six chapters, generally referred to as part two, include prophecies concerning the advent of Messiah, deliverance, final victory, and God's reign of peace.

Some scholars are of the opinion that the last six chapters belong to a much earlier anonymous author, a "Second Zechariah"; others, however, maintain that the so-called Second Zechariah lived at a much later period than the original Zechariah who, like his older contemporary Haggai, urged the immediate rebuilding of the Temple in Jerusalem during the years 520–518.

In the second year of King Darius, the word of the Lord came to Zechariah the prophet, bidding him tell the people: "Turn to me, and I will turn to you; be not like your fathers, who did not listen to me."

I raised my eyes and looked. There was a man with a measuring line in his hand! "Where are you going?" I asked him. He replied: "To measure Jerusalem, to see how broad and how long it should be." Another angel came forward and said: "Jerusalem shall be unwalled, like an open village, because of the multitude of men and cattle in it. For I, says the Lord, I will be a wall of fire around her, and I will be the glory within her. Sing and rejoice, O Zion, for I am coming, I will dwell in the midst of you, says the Lord."

Once more the angel came and waked me like a man roused from sleep, and he asked me: "What do you see?" I answered: "I see a lampstand, all of gold, with seven lights on it; there are two olive trees beside it, one to the right and the other to the left." Then I asked: "What are these, sir?" The angel replied: "These seven are the eyes of the

165

Lord; they range over the whole earth." I asked him: "What are these two olive trees?" He replied: "These are the two anointed who stand before the Lord of all the earth."

The word of the Lord came to Zechariah, saying: "Administer true justice; practise kindness and compassion toward each other; oppress not the widow, the orphan, the stranger or the poor; do not plot evil in your hearts against each other.

"Old men and old women shall again sit in the streets of Jerusalem. The streets of the city shall be full of boys and girls playing there. I will save my people from the land of the east and from the land of the west, and I will bring them home to dwell within Jerusalem; they shall be my people and I will be their God. I will sow peace and prosperity; the vine shall yield its fruit, the ground shall give its produce, and the skies shall drop their dew. I will save you, O house of Israel, and you shall be a blessing. Fear not, but let your hands be strong."

Thus says the Lord of hosts: "These are the things you must do: Speak the truth to one another; render judgments that are true and for the common good; do not plot evil in your hearts against one another, and never give yourselves to any perjury."

Thus says the Lord of hosts: "The fast of the fourth month, and the fast of the fifth, and the fast of the seventh, and the fast of the tenth shall become seasons of joy and gladness to the house of Judah, cheerful feasts. Only love truth and peace."

Malachi

מַלְאָכִי

Malachi, signifying "my messenger," is not a personal name but a pseudonym alluding to the promise: "Behold, I will send my messenger" (Malachi 3:1). The Socratic method of developing an idea through question and answer is a prominent feature of the style of Malachi, who often makes a statement and asks a question. This unidentified prophet, who was active about the middle of the fifth century before the common era, stresses personal religion, emphasizes mercy and faith. He deals with questions which have to be faced repeatedly, and analyzes the proper way of life. The book of Malachi, regarded as the finale of the Bible from a chronological viewpoint, contains the firm belief that ultimately all wrongs will be righted.

The word of the Lord to Israel through Malachi:

"I have loved you," says the Lord. But you ask: "How hast thou loved us?" "Is not Esau Jacob's brother?" says the Lord; "yet I loved Jacob and hated Esau. I laid waste his hill country and left his heritage to jackals of the desert.

"A son should honor his father, and a servant should honor his master. Now, if I am a Father, where is my honor? If I am a Master, where is my reverence?" says the Lord of hosts to you, O priests, who despise his name. The lips of a priest should treasure wisdom, and men should seek direction from his words. But you have turned aside from the way, you have caused many to stumble by your instruction; "you have violated the covenant of Levi," says the Lord of hosts; "so I too will make all the people despise and degrade you."

Have we not all one Father? Has not one God created us? Why then are we faithless to one another? "Take heed to yourselves, and let none be unfaithful to the wife of his youth; for I detest divorce and cruelty," says the Lord God of Israel.

167

"Behold, I send my messenger to clear the way for me; the Lord whom you seek will suddenly come to his temple; the messenger of the covenant, in whom you delight, is coming. But who can endure the day of his arrival, who can stand when he appears? He will sit as a refiner and purifier of silver, and he will cleanse the sons of Levi; he will refine them like gold and silver. Then the offering of Judah and Jerusalem will be pleasing to the Lord, as in the days of old. Return to me, that I may return to you," says the Lord of hosts.

"Behold, the day is coming, burning like an oven; all the arrogant and all evildoers shall be stubble; the day to come shall burn them up, leaving them neither root nor branch. But for you who revere my name, the saving sun shall rise with healing in its wings.

"Remember the Torah of my servant Moses, the rules and regulations that I gave him at Horeb for all Israel. Behold, I will send you Elijah the prophet, and he will turn the hearts of fathers to their children and the hearts of children to their fathers."

Psalms

תְּהִלִּים

The book of Psalms, consisting of 150 stirring hymns, is the first book in the third division of the Bible known as Hagiographa (Sacred Writings). The word *Psalms* is derived from the Greek version of the Bible, the Septuagint, where it is used in the sense of songs accompanied by the playing of musical instruments. The keynote of the psalms is simplicity of heart, faith in God and good conduct. In them we find the human heart in all its moods and emotions—in penitence, in danger, in desolation, and in triumph. The psalms are as varied as human life; they are enlightened in their ethics as they are lofty in their religious spirit.

Psalm 15 has the most perfect description of a good man. According to the Talmud, the six hundred and thirteen precepts of the Torah are summed up in this psalm, that is to say, the moral purpose of the Torah is clearly defined here.

Psalm 19 has been epitomized in the saying: "The starry sky above me and the moral law within me are two things which fill the soul with ever new and increasing admiration and reverence." According to Maimonides, this psalm contains a description of what the celestial spheres actually do; the heavens themselves are declaring God's wonders without words.

Psalm 23, portraying God's tender care and abundant love, has been the world's favorite psalm for many centuries. With quiet beauty and simple, unquestioning and unclouded confidence, the Psalm describes how all man's needs are met on his journey through life in a vast and dangerous world. God is presented first as a shepherd and next as a host, ever affording guidance and protection.

Psalm 27 consists of two parts. The first part expresses fearless confidence in the face of hostile armies, while the second part is the prayer of one in deep distress, beset by malicious accusers.

Psalm 34 is arranged alphabetically in the Hebrew text, each line begins with a letter of the alphabet in consecutive order. The essential message of the psalm is confidence and trust in God.

Psalm 39, of great pathos and beauty, has been said to be

"the finest of all the elegies in the Psalter." This short hymn reveals a variety of moods: faith, rebellion, despair, penitence, resignation and trust.

Psalm 90, contrasting the eternity of God with the brevity of human life, is ascribed to Moses and bears a resemblance to the book of Deuteronomy.

Psalm 104 is closely similar to the story of creation in Genesis. The psalmist celebrates God's glory as seen in the forces of nature. It has been declared that it is worthwhile studying the Hebrew language for ten years in order to read Psalm 104 in the original.

Psalm 107 has a universal appeal. It begins by calling upon the exiles, brought back to their homes, to give thanks. Then it describes God's goodness in taking care of lost travellers, prisoners, the sick, and sea-voyagers. At the end of each of the four stanzas, Psalm 107 uses the double refrain: "They cried out to the Lord in their trouble, and he delivered them from their distress. Let them thank the Lord for his kindness and his wonders toward men." Hence the talmudic statement that all who escape serious danger arising from illness, imprisonment or a perilous voyage, must offer public thanks.

The description of a storm at sea is the part of the psalm often recited by seafaring men. The storm is of exceptional violence, and the sailors realize in terror that they are in real danger. Their technical skill has become useless; they are at the mercy of the sea until the roar of the storm dies away, and nothing but a gentle, whispering wind remains.

Psalm One

Happy is the man who walks not in the counsel of the wicked, nor stands in the road of sinners, nor sits in the company of scoffers; but his delight is in the law of the Lord, and he meditates on it day and night.

He is like a tree planted by streams of water, that bears fruit in due season, with leaves that do not fade; whatever he does shall succeed.

Not so the wicked! They are like the chaff which the wind sweeps away. Hence, the wicked shall not stand when judgment comes, nor shall the sinful be among the upright.

Truly, the Lord favors the way of the just, but the way of the wicked shall perish.

170

Psalm Six

O Lord, punish me not in thy anger; chastise me not in thy wrath. Have pity on me, O Lord, for I languish away; heal me, O Lord, for my health is shaken. My soul is severely troubled; and thou, O Lord—how long?

O Lord, save my life once again; save me for the sake of thy grace. For in death there is no thought of thee; in the grave who can give thanks to thee?

I am worn out with my groaning; every night I drench my bed with tears. My eye is dimmed from grief; it grows old and weak because of all my foes.

Depart from me, all you evildoers! For the Lord has heard my weeping; the Lord accepts my prayer. All my foes shall turn back; they shall suddenly be put to shame.

Psalm Fifteen

O Lord, who may dwell in thy temple, who may reside in thy sanctuary? The blameless man who acts uprightly, and speaks truth in his heart. He neither slanders nor hurts nor insults his neighbor. He has contempt for a rogue, and honors those who revere the Lord. He keeps his word at his own risk, and does not retract. He lends money without interest, and does not accept a bribe against the innocent. He who does these things shall never be shaken.

Psalm Nineteen

The heavens proclaim the glory of God; the sky declares his handiwork. Day unto day pours forth speech, and night unto night reveals knowledge. There is no speech, there are no words; their voice is unheard. Yet their message extends through all the earth, and their words reach the end of the world.

The law of the Lord is perfect, refreshing the soul; the testimony of the Lord is trustworthy, making wise the simple. The precepts of the Lord are right, gladdening the heart; the commandment of the Lord is clear, enlightening the eyes. The Lord's faith is pure, enduring forever; the Lord's judgments are all true, all just. They

171

are more desirable than gold; sweeter are they than honey from the honeycomb.

Thy servant is careful of them; in keeping them there is great reward. But who can discern his own errors? Hold thou me guiltless of unconscious faults. Restrain thy servant also from wilful sins; let them not have dominion over me. Then I shall be blameless, I shall be clear of grave transgressions.

May the words of my mouth and the meditation of my heart be pleasing to thee, O Lord, my stronghold and my redeemer.

Psalm Twenty-three

The Lord is my shepherd; I am not in want. He makes me lie down in green pastures; he leads me beside refreshing streams. He restores my life; he guides me by righteous paths for his own sake. Even though I walk through the darkest valley, I fear no harm; for thou art with me. Thy rod and thy staff—they comfort me. Thou spreadest a feast for me in the presence of my enemies. Thou hast perfumed my head with oil; my cup overflows. Only goodness and kindness shall follow me all the days of my life; and I shall dwell in the house of the Lord forever.

Psalm Twenty-four

The earth and all it contains belong to the Lord! He has founded it upon the seas, and established it on the floods.

Who may ascend the mountain of the Lord? Who may stand within his holy place? He who has clean hands and a pure heart; he who strives not after vanity and swears not deceitfully.

Who is the King of glory? The Lord of hosts. He is the King of glory.

Psalm Twenty-seven

The Lord is my light and my aid; whom shall I fear? The Lord is the strength of my life; of whom shall I be afraid? Though war should rise against me, still will I be confident.

One thing I ask of the Lord, one thing I desire: that I may dwell in the house of the Lord all the days of my life, to behold the goodness of the Lord and to meditate in his temple.

O Lord, hear my voice when I call; be gracious to me and answer me. Teach me thy way, O Lord, and lead me in a straight path, in spite of my enemies. Deliver me not to the will of my adversaries.

Truly I trust to see the goodness of the Lord in the world of the living. Hope in the Lord! Be strong! Let your heart be brave! Hope in the Lord!

Psalm Thirty-three

Rejoice in the Lord, you righteous; it is fitting for the upright to give praise. The word of the Lord is right; all his work is done with faithfulness. He loves righteousness and justice; the earth is full of the Lord's kindness. By the word of the Lord the heavens were made, and all their host by the breath of his mouth.

Let all the earth revere the Lord; let all the inhabitants of the world stand in awe of him. For he spoke, and the world came into being; he commanded, and it stood firm.

From heaven the Lord looks down, and sees all of mankind. He fashions the hearts of all, he notes all their deeds. A king is not saved by the size of an army; a warrior is not rescued by sheer strength. Our soul waits for the Lord; he is our help and our shield. In him our heart rejoices; in his holy name we trust.

May thy kindness, O Lord, rest on us, even as our hope rests in thee.

Psalm Thirty-four

I bless the Lord at all times; his praise is ever in my mouth. Exalt the Lord with me, and let us extol his name together! I sought the Lord and he answered me; he delivered me from all my fears.

O consider and see that the Lord is good; happy is the man who takes refuge in him. Young lions may suffer want and hunger, but those who seek the Lord shall lack nothing.

Come, children, listen to me; I will teach you how to

revere the Lord. Who is the man that desires life, and loves a long life of happiness?

Keep your tongue from evil, and your lips from speaking falsehood. Shun evil and do good; seek peace and pursue it. The Lord is near to the broken-hearted, and saves those who are crushed in spirit.

A good man may have many afflictions, but the Lord delivers him from them all. The Lord saves the life of his servants; none of those who trust in him are ever desolate.

Psalm Thirty-nine

O Lord, let me know my end, the number of days that I have left; let me know how short-lived I am. Thou hast made my days no longer than a span; my lifetime is as nothing in thy sight. Every man, at his best, is an empty breath. Man walks about as a mere shadow, making much ado about vanity; he heaps up riches and knows not who will possess them.

What then can I expect, O Lord? My hope is in thee! Save me from all my sins; let me not become an object of reproach. Hear my prayer, O Lord, listen to my cry, answer thou my tears; for I am but a guest of thine, a sojourner, like all my forefathers. Have mercy upon me that I may recover my strength before I depart to be no more.

Psalm Forty-nine

Hear this, all you peoples; listen, all you inhabitants of the world, both low and high, rich and poor alike. My mouth speaks wisdom, and my heart's meditation is deep insight.

Why should I be afraid in days of evil, when the iniquity of my foes surrounds me, men who trust in their wealth, and boast of their great riches?

Even wise men die, the stupid and senseless perish alike, and leave their wealth to others. Man abides not in his splendor; he is like the beasts that perish.

Such is the fate of those who trust in themselves, the end of those who are pleased with their own mouthings. Like sheep they are destined to die. Death shall be their shepherd.

174

So fear not when a man grows rich, when the splendor of his house increases; for he will take nothing with him when he dies; his wealth will not follow him down to the grave. The man who lives in splendor but lacks understanding is like the beasts that perish.

Psalm Ninety

O Lord, thou hast been our shelter in every generation. Before the mountains were brought forth, before earth and world were formed,—from eternity to eternity thou art God.

Thou turnest man back to dust, and sayest: "Return, you children of man." A thousand years in thy sight are like a day that passes. Thou sweepest men away and they sleep. They are like grass that grows in the morning; in the evening it fades and withers.

All our days pass away in thy displeasure; we spend our years like a fleeting sound. The length of our days is seventy years, or, if we are strong, eighty years. It is speedily gone, and we fly away.

O teach us how to number our days, that we may get us a heart of wisdom. Have pity on thy servants. Gladden us in proportion to the days wherein thou hast afflicted us, the years wherein we have seen evil. May thy favor, Lord our God, rest on us; and establish thou the work of our hands.

Psalm Ninety-two

It is good to give thanks to the Lord, and to sing praises to thy name, O Most High; to proclaim thy goodness in the morning, and thy faithfulness at night.

Thou, O Lord, hast made me glad through thy work; I sing for joy at all that thou hast done. How great are thy works, O Lord! How very deep are thy designs! A stupid man cannot know, a fool cannot understand this. When the wicked thrive like grass, and all evildoers flourish, it is that they may be destroyed forever.

But thou, O Lord, art supreme for evermore. For lo, thy enemies, O Lord, shall perish; all evildoers shall be dispersed. The righteous will flourish like the palm tree;

175

they will grow like a cedar in Lebanon. Vigorous and fresh they shall be, to proclaim that the Lord is just! He is my Stronghold, and there is no wrong in him.

Psalm Ninety-four

Lord God of retribution, appear! Arise, thou Judge of the earth, render to the arrogant what they deserve. How long shall the wicked, O Lord, how long shall the wicked exult?

They speak arrogantly; all the evildoers act boastfully. They crush thy people, O Lord, and afflict thy heritage. The widow and the stranger they slay, and the fatherless they murder. They think the Lord does not see, the God of Jacob does not observe.

You fools, when will you understand? He who sets the ear, does he not hear? He who forms the eye, does he not see? He who punishes nations, shall he not punish you?

The Lord will not abandon his people, nor forsake his heritage. Judgment shall again conform with justice, and all the upright in heart will follow it.

They band themselves against the life of the righteous, and condemn innocent blood. But the Lord is my stronghold; my God is the rock of my safety. He will requite them for their crime, and destroy them for their wickedness.

Psalm One Hundred Four

Lord my God, thou art very great; thou art robed in glory and majesty. Thou wrappest thyself in light as in a garment; thou spreadest the heavens like a curtain. Thou makest winds thy messengers, the flaming fire thy servant.

Thou sendest forth streams into the valleys; they run between the mountains. They furnish drink for all the beasts of the field. Beside them the birds of the sky dwell; from among the branches they sing. Thou waterest the mountains from thy upper chambers; the earth is full of the fruit of thy works.

Thou makest grass grow for the cattle, and fodder for the working animals of man, to bring forth bread from the earth, and wine that cheers man's heart.

How manifold are thy works, O Lord! In wisdom hast thou made them all; the earth is full of thy creations. There is the sea, vast and broad, wherein are creeping things innumerable, creatures small and great. When thou takest away their breath, they die and turn again to dust. When thou sendest forth thy spirit they are created, and thou renewest the face of the earth.

Psalm One Hundred Seven

Give thanks to the Lord, for he is good; his mercy endures forever. Let the redeemed of the Lord say praise, for he has delivered them from the hand of the oppressor. He has gathered them from far lands, from east and west, from north and south. They wandered in the wilderness, on a desert road, without finding an inhabited town. They were hungry and thirsty, and were fainting away. Then they cried out to the Lord in their trouble, and he delivered them from their distress. He guided them in the right way, that they might reach an inhabited city. Let them thank the Lord for his kindness and his wonders toward men. He satisfies the longing soul, and gratifies the hungry heart.

Some sat in darkness and in gloom, bound in misery and iron, because they had rebelled against the words of God and scorned the counsel of the Most High. He humbled their heart by toil; they stumbled, with none to help. Then they cried out to the Lord in their trouble, and he delivered them from their distress. He delivered them from darkness and gloom, and broke their chains. Let them thank the Lord for his kindness and his wonders toward men. He breaks gates of bronze, and shatters iron bars.

Some, fools in their sinful ways, were sick and suffering because of their iniquities. They loathed all food, and reached the gates of death. Then they cried out to the Lord in their trouble, and he delivered them from their distress. He sent his word and healed them; he saved them from their graves. Let them thank the Lord for his kindness and his wonders toward men. Let them bring offerings of thanksgiving, recounting joyfully what he has done.

Those who crossed the sea in ships, trading in great waters, saw the works of the Lord and his marvels in the deep. He commanded and raised the stormy wind, which lifted the waves on high, soaring to the sky, sinking to the depths. Their soul melted away in distress. They reeled and staggered like drunken men, and were at their wit's end. Then they cried out to the Lord in their trouble, and he delivered them from their distress. He stilled the storm, and the waves were hushed. They rejoiced because the waves were calmed; he brought them to their desired haven. Let them thank the Lord for his kindness and his wonders toward men. Let them extol him in crowds of people; let them praise him in the council of the elders.

He turns rivers into a desert, fountains into parched land, and a fruitful country into a salt waste, because of the wickedness of its inhabitants. He turns a desert into pools of water, and dry land into fountains; there he settles the hungry, who establish a town for habitation. They sow fields and plant vineyards, which yield fruits for harvest. He blesses them and they multiply greatly; he does not diminish their herds. And when they are decreased and brought low through oppression, evil and distress, he pours contempt on lords and sets them in a pathless waste astray. But he lifts the needy from their affliction, and makes their families [as numerous] as a flock. Let the upright see this and rejoice, and all wickedness shut its mouth. Whoso is wise, let him observe these things and consider the gracious acts of the Lord.

Psalm One Hundred Fourteen

When Israel went out of Egypt, Judah became God's sanctuary and Israel his dominion. The sea beheld and fled; the Jordan turned backward; the mountains skipped like rams, and the hills like lambs.

What ails you, O sea, that you flee? Why, O Jordan, do you turn backward? You mountains, why do you skip like rams? You hills, why do you leap like lambs?

Tremble, O earth, at the Lord's presence, at the presence of the God of Jacob, who turns the rock into a pool of water, the flint into a flowing fountain.

Psalm One Hundred Eighteen

Out of distress I called upon the Lord; he answered me by setting me free. The Lord is with me; I have no fear. What can man do to me? The Lord is my helper; I shall see the defeat of my foes.

It is better to seek refuge in the Lord than to trust in man. It is better to seek refuge in the Lord than to trust in princes.

They swarmed like bees about me, but they were extinguished like a fire of thorns; relying on the Lord, I routed them. The Lord is my strength and my song; he has delivered me indeed. The right hand of the Lord does valiantly; the Lord's right hand triumphs. I shall not die, but live to recount the deeds of the Lord. The Lord has indeed punished me, but he has not left me to die. Open for me the gates of righteousness, that I may enter and praise the Lord. This is the gateway of the Lord; the righteous alone may enter.

Psalm One Hundred Twenty-one

I lift my eyes to the hills; oh, whence will my help come? My help comes from the Lord who made heaven and earth.

He will not let your foot slip; he who guards you does not sleep. Behold, he who keeps Israel neither slumbers nor sleeps.

The Lord is your keeper; the Lord is your shelter upon your right hand. The sun shall not harm you in the day, nor the moon by night.

The Lord will keep you from all evil; he will preserve your life. The Lord will protect you as you come and go, henceforth and forever.

Psalm One Hundred Twenty-five

Those who trust in the Lord are like Mount Zion which cannot be shaken, but abides forever. The mountains are round about Jerusalem, and the Lord is round about his people, henceforth and forever. Do good, O Lord, to those who are good, to those who are upright in heart. Peace be in Israel!

Psalm One Hundred Twenty-six

When the Lord brought the exiles back to Zion, we were like those who dream. Our mouth was filled with laughter, and our tongue with ringing song; then it was said among the nations: "The Lord has done great things for them." The Lord had done great things for us, and we rejoiced. Restore our fortunes, O Lord, like streams in the Negev. Those who sow in tears shall reap in joy.

Psalm One Hundred Twenty-eight

Happy is everyone who reveres the Lord, who walks in his ways. When you eat the toil of your hands, you shall be happy and at ease. Your wife shall be like a fruitful vine in your house; your children like olive plants, around your table. The Lord bless you from Zion; may you see the welfare of Jerusalem all the days of your life; may you live to see your children's children. Peace be upon Israel!

Psalm One Hundred Thirty

Out of the depths I call to thee. O Lord, hear my voice; let thy ears be attentive to my supplications. If thou, O Lord, shouldst keep strict account of iniquities, who could live on? But there is forgiveness with thee, that thou mayest be revered.

I hope in the Lord, my whole being hopes; I wait for his word. My soul waits for the Lord more eagerly than watchmen for the dawn. O Israel, put your hope in the Lord, for with the Lord there is kindness; with him there is great saving power. He will redeem Israel from all its iniquities.

Psalm One Hundred Thirty-seven

By the rivers of Babylon we sat down and wept when we remembered Zion. There upon the willows we hung our harps. Our captors demanded of us songs, saying: "Sing us some of the songs of Zion!"

How shall we sing the Lord's song in a foreign land? If ever I forget you, O Jerusalem, may my right hand wither! May my tongue cleave to my palate, if I ever stop think-

180

ing of you, if ever I do not set Jerusalem above my greatest joy!

Psalm One Hundred Thirty-nine

O Lord, thou hast searched me and dost know me. Thou knowest me sitting or rising; thou dost discern my very thoughts from afar. Even before a word is on my tongue, O Lord, thou knowest it all. Thou art on every side, behind me and before, laying thy hand on me.

Where could I go from thy spirit? Where could I flee from thy presence? If I ascend to heaven, thou art there! If I make my bed in the netherworld, thou art there! If I dwell in the uttermost parts of the sea, even there thy hand shall lead me, thy right hand shall hold me.

Thou didst form my being, didst weave me inside my mother. I praise thee for the awe-inspiring wonder of my birth; thy work is wonderful! Search me, O God, and know my heart; try me and test my thoughts; do thou lead me in the way everlasting!

Psalm One Hundred Forty-four

Blessed be the Lord, my stronghold, who trains my hands for war, my fingers for battle. He is my refuge and my deliverer.

O Lord, what is man that thou shouldst regard him? What is mortal man that thou shouldst consider him? Man is like a breath; his days are like a passing shadow.

O Lord, flash lightning and scatter my foes; send forth thy arrows and destroy them. Send down thy help from on high; rescue me from the great floods, from the hands of barbarians.

May our sons be like full grown plants, our daughters like sculptured pillars in a palace. May our barns be filled with all kinds of produce; may our sheep increase by tens of thousands. May there be no riot, no cry of distress in our streets. Happy are the people whose God is the Lord!

Psalm One Hundred Forty-five

I extol thee, my God, O King, and bless thy name forever and ever. One generation praises thy works to another, and

181

recounts thy mighty acts. They spread the fame of thy great goodness, and sing of thy righteousness.

Gracious and merciful is the Lord, slow to anger and of great kindness. The Lord is good to all, and his mercy is over all his works.

Thy kingdom is a kingdom of all ages, thy dominion is for all generations.

The Lord upholds all who fall, and raises all who are bowed down.

The eyes of all look hopefully to thee, and thou givest them their food in due season. Thou openest thy hand, and satisfiest every living thing with favor.

The Lord is righteous in all his ways, and gracious in all his deeds. The Lord is near to all who call upon him sincerely. The Lord preserves all who love him, but all the wicked he destroys.

Let all creatures bless his holy name forever and ever.

Psalm One Hundred Forty-six

Praise the Lord! Praise the Lord, O my soul! I will praise the Lord as long as I live; I will sing to my God as long as I exist.

Put no trust in princes, in mortal man who can give no help. When his breath goes, he returns to the dust, and on that very day his designs perish.

Happy is he who has the God of Jacob as his help, whose hope rests upon the Lord his God, Maker of heaven and earth and sea and all that is therein. The Lord sets the captives free.

The Lord opens the eyes of the blind, raises those who are bowed down, and loves the righteous. The Lord protects the strangers, and upholds the fatherless and the widow; but the way of the wicked he thwarts.

The Lord shall reign forever; your God, O Zion, for all generations. Praise the Lord!

Psalm One Hundred Forty-seven

Praise the Lord! It is good to sing to our God, it is pleasant; praise is comely. The Lord rebuilds Jerusalem;

182

he gathers together the dispersed people of Israel. He heals the broken-hearted, and binds up their wounds.

Great is our Lord and abundant in power; his wisdom is infinite. The Lord raises the humble, casts the wicked down to the ground, provides rain for the earth, and causes grass to grow upon the hills. He gives food to the cattle, and to the crying young ravens.

Praise the Lord, O Jerusalem! Praise your God, O Zion! He has fortified your gates; he has blessed your children. He sends forth his command to the world; his word runs very swiftly. He declares his word to Jacob, his statutes and ordinances to Israel. He has not dealt so with any of the heathen nations; his ordinances they do not know. Praise the Lord!

Psalm One Hundred Forty-nine

Praise the Lord! Sing a new song to the Lord; praise him in the assembly of the faithful. Let Israel rejoice in his Maker; let the children of Zion exult in their King. Let them praise his name with dancing; let them make music to him with drum and harp. For the Lord is pleased with his people; he adorns the meek with triumph. Let the faithful exult in glory; let them sing upon their beds. Let the praises of God be in their mouth, and a double-edged sword in their hand, to execute vengeance upon the heathen, punishment upon the peoples; to bind their kings with chains, and their nobles with fetters of iron; to execute upon them the written judgment. He is the glory of all his faithful. Praise the Lord!

Psalm One Hundred Fifty

Praise the Lord! Praise God in his sanctuary; praise him in his glorious heaven. Praise him for his mighty deeds; praise him for his abundant greatness. Praise him with the blast of the horn; praise him with the harp and the lyre. Praise him with the drum and dance; praise him with strings and flute. Praise him with resounding cymbals; praise him with clanging cymbals. Let everything that has breath praise the Lord. Praise the Lord!

Proverbs

מִשְׁלֵי

The book of Proverbs, together with the books of Job and Ecclesiastes, belongs to the Wisdom Literature of the Bible. It contains maxims and aphorisms for the better conduct of everyday life. In Proverbs, the ideal of life is a composite of honesty, diligence, helpfulness toward the distressed and consideration for one's fellow man. At the end of the book there is the poem which describes the perfect wife, trusted by her husband, obeyed by her servants, and admired by everyone. She is kind to the poor and gentle to all. She is self-respecting and dignified. Husband and children prize her as the source of their happiness.

Hear, my son, your father's instruction, and reject not your mother's teaching.

Happy is the man who gathers wisdom; no treasure can compare with it.

Go to the ant, you sluggard; look at her ways and learn wisdom. Though she has no leader, no ruler nor chief, she prepares her food in the summer, and gathers sustenance during the harvest season.

How long will you sleep, you sluggard? When will you rise from your slumber?

A little sleep, a little slumber, a little folding of the hands to rest, and poverty will pounce on you, want will overpower you.

Six things the Lord hates; seven he loathes: haughty eyes, a lying tongue, hands that shed innocent blood, a mind that plots wicked plans, feet that are quick to run after evil, a false witness who tells lies, and one who sows discord among brothers.

Can a man carry fire in his bosom without burning his clothes? Can one walk upon hot coals without scorching his feet? So is he who touches a neighbor's wife; he shall not go unpunished.

Do not reprove a scoffer, for he will hate you; reprove a man of sense, and he will love you.

Reverence for the Lord is the first thing in wisdom.

A sensible son is a joy to his father; a senseless son is a grief to his mother.

Where words abound, sin is not lacking; he who controls his tongue is a wise man.

The good man is delivered from trouble; the bad man takes his place.

A good man cares for the life of his beast; the bad man has a cruel heart.

The way of a fool is right in his own eyes, but a wise man listens to advice.

There are those whose reckless words wound like a sword, but the tongue of the wise brings healing.

A cautious man conceals his knowledge, but a fool comes out with his folly.

Worry weighs a man down; a kind word cheers him up.

He who guards his lips guards his life; he who talks freely comes to ruin.

One man pretends to be rich, though he has nothing; another pretends to be poor, though he has great wealth.

Wealth won in haste will dwindle, but he who gathers little by little will increase it.

Associate with wise men and you will be wise; a companion of fools will suffer harm.

He who spares the rod hates his son; the man who loves his son disciplines him.

The simpleton believes every thing; the prudent man watches where he goes.

In a multitude of people there is glory for a king; in a scarcity of people there is ruin for a prince.

He who oppresses a poor man insults his Maker; he who is kind to the poor honors his Maker.

Righteousness exalts a nation; evil brings a people low.

A soft answer turns wrath away, but a harsh word stirs up anger.

For the depressed every day is hard, but the cheerful heart enjoys a continual feast.

Better a little with reverence for the Lord than a great treasure with worry.

Better a dish of vegetables with love than the best beef served with hatred.

Pride ends in disaster, haughtiness means a downfall.

Better be modest among the poor than divide plunder with the proud.

He who is slow to anger is better than the mighty; he who controls himself is better than a conqueror.

Better a morsel of dry bread and peace than a house full of feasting and quarrels.

A rebuke goes deeper into a man of sense than a hundred lashes into a fool.

Even a fool may pass for wise if he says nothing; with closed lips he may be counted intelligent.

To answer a question before hearing it is foolish and shameful.

Many seek the favor of a generous man; all are friends of a man who gives presents.

Even a child makes himself known by his acts.

Better live in a lonely desert than beside a nagging, fretful woman.

Reputation is better than riches; esteem means more than silver and gold.

Train a child in the way he should go, and he will not leave it even when he grows old.

You see a man skillful in his work? He will stand before kings.

Do not eat the bread of a niggardly man; "eat and drink" he says to you, but his heart is not with you.

Never talk to a fool, for he will despise your words of wisdom.

Do not rejoice when your enemy falls, do not exult when he is overthrown.

Like clouds and wind without rain is a man who does not give what he promises.

Go seldom to your neighbor's house; he may grow tired of you and hate you.

186

If your enemy is hungry give him food; if he is thirsty give him water.

Like snow in summer and rain in harvest, so honor is unbecoming to a fool.

You see a man who is wise in his own eyes? There is more hope for a fool than for him.

The sluggard says: "There is a lion in the street."

As the door turns on its hinges, the lazy man turns upon his back.

Never boast about tomorrow; you never know what the day may bring.

The wicked flee when no one pursues, but the righteous are bold as lions.

He who hates unjust gain will prolong his life.

He who gives to the poor will not come to want.

The man who flatters his neighbor spreads a net for his feet.

A fool gives full vent to his temper, but a wise man restrains it.

Open your mouth, defend the rights of the poor and the needy.

The Ideal Wife

Who can find a good wife?
She is worth far more than rubies.
Her husband trusts in her,
And he never lacks gain.
She brings him good, and not harm,
All the days of her life.
She seeks out wool and flax,
And works willingly with her hands.
She is like the merchant ships—
She brings her food from afar.
She rises while it is yet night,
And gives food to her household,
And rations to her maids.
She considers a field and buys it;
With her earnings she plants a vineyard.
She girds herself with strength,
And braces her arms for work.

She finds that her trade is profitable;
Her lamp goes not out at night.
She sets her hands to the distaff;
Her fingers hold the spindle.
She stretches out her hand to the poor;
She reaches out her arms to the needy.
She is not afraid of the snow for her
    household,
For all her household is clad in scarlet
    wool.
She makes her own tapestries;
Her clothing is fine linen and purple.
Her husband is known at the gates,
As he sits among the elders of the land.
She makes linen cloth and sells it;
She supplies the merchants with belts.
Dignity and honor are her garb;
She smiles, looking at the future.
She opens her mouth with wisdom,
And kindly counsel is on her tongue.
She looks after her household;
She eats not the bread of idleness.
Her children rise and bless her,
And her husband praises her, saying:
"Many women do worthily,
But you excel them all."
Charm is deceptive, and beauty is vain;
Only a God-fearing woman shall be
    praised.
Give her due credit for her
    achievement;
Let her own works praise her at the gates.

Job　　　　　　　　　　　　　　　　אִיּוֹב

The book of Job deals with the problems of human suffering and contains some of the deepest thoughts that have come down from antiquity. Written in poetry, which is always more difficult than prose, the book of Job is not known and read as it deserves to be.

The forty-two chapters consist of three parts: a prologue, a poem, and an epilogue. The poem contains the debates between Job and his three friends; a speech by a bystander named Elihu; an address by God and a penitent confession by Job. In true humility, Job acknowledges the divine supremacy and learns the value of perfect trust and patience. God vindicates him and does not forsake him.

In chapter thirty-one, the virtues enumerated by Job are: a blameless family life, consideration for the poor and weak, charity, modesty, generosity, hospitality to strangers, honesty and just dealings.

The function of Satan, the Adversary, is described in the prologue as that of testing the sincerity of man's character. In talmudic literature, Satan was transformed into the *yetser ha-ra,* the evil impulse, whose function it is to strengthen man's moral sense by leading him into temptation. Man's heart is pictured as an arena where the good and evil wrestle in perpetual conflict.

In midrashic literature, Job is represented as a most generous man. He built an inn at the crossroads with four doors opening in four directions, so that transients might have no trouble in finding an entrance. He took the greatest care to keep himself aloof from every unseemly deed. However, Rabbi Yohanan ben Zakkai used to say that Job's piety was only the result of his fear of punishment (Sotah 27a). Job's chief complaint was, according to a talmudic opinion, that although man is driven to sin by the *yetser ha-ra* or evil impulse, yet he is punished. But Eliphaz answered him that if God created the *yetser ha-ra,* he also created the Torah by which a man can subdue the evil impulse (Baba Bathra 16a). The Rabbis ascribed the book of Job to Moses.

189

Once there was a man in the land of Uz, whose name was Job, a blameless and upright man who revered God and shunned evil. He had seven sons and three daughters, and possessed seven thousand sheep, three thousand camels, five hundred pair of oxen, five hundred donkeys, and a large number of servants. He was the greatest man in all the East.

One day the heavenly beings presented themselves before the Lord, and among them was Satan. "Whence do you come?" said the Lord to Satan. Satan answered: "From roaming and roving about the earth." And the Lord said to Satan: "Have you noticed my servant Job, a perfect and upright man who reveres God and shuns evil?" Satan replied: "But is it for nothing that Job reveres God? Hast thou not hedged him safely round about, his house and all that belongs to him? Thou hast blessed the labor of his hands, and his wealth is spread abroad in the land. Only put out thy hand and touch whatever he has; surely he will blaspheme thee to thy face!" Then said the Lord to Satan: "Well, all that he has is in your power; but lay no hand upon the man himself." Then Satan went away from the presence of the Lord.

One day, when Job's sons and daughters were eating and drinking in the house of their eldest brother, a messenger came to Job and said: "The oxen were plowing, the donkeys were grazing close by, when the Sabeans made a raid and carried them off; they killed the servants and I alone have escaped to tell you.". He was still speaking when another came and said: "Lightning fell from the sky and consumed the flocks and the servants; I alone have escaped to tell you." He was still speaking when another came and said: "The Chaldeans formed three divisions and made a raid upon the camels. They carried them off and killed the servants; I alone have escaped to tell you." He was still speaking when another came and said: "Your sons and daughters were eating and drinking in the house of their eldest brother, when a mighty wind came from the wilderness and struck the four corners of the house. It fell upon the young people, and they were killed; I alone have escaped to tell you."

Then Job arose, tore his mantle, shaved his head and fell to the ground crying: "Naked I came from my mother's womb, and naked I shall return; the Lord gave and the Lord has taken away; blessed be the name of the Lord." In all this, Job did not sin nor did he give offense to God.

Again on another day the heavenly beings presented themselves before the Lord, and among them was Satan. "Whence do you come?" said the Lord to Satan, and Satan answered: "From roaming and roving about the earth." And the Lord said to Satan: "Have you noticed my servant Job, a perfect and upright man, who reveres God and shuns evil? He still holds to his integrity, though you have led me to ruin him without cause." But Satan answered: "His own skin has been saved! A man will give all that he has to preserve his life. Only put out thy hand and touch his flesh and bones; surely he will blaspheme thee to thy face." And the Lord said to Satan: "Behold, he is in your hands; only spare his life."

Satan went away from the presence of the Lord, and he smote Job with leprosy from the soles of his feet to the crown of his head. Job took a potsherd with which to scrape himself as he sat among the ashes. His wife said to him: "Do you still hold fast to your integrity? Blaspheme God, and die." But he said to her: "You speak like a worthless woman. Shall we receive good at the hand of God, but not receive evil?" In all this, Job did not sin with his lips.

When Eliphaz, Bildad and Zophar, the three friends of Job, heard of all the trouble that had befallen him, they came to comfort him. When they saw him from a distance and could not recognize him, they wept aloud. For seven days and seven nights they sat beside him on the ground, and no one spoke a word to him, for they saw that his suffering was very great.

After this Job opened his mouth and cursed the day of his birth: "Perish the day I was born! Why did I not die at birth? I would have been lying still, I would have slept in peace, with the kings and counselors of the world. High and low are there alike, and the slave is free from his master. Why is light given to him who is in misery, and life to men in bitter despair, who long for death, but it comes not?"

Then Eliphaz replied: "If one ventures a word with you, will you be offended? Yet who can keep from speaking? Think now, what guiltless man has ever perished? When have the just ever been swept away? As I see it, men reap the evil that they plow, the trouble that they sow. Can mortal man be just before God? Can man be pure before his Maker? Were I in your place, I would turn to God who does great things beyond our understanding. He gives rain upon the earth and sends waters upon the fields; he sets on high those who are lowly, and those who mourn are exalted to victory. In famine he will rescue you from death, and in war from the power of the sword. You shall come to the grave in ripe old age, as a shock of grain comes to the threshing floor in the harvest season."

Job answered: "Would that God were pleased to crush me! What strength have I to hold out? Is my strength the strength of stones? Is my flesh made of bronze? Teach me, I will be silent; make me understand where I have gone wrong.

"I am forced to live through empty months, and nights of misery are allotted to me. I lie down thinking, 'When shall I arise?' The night is long, and till the day dawns I keep tossing to and fro. I will not restrain my mouth; I will speak in the anguish of my spirit; I will complain in the bitterness of my soul. When I think, 'My bed will comfort me, my couch will ease my complaint,' then thou scarest me with dreams, terrifying me with nightmares, till I would fain be strangled, I would prefer death to my being. Let me alone, for my days are but a breath. What is man, that thou dost make so much of him, punishing him every morning, testing him moment by moment? If I sin, what harm is that to thee? Why dost thou not pardon my transgression, why not let my sin pass?"

Then Bildad replied: "How long will you talk like that? Does God pervert justice? If you are pure and upright, he will reward you and prosper your righteous house. And though your beginning was small, he will amply enrich

192

you in the end. God will not reject a blameless man; he will yet fill your mouth with laughter and shouts of joy."

Then Job answered: "Yes, it is true; I know it; but how can a man be just before God? Though I am innocent, I cannot answer him; I must appeal for mercy to my accuser. Though I am blameless, he would prove me wrong. He destroys the blameless and the bad alike. The world is handed over to the wicked; he makes the rulers of men blind to justice! I am bound to be held guilty; why, then, should I struggle in vain? I am sick of life; I will give free utterance to my complaint; I will speak in the bitterness of my soul. I will say to God: 'Do not condemn me; let me know why thou dost quarrel with me. Does it seem good to thee to oppress and to despise the work of thy hands? Thy hands fashioned and made me; and wilt thou try to destroy me? Remember that thou madest me like clay; and wilt thou grind me into dust again?' "

Then Zophar replied: "Should a multitude of words go unanswered? Are men to be silenced by your babbling? When you mock, shall no one rebuke you? If God would only speak, and open his lips against you, you would know that God exacts of you less than your guilt deserves. If you will turn your mind to God, banishing sin from your life and evil from your house, you will be calm and fearless. You will forget your misery, remembering it no more than waters that have flowed away. Your life will be brighter than the noonday, your darkness will be like the dawn. You will lie down, and none will disturb you; and many will entreat your favor."

Then Job spoke: "No doubt you are the wise men, and wisdom will die with you. But I have understanding as well as you. Men at ease sneer at the unfortunate; when men stumble, there is contempt for them. The homes of robbers are at peace; those who provoke God are secure. I have seen all this; my ear has heard and understood it. What you know, I know too. But I would appeal to the Almighty; I desire to argue my case with God. You white-wash everything with lies. If only you would keep silent, you might pass for wise men. Will you speak falsely for

God? Will you show partiality toward him? Can you deceive him as one deceives a man?

"Let me have silence and I will speak, and let come on me what may. What are my iniquities? Let me know my offense and my sin. Why dost thou hide thy face and count me as thy enemy? Wilt thou frighten a driven leaf? Wilt thou pursue a withered straw? Man wastes away like a rotten thing, like a garment that is moth-eaten. Man born of woman lives but a few days and is full of trouble. He comes forth like a flower and withers; he is a fleeting shadow. There is hope for a tree that is felled; it may flourish yet again. Though its root decays in the soil, though its stump is dead in the ground, it may bud at the scent of water and put forth branches like a young plant. But man dies, and his strength is gone; man breathes his last, and where is he? Man lies down and rises not again; till the skies are no more he will not awake, he will not stir from his slumber. If only man might die and live again.

"But the mountain falls and crumbles away, the rock is removed from its place; stones are worn out by waters, torrents wash the soil away; even so thou destroyest the hope of man. Thou dost overpower him, and he has to go. His sons come to honor, but he does not know it; they are brought low, but he does not perceive it.

"Terrors are let loose on me; like a cloud my welfare has disappeared. My soul within me melts with sorrow; days of affliction lay hold of me. The night racks my bones; the pain that gnaws me never slumbers. God has plunged me into the mire, I am reduced to dust and ashes. I cry to thee and thou dost not answer me. Thou hast turned cruel to me; thou tossest me before the wind. I hoped for good, and evil came; I waited for the light, and darkness fell.

"If ever my step turned from the right way, if ever my heart went after my eyes, if ever I took to fraud, may others eat up what I sow, may my crops be uprooted.

"I never ignored the rightful claim of my servants when they complained against me—did not my Maker make my servant too, forming us both alike? I never begrudged a poor man anything, or caused a widow to pine in want or ate my food alone without sharing it with the fatherless.

For, like a father, God has brought me up, caring for me since ever I was born.

"If ever I saw anyone perish for lack of clothing without giving him fleece from my sheep; if ever I lifted up my hand against the fatherless; then let my shoulder drop from its socket, my arm snap from the collar-bone!

"If ever I relied on gold, or rejoiced because my wealth was great; if ever I exulted over my foe's ruin when evil overtook him, or practised the sin of cursing him and praying for his death; if ever I concealed my sins from men, covering up my guilt; if ever I was afraid of the great multitude and kept quiet within doors—well, here I enter my own plea of innocence.

"If ever my land accused me, if the furrows complained with tears that I ate the products without paying, and snuffed out the life of those who owned the land, may thorns grow up instead of wheat, and weeds instead of barley."

The three men ceased speaking to Job, because he considered himself in the right. Elihu became angry with Job. His anger was kindled also against Job's three friends, because they had found no answer to Job's railing against God. Elihu had waited to speak to Job because the men were older than he, but now he spoke:

"I am young and you are old, so I was timid and afraid to tell you my opinion. However, it is the spirit in men, the breath of the Almighty, that makes them understand. The old are not always wise, nor do the aged always understand what is right. Therefore I say: Listen to me; let me also express my opinion. I waited while you spoke, I listened to your arguments; I paid attention carefully to you, but none of you confuted Job. I must speak, that I may find relief; I must open my lips and answer. I will show partiality to no man. I will not flatter anyone. I do not know how to flatter.

"Give heed, O Job, listen to me; be silent, and I will speak. If you have anything to say, answer me; speak, for I desire to justify you. If not, be silent, and I will teach you wisdom. Far be it from God to do evil, far be it from the Almighty to do wrong. He makes man answer for his deeds, and fare exactly as he may deserve. Were he to withdraw his spirit, were he to gather in his breath, all flesh would perish at once, and man would return to dust. Could one who is opposed to justice govern? Would you denounce him who is righteous and mighty, who never favors princes, and who never prefers the rich to the poor? All men are the work of his hands. In a moment they are dead; in the middle of the night people are shaken and pass away; the mighty are taken away by an unseen hand.

"God's eyes are upon the ways of man, he watches every step that a man takes. There is no darkness, there are no black shadows, where evil-doers can hide themselves. He shatters the mighty and sets others up in their place. He strikes them down for their wickedness in the sight of men, because they turned aside from following him and heeded none of his ways. They caused the poor to cry to him, and he heard the groaning of the oppressed.

"Look at the heavens and see, behold the skies above. If you have sinned, how does it affect him? What are your many misdeeds to him? If you are upright, what do you give to him? What does he receive from your hand? Behold, God is exalted in his power; who is a teacher like him? Who can prescribe for him his way? Who can say: 'Thou hast done wrong?'

"Behold, God is great, and we know him not. He draws up water from the sea, and pours the rain down from the clouds, and provides food in abundance. Can any one understand the spreading of the clouds, the thunderings of his pavilion? He hurls the lightning from an unseen hand, and commands it to strike the mark. The thunder tells of him whose anger blazes against iniquity. To the snow he says: 'Fall on the earth,' and to the downpour and the rain: 'Be strong.' Then the beasts go into their lairs, and remain in their dens. Storms blow out of the south, and cold comes from the north. By the breath of God ice is formed, and the broad waters are frozen fast. He loads the thick cloud with moisture, and from the clouds his lightning scatters, turning as he directs it, doing whatsoever he commands it over all the world.

"Listen to this, O Job; stop and consider the wonders of God. Do you know how God makes the lightning of his cloud to flash? Do you know how the clouds are poised? Tell us what we shall say to him; we cannot argue with our darkened minds. The Almighty is beyond our reach; he is great in power and justice; he violates no right. He has no regard for those who are wise in their own conceit."

Then the Lord answered Job out of the whirlwind, saying: "Who is this that darkens my design by thoughtless words? Gird up your loins like a man, answer me the questions I will ask you. When I founded the earth, where were you then? Tell me, if you have understanding. Who fixed its measurements—do you know that? Have you discovered the fountains of the sea? Have you set foot upon the depths of ocean? Have you ever entered the storehouses of the snow? Have you ever seen the arsenals of hail? Do you know the laws of the heavens? Can you describe their sway over the earth? Can you lift up your voice to the clouds, that a flood of waters may cover you? Can you send out lightnings on a mission? Do they say humbly to you: 'Here we are'? Who provides for the raven its prey, when its young ones cry to God for lack of food?

"Do you know how wild goats breed upon the hills? Do you know the time when they bring forth? They bend down as they bring forth their young—robust offspring, thriving in the open; they run off and return not to the herd. Can you give strength to the horse? Do you make him leap like the locust, with majesty and terrible snorting? He mocks at fear and is not frightened, but on he charges in wild rage, he cannot stand still at the sound of the trumpet. Is it by your wisdom that the hawk soars and spreads its wings for the south? Does your word make the eagle fly high to nest aloft among the hills? Will the faultfinder still argue with the Almighty? He who argues with God, let him answer it."

Then Job replied to the Lord: "I am of small account; how shall I answer thee? I put my hand over my mouth. I will not answer. I know that thou canst do all things, and that nothing is too difficult for thee. I have said what I did not understand, things too wonderful for me, things which I did not know. I despise myself, in dust and ashes I repent."

Then the Lord said to Eliphaz: "My anger is hot against you and your two friends, because you have not spoken sincerely of me, as my servant Job has."

The Lord restored the fortunes of Job when he had prayed for his friends, and the Lord doubled all that Job had possessed before. His brothers and sisters and all who had known him before came and ate bread with him in his house; they comforted him for all the evil that the Lord had brought upon him.

In the end, the Lord made Job more prosperous than he had been before. He had fourteen thousand sheep, six thousand camels, a thousand pair of oxen, and a thousand donkeys. He had also seven sons and three daughters. In all the land there were no women as beautiful as Job's daughters. Job lived to see his grandsons and great-grand-sons—four generations. Then Job died, old, after a full life.

Song of Songs שִׁיר הַשִּׁירִים

The Song of Songs has been accepted throughout the ages as an allegory of the relations between God and Israel. Some nineteen centuries ago, Rabbi Akiba declared that the Song of Songs is the holiest of all the sacred writings. According to the Targum, the Song of Songs portrays the history of Israel. It has been regarded also as a representation of the affection of Israel for the Sabbath.

O kiss me with your lips, for your caresses are better than wine. Sweet is the fragrance of your perfumes; your very self is a precious perfume; therefore do maidens love you.

I am dark but lovely, maidens of Jerusalem. Do not stare at me because I am dark, for the sun has tanned me. My brothers were angry with me, so they made me keeper of the vineyards, and I did not look after my own vineyard.

Tell me, you whom my soul loves, where you feed your flocks, where you bring them to rest at noon. Why should I have to wander among your companions' flocks?

You are beautiful, my love, you are beautiful; your eyes are like doves. Like a lily among thorns, so is my loved one among maidens.

Like an apple tree among trees of the forest, so is my beloved among youths. In his shadow I long to sit; his fruit is sweet to my taste.

I hear the voice of my beloved! Here he comes, leaping across the mountains, bounding over the hills! My beloved is like a gazelle, like a young deer. There he stands, behind our wall, gazing through the windows, peering through the lattice.

My beloved called and said to me: Rise, my love, my beauty, come away. For, lo, the winter is over, the rain is past and gone; the flowers appear on the earth, the time of song has come! The call of the turtle-dove is heard in our land; the fig tree is ripening its early figs, and the vines in blossom give forth their fragrance. Rise, my love, my beauty, come away. O my dove, in the clefts of the rock, in the cover of the cliff, let me see your form, let me hear your voice; for sweet is your voice, and your form is lovely.

On my bed at night I looked for him whom my soul loves; I searched for him, but I did not find him. I will rise, I said, and go through the city—I will seek him whom my soul loves.

I looked for him, but I did not find him. I asked the watchmen: "Have you seen him whom my soul loves?" Scarcely had I left them than I found him. I held him and would not let go of him until I had brought him into my mother's house.

You are beautiful, my love, you are beautiful! Your eyes are dove-like behind your veil; your hair is like a flock coming down from Mount Gilead. Your teeth are like a flock of sheep all shaped alike, which have come up from being washed; they are evenly matched, and not one is missing. Your lips are like a thread of scarlet, and your mouth is lovely.

I was asleep, but my heart was awake. Hark! My beloved is knocking. "Open to me, my sister, my love, my dove, my innocent one; for my hair is drenched with dew, my locks with the drops of night."

I opened to my beloved, but he had turned away and was gone. I searched for him, but could not find him; I called him, but he did not answer. The watchmen struck me and wounded me, the guardians of the walls stripped me of my mantle.

Where has your beloved gone, O fairest of women? Where has he turned, that we may seek him with you?

My beloved has gone down to his garden, to the flower-beds of balsam, to gather lilies. I am my beloved's, and he is mine.

Come, let us go into the fields, let us stay in the villages. Let us go early to the vineyards, to see whether the grape-

200

vine has budded, whether the vine blossoms have opened, whether the pomegranates are in flower. There I will give my love to you.

O that you were my brother! I would meet you in the street and kiss you, and none would despise me. I would bring you into my mother's house; I would give you some wine to drink, some of my pomegranate juice.

Love is strong as death itself; its flashes are flashes of fire, a flame of the Lord. Floods cannot quench love, rivers cannot drown it. If a man offered all his wealth for love, he would be utterly scorned.

Make haste, my beloved! Be like a gazelle, or like a young deer, on the mountains of spices.

Ruth

רוּת

The book of Ruth takes its name from Ruth who clung to her mother-in-law Naomi with all the unselfishness of true-hearted affection. The narrative is one of idyllic beauty. It is the most charming short story in the Bible, and presents a pleasing picture of life in Israel during the period of the judges.

Naomi is an example of faithfulness and loyalty, self-sacrifice and moral integrity. Widowed and bereft of her two sons, Naomi returned to Bethlehem from Moab, where they had lived during a famine in Judea. Anxious to provide for Ruth and to see her married, she successfully arranged the marriage of Ruth to Boaz.

About two-thirds of the narrative is in dialogue. In the Hebrew Bible, the book of Ruth is placed among the five *Megilloth* or Scrolls (Song of Songs, Ruth, Lamentations, Ecclesiastes, Esther), which are recited in the synagogue on special occasions.

The book of Ruth is recited annually on Shavuoth (Pentecost), the harvest festival commemorating the giving of the Torah, because the scene of its story is the harvest field and its leading character embraces Judaism.

In the time when the judges ruled, there was a famine in the land of Judah; so a man named Elimelech from Bethlehem went to live in Moab, he and his wife Naomi and their two sons. Elimelech died, and Naomi was left with her two sons, Mahalon and Kilion, who married Moabite women, one named Orpah, and the other—Ruth. After about ten years, both Mahalon and Kilion died, so that the woman was bereft of her two children as well as her husband.

When she heard that the Lord had remembered his people in Judah and given them food, she left Moab together with her daughters-in-law to return to her own country. But, as they were setting out, Naomi said to her two daughters-in-law: "You go back, each of you to her mother's house. May the Lord treat you as kindly as you have treated the dead and me. May the Lord help each of you find a home in the house of her husband." Then she kissed them. "No," they replied, "we will go back with you to your people."

"Turn back, my daughters," Naomi said, "why should you go with me? Have I any more sons to be husbands to you? No, my daughters, my plight is worse than yours; the hand of the Lord has gone forth against me." Again they wept; Orpah kissed her mother-in-law goodby, but Ruth clung to her.

Naomi said: "Look, your sister-in-law has turned back to her people and to her gods; turn back after her." But Ruth said: "Entreat me not to leave you and to turn back from following you; wherever you go, I will go; wherever you stay, I will stay; your people shall be my people, and your God shall be my God; wherever you die, I will die, and there will I be buried. May the Lord punish me time and again if anything but death parts me from you!" When Naomi saw that she was determined to go with her, she said no more.

The two went on until they came to Bethlehem. Upon their arrival in Bethlehem the whole town was stirred, and the women said: "Is this Naomi?" But she said to them: "Do not call me Naomi; call me Mara, for the Almighty has dealt very bitterly with me. I left here when I was rich, and the Lord has brought me back empty-handed."

The barley harvest was just beginning when Naomi and Ruth reached Bethlehem. So Ruth said to Naomi: "Let me go to the fields and glean ears of corn after one who will be kind to me." "Go, my daughter," Naomi answered. So Ruth went and gleaned in the fields after the harvesters, and she happened to come to the field belonging to Boaz, a kinsman of Naomi's husband. Just then Boaz came out from Bethlehem and said to the harvesters: "May the Lord be with you!" They replied: "May the Lord bless you!"

"Whose girl is this?" Boaz asked the foreman of the

harvesters. The foreman replied: "It is the Moabite girl who came back with Naomi. She asked to be allowed to glean among the sheaves after the harvesters, and she has been working ever since morning, without resting even for a moment."

Then Boaz said to Ruth: "Now listen, my daughter. Do not go to glean in another field; do not leave this one, but stay close to my maidservants. Keep your eyes on the field they are reaping and follow them. Whenever you are thirsty, go to the water jars and drink. I have been well informed of all that you have done for your mother-in-law since the death of your husband, of how you left your father and mother and the land of your birth and came to a people who were strange to you. May the Lord reward you for what you have done; may you receive full recompense from the Lord God of Israel, under whose wings you have taken refuge."

She answered: "Thank you, my lord, for speaking kindly to me, even though I am not one of your own servants."

At mealtime Boaz said to her: "Come here and eat some of our bread; dip your slice in the vinegar." So she sat beside the harvesters, and he handed her roasted grains. She ate till she was satisfied, and had some left over. When she got up to glean, Boaz gave orders to his servants: "Let her glean even among the sheaves, and do not be rude to her."

So she gleaned in the field till evening. Then she beat out what she had gleaned and took it away with her to the town. Her mother-in-law asked her: "Where did you glean today? Where did you work? A blessing on the man who was friendly to you!" So she told her mother-in-law that the man's name was Boaz. Then Naomi said: "May he be blessed by the Lord, who has not ceased to be kind to the living and to the dead! The man is a relative of ours; he is one of our near kinsmen."

"Furthermore," said Ruth, "he told me to keep close to his servants till they have finished all his harvesting." But Naomi said: "It is well, my daughter, that you go out with his girls, so as not to be molested in another field." So she kept close to the girls of Boaz as she gleaned until the end of the barley and wheat harvests.

Then Naomi said to her: "Boaz is winnowing barley to-night at the threshing floor. Wash yourself, put on your best clothes, and go down to the threshing floor, but do not reveal your presence to the man until he has finished eating and drinking. Note the place where he lies down; then uncover his feet and lie down there; and he will tell you what to do."

She went down to the threshing floor and did just as her mother-in-law had told her. At midnight the man was startled; he discovered a woman lying at his feet. "Who are you?" he asked. She replied: "I am Ruth; take me in marriage, for you are a close relative." And he said: "May the Lord bless you, my daughter. Have no fear, my daughter, I will do for you all that you ask. It is true that I am a kinsman, but there is a nearer kinsman than myself. If he will do his duty, good and well; if not, I will."

So she lay at his feet until morning, then she went back to the city. "How did you fare, my daughter?" her mother-in-law asked. And she told her all that Boaz had done for her, saying: "He gave me these six measures of barley, for he said that I must not go back empty-handed."

Boaz found the kinsman and asked him if he would buy the parcel of land which belonged to Elimelech. "I will," the man replied. Then Boaz said: "When you buy the field from Naomi, you are also buying Ruth, the widow, so as to carry on the name of her dead husband along with his inheritance." But the kinsman answered: "I cannot, for fear of injuring my own inheritance. Take over my right of redemption yourself, for I cannot redeem the property."

Boaz married Ruth, and she bore a son. Then the women said to Naomi: "Blessed be the Lord who has not left you this day without a kinsman! May the boy's name be renowned in Israel! He will renew your life and nourish your old age, for he is the child of your daughter-in-law, who loves you and is better than seven sons to you." They named the baby Obed. He was the father of Jesse, who in turn was the father of David.

Lamentations

The book of Lamentations consists of five lyric poems describing the fall of Jerusalem in 586 before the common era. In the Hebrew Bible, four of these dirges are alphabetical acrostics. The fifth poem, even though it is not an alphabetical acrostic, has twenty-two verses, corresponding to the number of letters in the Hebrew alphabet.

These poems are among the finest examples of biblical Hebrew. They are attributed to Jeremiah who was an eye-witness to the agony of Jerusalem and the despair of its inhabitants during the invasion of Nebuchadnezzar, when Solomon's Temple was destroyed after it had been in existence for four hundred and ten years.

The Greek version of the Bible, known as the Septuagint, begins the book of Lamentations with these words: "After Israel was carried into captivity, and Jerusalem was laid waste, Jeremiah sat down and wept, and sang this song of woe over Jerusalem." The book is recited in the synagogues on the ninth day of Av, the day on which the Temple was destroyed.

How lonely is the city, once so full of people! She has become like a widow, once so great among the nations! She weeps bitterly in the night. Of all her friends there is none to comfort her. They have all betrayed her. They have become her enemies.

Judah has gone into exile; she finds no rest; her pursuers have all overtaken her in the midst of her distress. Jerusalem recalls all the precious things that were hers; the enemy has laid his hands on all her treasures; she has seen pagans invade her sanctuary. All her people are moaning in their search for bread; they trade their treasures for food to keep themselves alive.

You who pass by, look all of you and see if there is any

sorrow like my sorrow which was brought upon me by the Lord on the day of his wrath. For all this I weep, tears stream from my eyes; my children are desolate, for the enemy has prevailed. Zion stretches out her hands, but there is none to comfort her.

Cry aloud to the Lord, O Zion! Pour out your heart like water before the Lord! Look, O Lord, and see! All over the streets they lie, both young and old. My maidens and my young men have fallen by the sword; not one escaped or survived on the day of thy anger.

The kindnesses of the Lord never cease, his mercies never fail; they are new every morning; great is thy faithfulness! The Lord is good to those who look hopefully to him, to a soul that seeks him. It is good to wait in silence for the salvation of the Lord.

Why should a man complain when he is punished for his sins? Let us scan and test our ways, let us return to the Lord! Let us lift up our hearts and hands to God in heaven. Without cause, my enemies have hunted me like a bird.

Happier were the victims of the sword than the victims of hunger. Compassionate women have cooked their children with their own hands; they became their food at the downfall of my people. The Lord lit a fire in Zion which consumed its foundations. Our eyes failed as we looked vainly for help.

Our pursuers were swifter than the vultures of the air; they hunted us on the hills, they lay in wait for us in the wilderness. Remember, O Lord, what has befallen us; look and see our disgrace! Our heritage has been turned over to strangers; we have become orphans and are fatherless.

Our fathers sinned and are no more; and we must bear their guilt. Slaves rule over us; there is none to free us from their power. But thou, O Lord, dost reign forever; thy throne endures through all generations. Restore us, O Lord, and let us return to thee. Renew our days as of old.

Ecclesiastes

The book of Ecclesiastes was composed by Koheleth, who is traditionally identified with King Solomon. It contains twelve chapters of maxims and wise observations on the purpose of life.

Koheleth counsels patience, endurance and discretion. He examines the value of wisdom, wealth, and pleasure, and finds life unsatisfying. He declares that wealth does not yield happiness. It is often lost even before it is enjoyed. At death, it is left to people who have not toiled to acquire it; hence, all is a vain pursuit.

How are we to gain happiness? Shall we follow wisdom or unrestrained pleasure? Human existence is monotonous: there is nothing new in the entire world. We should therefore alternate wholesome work with reasonable pleasures of life while we can, since there is no telling when the end comes.

This book concludes with this counsel: "Revere God and keep his commandments, for this is the whole duty of man." Koheleth is recited in the synagogues on the eighth day of the Sukkoth festival.

Vanity of vanities, says Koheleth, all is vain. What does a man gain from all his toil under the sun? One generation goes and another comes, but the earth remains forever. The sun rises and the sun sets, only to rise again. All the rivers flow into the sea, but the sea is never full. There is nothing new under the sun. Men may say of something: "See, this is new!"—but it existed long ago before our time.

I was king of Israel in Jerusalem. I set my mind to search and survey all that is done under the sun. It is a sorry task given to the sons of men by God! I have seen all the things done under the sun—they are vain and futile. The more you know, the more you suffer; an increase of knowledge is an increase of sorrow.

I built mansions, planted vineyards, and laid out gardens and parks. I made pools to water the trees in my

208

plantations; I acquired servants; I amassed silver and gold. Richer and richer I grew, more than any before me in Jerusalem. My wisdom also remained with me. I denied myself nothing that I desired. I withheld no pleasure from my heart. But when I turned to look at all I had achieved, at my toil and trouble—it appeared all vain and unreal. There was nothing to be gained under the sun. Then I saw that wisdom excels folly as light excels darkness.

There is a time for everything: a time to be born and a time to die; a time to plant and a time to uproot; a time to kill and a time to heal; a time to break down and a time to build up; a time to weep and a time to laugh; a time to mourn and a time to dance; a time to cast away stones and a time to gather stones; a time to embrace and a time to repel; a time to seek and a time to discard; a time to keep and a time to throw away; a time to rend and a time to mend; a time to keep silent and a time to speak; a time to love and a time to hate; a time for war and a time for peace.

I know that there is nothing better for men than to be happy and enjoy themselves as long as they are alive. It is indeed God's very gift to man that he should eat and drink and be happy as he toils.

There is one fate for man and beast; as the one dies so the other dies; the same breath is in all of them. All go to one place; all are from the dust, and all return to the dust. Who knows whether the spirit of man goes upward and the spirit of the beast goes down to the earth? So I saw that it is best for man to enjoy his work and be happy.

I looked again and saw all the oppression that prevails under the sun. So I thought that the dead are more fortunate than those who are still alive. I saw another futile thing under the sun—a person who has no one, either son or brother, yet there is no end to all his toil. He cannot satisfy himself with what he gains, and he never asks himself: "For whom am I toiling and depriving myself of pleasure?" Two are better than one—if either of them should fall the other will raise him up; but woe to him who is alone.

Never be rash with your mouth. Better not vow at all than vow and fail to pay.

A lover of money will never be satisfied with his money.

Sweet is the sleep of the worker, whether he eats much or little; but the surfeit of the rich man does not let him sleep.

Naked he came from his mother's womb, and naked he must return; for all his toil he has nothing to take with him. What does he gain by all his toil for the wind, spending all his days in darkness and grief, in much anger and sickness and distress?

There is an evil that lies heavy upon mortals: a man to whom God gives riches, wealth and honor, and he lacks nothing of all that he desires, yet God does not permit him to enjoy it, but a stranger enjoys it.

A good name is better than precious oil.

It is better to hear the rebuke of the wise than the praise of fools.

Let your garments be always spotless.

Cast your bread upon the waters; after many days you shall find it.

As you do not know how the wind blows, nor how a child within the womb grows, so you do not know how God works, God who makes everything.

Sweet is the light of life; it is pleasant for the eyes to see the sun.

If a man lives many years, let him have joy throughout all of them; let him remember that the days of darkness will be many.

Rejoice in your youth, young man; follow your heart's desire and the sight of your eyes, but know that for all this God will bring you to account.

Remove all worries from your mind, and keep your body free from pain.

Remember your Creator in the days of your youth, before the evil days come and the years approach of which you will say: "I have no joy in them." Revere God and keep his commandments, for this is the whole duty of man.

Esther

The book of Esther, one of the most cherished works in Jewish literature, is the last of the five sacred scrolls that are part of the third division of the Bible known as Hagiographa (Holy Writings). The scroll of Esther tells the story of a Jewish girl who used her influence as queen of Persia to save her people from a general massacre which Haman had plotted against them on purely racial grounds. It is a tale of plot and counterplot, showing the downfall of the arrogant and the vindication of the innocent.

Queen Esther is depicted as dutiful toward Mordecai, her guardian, and faithful to her people. Haman, with his vanity, malice and cruelty, is a masterpiece of portraiture. His fate reminds us that pride goes before a fall. Ahasuerus, who agrees to Haman's plot without thought, is painted as a pompous and feeble-minded monarch. Some scholars identify him with Xerxes, who reigned from 486 to 465. Others believe him to be Artaxerxes II, who reigned from 404 to 361, and who is mentioned in Ezra 4:6.

Explaining the origin of the social and convivial festival of Purim, the scroll of Esther is recited aloud in the synagogues at the eve of Purim and again the next morning. The feast of Purim, universally observed by the Jewish people even to this day, has been considered strong evidence that the book of Esther is an historical document. Though the name of God is not mentioned in the book, the author clearly implies that God used Mordecai and Esther as instruments for the deliverance of a persecuted people.

King Ahasuerus, who reigned over a hundred and twenty-seven provinces from India to Ethiopia, gave a banquet to the nobles and officers of the army and displayed his royal treasures. The banquet lasted one hundred and eighty days, and was followed by a seven-day banquet for all the people in Shushan, the capital. Queen Vashti also gave a banquet for the women. On the seventh day, when the king's heart was merry with wine, he commanded Queen Vashti to appear in order to show off her beauty, but Queen Vashti refused to go before the court. Enraged, the king asked his wise men what should be done with her. "Let the king assign her royal position to a better woman," Memucan advised, and the king acted accordingly. He also sent letters to every province directing that every man should be lord in his own house.

There was a Jew in Shushan by the name of Mordecai. He had adopted his orphaned cousin Esther and brought her up as his own daughter. Beautiful and lovely, she was taken into the royal house where she became a favorite. She said nothing about her people or her descent, for Mordecai had told her not to reveal it. The king loved Esther more than all his wives and he made her queen instead of Vashti.

After these events, King Ahasuerus promoted Haman and advanced him above all his officers. All bowed low before Haman, but Mordecai would not bow to him. This infuriated Haman so much that he decided to destroy all the Jews throughout the empire of Ahasuerus. He said to the king: "There is a certain people dispersed in every province of your kingdom whose laws are different from those of other people and they do not obey the king's laws. The king should not tolerate them in the land. If it please the king, let it be decreed that they be destroyed, and I will pay ten thousand talents of silver into the royal treasury."

"Keep your money," the king said to Haman, "and do what you like with the people." Then instructions were sent to all the king's provinces to massacre and destroy all the Jews, young and old, women and children in one day, the thirteenth day of the month of Adar. The king and Haman sat down to drink, but the city of Shushan was perplexed.

When Mordecai learned all that had been done, he rent his garments, put on sackcloth and went about the city, crying bitterly. There was great mourning among the Jews in every province, wherever the king's command was heard. Esther ordered Hathach to go and find out from Mordecai what was the meaning of it all. Mordecai told him all that had happened and gave him a copy of the decree, which he was to show to Esther, charging her to intercede with the king on behalf of her people.

When Hathach told Esther what Mordecai had said, she gave him this message for Mordecai: "Everybody knows that there is one penalty for any person who goes to the king without being summoned; it is death. I have not been summoned for thirty days." Whereupon Mordecai replied: "Do not imagine you will escape inside the royal palace any more than the rest of the Jews on the outside. If you keep silent at a time like this, relief and deliverance will arise from another quarter; but you will perish, you and your father's house. Who knows whether it was not for a time like this that you have been raised to royalty."

Then Esther sent this reply to Mordecai: "Go gather all the Jews of Shushan and fast on my behalf; eat and drink nothing for three days and three nights; I and my maids will fast likewise. Then I will go to the king, though it is against the law; and if I perish, I perish." Mordecai did as Esther ordered him.

On the third day Esther stood in the inner court of the royal palace. When the king saw Esther standing in the court, he held out the golden scepter to her; Esther approached and touched it. "What is your wish, Queen Esther," the king asked, "what is your request? It shall be given you were it even half of my kingdom." Esther said: "If it please the king, let the king and Haman come today to a banquet which I have prepared for the king."

"Bring Haman at once," the king ordered, "that we may do as Esther desires." So the king and Haman came to the banquet that Esther had prepared. As they were drinking wine, the king said to Esther: "What is your petition? It shall be granted; were it even half of my kingdom, it shall be fulfilled." But Esther replied: "My petition and my request—well, if it please the king, let the king and Haman come tomorrow to the banquet which I will prepare for them; tomorrow I will do as the king has said."

That day Haman was joyful and glad of heart. He told his friends and his wife Zeresh: "Queen Esther invited no one except myself along with the king to the banquet she had prepared, and she has invited me again tomorrow together with the king. But all this does me no good as long as I see Mordecai the Jew sitting at the king's gate." Then his wife and all his friends said to him: "Let a gallows be made, and in the morning tell the king to have Mordecai hanged upon it; then go merrily with the king to the banquet." This pleased Haman, and he had the gallows made.

On that night the king could not sleep, so he had the book of records brought and read in his presence. It was found that Mordecai had saved the king's life. The king asked: "What honor, what dignity has been bestowed on Mordecai for this?" "Nothing has been done for him," the king's attendants replied. Then the king asked: "Who is in the court?" Haman had just entered the outer court to speak to the king about hanging Mordecai. So the king's attendants said: "Haman is standing in the court." And the king said: "Let him come in."

Haman came in, and the king asked him: "What should be done to the man whom the king delights to honor?" Haman said to himself: "Whom would the king delight to honor more than me?" So he said to the king: "For the man whom the king delights to honor, let a royal robe be brought which the king has worn, and a horse on which the king has ridden, with a royal crown upon its head; let the robe and the horse be entrusted to one of the king's noblest officials. He shall see that the man whom the king delights to honor is arrayed and led on horseback through the streets of the city, proclaiming: 'This is done for the man whom the king delights to honor.'"

The king said to Haman: "Make haste, take the robe and the horse, as you have said, and do all this to Mordecai the Jew; leave out nothing of what you have spoken." So Haman took the robe and the horse and arrayed Mordecai and led him on horseback through the streets of the city, proclaiming: "This is done for the man whom the king delights to honor."

Then Haman hurried home lamenting, and told his wife Zeresh and all his friends everything that had befallen him.

They said to him: "If Mordecai, before whom you have begun to fall, is of the Jewish people, you will never defeat him, but you will keep falling before him." Just as they were talking, the king's attendants arrived and hurried Haman to the banquet that Esther had prepared.

So the king and Haman came to feast with Queen Esther. On the second day of the banquet, the king again asked Esther: "What is your petition, Queen Esther? It shall be granted you. What is your request? Were it half my kingdom, it shall be fulfilled." Queen Esther replied: "If I have found favor in your sight, O king, and if it pleases the king, let my life be given me—that is my petition! Grant me my people—that is my request! I and my people are to be destroyed, to be slain, to be annihilated." King Ahasuerus asked Esther: "Who is it? Where is the man who has dared to do this?" Esther replied: "A foe, an enemy, this wicked Haman!"

Haman trembled before the king and the queen. The king rose in fury from the feast and went into the palace garden. Haman came forward to beg Queen Esther for his life, for he saw that the king had determined evil against him. When the king came back from the palace garden, Haman had fallen on the couch where Esther sat! "Will he even violate the queen in my presence, in my own house?" said the king. One of the royal attendants, Harbonah, said: "At Haman's house a gallows is standing, which he prepared for Mordecai who saved the king's life." "Hang him on that!" the king ordered. So they hanged Haman on the gallows which he had prepared for Mordecai.

Then Esther spoke again to the king; she fell at his feet and begged him with tears to avert the evil design of Haman against the Jews. She said: "If it please the king, let an order be written to revoke the letters sent out by Haman, in which he commanded the destruction of the Jews throughout the king's empire. How can I bear to witness the calamity that befalls my people? How can I endure the destruction of my kindred?" Thereupon King Ahasuerus said to Esther and Mordecai: "Write as you please about the Jews, write it in the name of the king and seal it with the signet of the king."

215

The king's secretaries were summoned, and an edict was written to the governors and officials of the provinces, from India to Ethiopia, to every province in its own script and to every people in its own language, and also to the Jews in their script and their language. The writing was in the name of King Ahasuerus and sealed with the king's signet ring. Letters were sent by mounted couriers riding on swift horses. By these the king gave the Jews permission to gather and defend their lives on the thirteenth day of the twelfth month, which is the month of Adar.

The couriers rode out in haste, and the decree was issued in Shushan. The Jews had light and joy and gladness and honor. In every province and in every city, wherever the king's edict arrived, there was gladness and joy among the Jews. Indeed, many pagans became Jews.

Mordecai sent despatches, giving to the Jews in every city the king's permission to defend their lives and destroy any armed forces that might attack them. On the thirteenth day of Adar, the Jews triumphed over their adversaries. In Shushan they fought for their lives on the thirteenth and the fourteenth, resting on the fifteenth and making that a day of feasting and rejoicing and sending gifts to one another.

Mordecai charged all the Jews to keep both the fourteenth and the fifteenth of the month of Adar, every year, as days of feasting and rejoicing. These days are called *Purim* after *pur*, lot, for Haman had cast the lot to destroy and annihilate the Jews, but his wicked plot recoiled upon his own head. Mordecai was great and popular among the Jews, for he sought their welfare and peace.

216

Daniel

דָּנִיֵּאל

The book of Daniel is made up of two parts. The first six chapters, written chiefly in Aramaic, tell of the miraculous deliverance of Daniel and his three friends who were exiled to Babylon by Nebuchadnezzar before the fall of Judea; they also include Daniel's interpretations of Nebuchadnezzar's dreams.

Daniel lived at the royal court and survived till the days of Cyrus, the Persian conqueror of Babylon, who authorized the return of the Jewish exiles and permitted them to rebuild the Temple at Jerusalem in 538.

The story of Daniel's three friends who were cast into the burning furnace is similar to the incident of Abraham and Nimrod. The last six chapters, written chiefly in Hebrew, consist of visions concerning four great empires, probably Babylon, Persia, Greece, and Syria.

Belshazzar is referred to as the son of Nebuchadnezzar, even though cuneiform inscriptions make it clear that he was the eldest son of and co-regent with Nabonidus, the last king of the Babylonian empire (556–539). Belshazzar was probably a descendant of Nebuchadnezzar, and in the Bible the word for "son" sometimes denotes "descendant."

The four Aramaic words, which were written by a mysterious hand on the wall at Belshazzar's feast, may have appeared in the form of anagrams. According to the Talmud, the inscription *mene mene tekel upharsin,* which could not be read by anyone except Daniel, appeared like this:

M M T L R
E E E U S
N N K P I
E E E A N

The initial "u" of the word *upharsin* is a conjunction, meaning *and.* After such a conjunction, the letter "p" changes to "ph," in keeping with rules of Hebrew grammar. The word *parsin* is the plural of *peres,* which denotes division and is spelled exactly like the Hebrew word for Persia. Hence, instead of *upharsin* the word should be transliterated *uparsin.*

King Nebuchadnezzar commanded his chief officer to bring to him some youths of Jewish nobility. They were to be handsome and intelligent, scholarly and competent, and able to serve in the royal palace. They were to be trained for three years before entering the king's service. Among these young men were Daniel, Hananiah, Mishael, and Azariah, who were renamed Belteshazzar, Shadrach, Meshach, and Abednego.

Daniel, who refused to defile himself by eating the king's food, said to the steward: "Let us have vegetables to eat and water to drink for ten days, and you will then compare our appearance with that of the youths who eat the king's fare." The steward agreed and did as they asked. At the end of ten days, they looked better and healthier than the youths who ate the king's fare. So he withheld meat and wine and served them vegetables. At the end of their training the four young men became the personal attendants of Nebuchadnezzar, who found them ten times better than all the magicians in his realm.

Nebuchadnezzar often had strange dreams. His spirit was troubled and he could not sleep. The king asked Daniel: "Can you explain the dream I have had and what it means?" Daniel answered: "There is a God in heaven who reveals mysteries, and he has disclosed to King Nebuchadnezzar what is to happen in days to come. You saw, O king, a mighty statue of exceeding brightness standing before you, terrible to behold. The head of this statue was made of fine gold, its breast and arms of silver, its belly and thighs of bronze, its legs of iron, and its feet were part iron and part clay. As you looked, a stone struck the feet of the image and shattered them to pieces; then the iron, the clay, the bronze, the silver, and the gold were shattered, and the wind swept them away so that not a trace of them remained. But the stone that struck the image became a great mountain and filled the whole earth.

"This was the dream; now we will tell the king what it means. You, O king, are the golden head. After you shall arise another kingdom, less powerful; then a third kingdom of bronze, which shall rule over all the earth. The fourth kingdom shall be strong as iron; it shall be a divided kingdom, for you saw iron mixed with the clay. The divided kingdom will not hold together, just as iron does not mix with clay. In the days of these kings, God will set up a kingdom which shall never be destroyed. It will smash all the kingdoms and bring them to an end. For you saw a stone cut out of the mountain by no human hand and it broke to pieces the iron, the bronze, the clay, the silver, and the gold. Great God has revealed to the king what shall happen in the future."

Then King Nebuchadnezzar gave Daniel high honors and many great gifts. He made him ruler over the entire province of Babylon and prefect over all the wise men of Babylon.

King Nebuchadnezzar once made a golden image, ninety feet high and nine feet broad. He summoned the officials of the provinces to appear at its dedication. When they arrived and stood before the image, the herald proclaimed aloud: "When you hear the sound of the horn and other kinds of music, you are commanded to fall down and worship the golden image that King Nebuchadnezzar has set up. Whoever does not bow down and worship shall instantly be cast into a fiery furnace." So, whenever the people heard the sound of the horn and the rest of the music, they knelt down and worshiped the golden image.

Some Chaldeans maliciously accused Shadrach, Meshach and Abednego of defying the king's orders. They said to King Nebuchadnezzar: "These men have paid no heed to you, O king; they do not serve your gods, and they do not worship the golden image which you have set up." At this, Nebuchadnezzar was filled with fury, and his face became distorted with rage. He ordered the soldiers to bind Shadrach, Meshach and Abednego and cast them into the burning furnace. So hot was the furnace the flames killed the men who lifted Shadrach, Meshach and Abednego; but these three fell bound into the flames of the furnace.

Then King Nebuchadnezzar became alarmed, and said: "I see four men walking in the midst of the flames, and they are not hurt. The appearance of the fourth is like that of an angel." Nebuchadnezzar went towards the door of the fiery furnace, calling: "Shadrach, Meshach and

Abednego, servants of the Most High God, come forth and come to me!" The three came out of the fire, and when the governors and the king's ministers gathered round, they saw that the fire had had no effect upon their bodies; their hair had not been singed, and there was no smell of burning about them.

Nebuchadnezzar said: "Blessed be the God of Shadrach, Meshach and Abednego! He has sent his angel to save his servants who trusted in him and surrendered their bodies to the fire rather than serve any god other than their own God." Then the king promoted them in the province of Babylon.

King Nebuchadnezzar to all the nations of the world: "I was at ease in my house, when I saw a dream which alarmed me. I told it to Daniel, saying:

"I saw a tree in the midst of the earth, and its height was great. The tree grew and became strong, till its top reached to heaven and was visible to the very end of the earth. Its leaves were lovely and its fruit was abundant; the beasts of the field took shelter in its shadow, and the birds of the air dwelt in its branches; it provided food for all. And an angel came down from heaven and called aloud: 'Hew down the tree and cut off its branches; shake off its leaves and scatter its fruit. Let the beasts flee from under it and the birds from its branches. Yet leave the stump of its roots in the earth, with a band of iron and bronze round it, amid the tender grass of the field. Let him be drenched with the dew of heaven. Let him share the grass of the earth with the beasts. Let his mind be changed from man's, and let a beast's mind be given to him.'

"I, King Nebuchadnezzar, had this dream. Now, Belteshazzar, tell me what it means. All the wise men of my kingdom are unable to tell me its meaning, but you are able, for the divine spirit is in you."

Then Daniel, whose name was Belteshazzar, replied: "My lord, may the dream be for those who hate you, and its interpretation for your enemies! The tree you saw, which grew and became strong till it was high as heaven and visible to all the word, the tree whose leaves were lovely and whose fruit was rich, providing food for all, the tree under

220

which the beasts of the field sheltered and in whose branches the birds of the air dwelt—it was you, O king! You have grown and become strong. Your power and your dominion stretch to the world's end. O king, it is a decree of the Most High, that you shall be driven from among men, and your dwelling shall be with the beasts of the field. You shall be made to eat grass like an ox, and you shall be drenched with the dew of heaven, and seven years shall pass over you, till you learn that the Most High rules the kingdom of men, and that he gives power to anyone he chooses. Therefore make an end of your sins by practising justice and showing mercy to the oppressed."

Now all this came upon King Nebuchadnezzar. Twelve months later he was walking on the roof of the royal palace in Babylon, saying to himself: "This great Babylon I have built by my vast power and for my glorious majesty." The words had not left his lips when a voice fell from heaven: "O King Nebuchadnezzar, here is your sentence: your kingdom is taken from you! You shall be driven from among men and shall dwell with the beasts of the field; you shall be forced to eat grass like an ox, and seven years shall pass over you until you have learned that the Most High reigns over the realm of men, and gives it to anyone he chooses."

The sentence was carried out instantly upon Nebuchadnezzar. He was driven away from among men. He ate grass like an ox, and his body was drenched with the dew of heaven until his hair resembled the feathers of an eagle, and his nails looked like the claws of a bird.

"When the time had passed, I, Nebuchadnezzar lifted my eyes to heaven, and my reason returned to me. I regained my majesty and splendor and was firmly seated on my throne. Now I praise and honor the King of heaven, for all his deeds are right and his ways are just, and those who walk in pride he is able to humble."

King Belshazzar made a great banquet for a thousand of his lords. Carried away by the wine he drank, Belshazzar commanded that the gold and silver vessels which his father Nebuchadnezzar had taken from the temple in Jerusalem be brought before him. The sacred vessels were brought, and the king, his lords, wives and concubines, drank from them.

That very hour, the fingers of a man's hand appeared and wrote upon the wall of the royal palace, and the king saw the hand as it wrote. The king's color changed, his thoughts alarmed him. His knees knocked against each other. Not one of all the king's wise men could read the writing or explain the meaning of it to him.

Daniel was then brought into the king's presence. He said: "O king, God gave Nebuchadnezzar, your father, greatness and glory and majesty; all nations trembled before him. But when he became arrogant, when his spirit became defiant, he was deposed from his royal throne and deprived of his glory; he was driven away from among men, and his mind was made like that of a beast. He ate grass like an ox, until he learned that the Most High God rules the kingdom of men and that he sets over it whom he chooses. Yet you, his son, O Belshazzar, have not humbled your heart. Though you knew all this, you lifted yourself up against the Lord of heaven. The vessels of his house were brought before you, and you and your lords, your wives and your concubines have drunk wine from them! You have praised the gods of silver and gold which do not see or hear or know; but the God in whose hand is your breath of life and all your destiny you have not honored.

"This is the writing that was inscribed upon the wall: *Mene, Mene, Tekel, Uparsin*. The meaning of it is: *Mene* (numbered), God has numbered the days of your kingdom and brought it to an end; *Tekel* (weighed), you have been weighed in the scales and found wanting; *Peres* (divided), your kingdom is divided and given to the Medes and Persians."

That very night Belshazzar, the Chaldean king was slain, and Darius the Mede captured the kingdom.

The windows in Daniel's room were opened toward Jerusalem, and three times a day he got down upon his knees and prayed to God. Daniel's foes surged in and found him offering prayers and supplications to his God. They went before King Darius and asked: "Did you not sign an edict that any man who makes petition to any god or man

222

within thirty days, except to you, O king, shall be cast into the den of lions?"

"It is true," the king replied. Then they said to the king: "Daniel pays no heed to you, O king; he recites his prayers three times a day to his own god."

When the king heard these words, he was greatly distressed. He worked hard until sundown trying to save Daniel's life, but the men reminded the king that, according to the statutes of the Medes and the Persians, no law laid down by the king could be changed. So Daniel was cast into the den of lions. A stone was brought and laid upon the opening of the den, and the king sealed it with his own signet and with the signet of his lords. Then the king went to his palace, and spent the night fasting.

At daybreak, the king went in haste to the den of lions. When he came near the den, he cried in a tone of anguish: "O Daniel, has your God been able to deliver you from the lions?" Daniel replied: "O king, live forever! My God has sent his angel and shut the mouths of the lions; they have not hurt me. He has found me innocent; nor have I done you any wrong, O king." The king was exceedingly glad, and commanded that Daniel be lifted out of the den. The men who had accused Daniel were then brought and cast into the den of lions; and before they reached the bottom of the pit, the lions crushed their bones to pieces.

Ezra עֶזְרָא

The books of Ezra and Nehemiah are counted as a single book because they owe their existence to a single compiler. This combined work is called *Ezra* in the Talmud. It is the main authority for that period of Jewish history with which it deals. A considerable part of Ezra-Nehemiah contains the memoirs left by the two leaders who organized Jewish life in Judea.

The book of Ezra describes the activities of a new figure in Judaism—the scribe, who took the place of the prophet after the return of the Jews from the Babylonian captivity. The scribes made available copies of the Scriptures, and carefully interpreted and taught them to the people.

Accompanied by fifteen hundred exiles, Ezra, the scribe, arrived in Jerusalem in 450. According to talmudic tradition, Ezra was the founder of the Great Assembly, a body of spiritual leaders, described as the successors to the prophets in keeping alive the knowledge of the Torah.

The book of Nehemiah, however, is written mostly in the first person singular. It tells of the experiences of Nehemiah, a cupbearer of the Persian king, Artaxerxes, who was twice governor of Jerusalem in 445 and 433. The noble character of Nehemiah, his strong self-reliance combined with a serene trust in God, are vividly portrayed in the story of his zealous endeavors to restore the ruined city of Jerusalem and rebuild its walls.

The Lord inspired Cyrus king of Persia to issue a proclamation permitting the Jews of his realm to return to Jerusalem and rebuild the temple.

The tribes of Judah and Benjamin, the priests and the Levites, prepared to go. Their neighbors helped them with silver and gold, goods and beasts of burden and costly things—all freely offered. The entire company numbered forty-two thousand three hundred and sixty, besides seven thousand three hundred and thirty-seven servants and two hundred singers. They had seven hundred and thirty-six horses, two hundred and forty-five mules, four hundred and thirty-five camels, and six thousand seven hundred and twenty donkeys.

They hired masons and carpenters to rebuild the temple. They traded food, drink, and oil with the Sidonians and Tyrians for cedars brought down from Lebanon to the seacoast at Jaffa. Zerubbabel appointed Levites to superintend the work on the house of the Lord. When the builders laid the foundation of the temple, the priests and the Levites came forward with trumpets and cymbals to praise the Lord with the refrain: "He is good, his kindness endures forever." All the people raised a mighty shout as they praised the Lord. But many of the priests and Levites, old men who had seen the first temple, wept aloud at the sight of this house.

When the enemies of Judah and Benjamin heard that the returned exiles were building a temple, they came and said to Zerubbabel and the heads of the tribes: "Let us build with you, for we worship your God as you do; we have been sacrificing to him ever since the king of Assyria brought us here." But Zerubbabel and the other leaders told them: "You can have nothing to do with building a house to our God; we will build it ourselves, as King Cyrus has commanded us."

The people of the land harassed the men of Judah and terrorized them. In a letter to Artaxerxes king of Persia, they wrote: "Be it known to the king that the Jews have come to Jerusalem. They are rebuilding that rebellious and wicked city. Be it known to the king that if this city is rebuilt, they will not pay tribute, tax, or toll, and the royal revenue will suffer; you will also lose all your territory west of the Euphrates." This put an end to the work on the temple. The rebuilding of the temple did not begin again until the second year of the reign of Darius, king of Persia.

Zerubbabel and Jeshua, aided by the prophets Haggai and Zechariah, started once more to rebuild the temple of God at Jerusalem. Then came the governor of the province, and his associates and asked: "Who gave you permission to build this temple? What are the names of the men who are building here?" However, they did not stop the construction but reported the matter to Darius, who replied with these instructions:

"Let the governor and the elders of the Jews rebuild the house of God on its site. The cost is to be covered from the royal treasury without delay. Day by day without fail, let them have whatever they require, that they may offer sacrifices and pray for the life of the king and his children." The governor and his associates acted promptly on the king's instructions and the elders of the Jews built and prospered. The temple was finished in the sixth year of the reign of King Darius.

The people of Israel, the priests and the Levites and the rest of the returned exiles, celebrated the dedication of this house of God with joy. On the fourteenth day of the first month the returned exiles observed the Passover. For seven days the festival of unleavened bread was celebrated with joy, for the Lord had made them joyful by turning the heart of the king of Assyria towards them, to encourage them in their work on the temple of the God of Israel.

It was after this that Ezra, who was a scribe skilled in the Torah of Moses, came from Babylon to Jerusalem accompanied by Israelites, priests, Levites, singers, wardens and temple attendants. He had set his heart upon studying the Torah, upon obeying it and upon teaching it in Israel.

Then the leaders approached Ezra and said: "The people of Israel and the priests and the Levites have not separated themselves from the abominable practices of the Canaanites, the Ammonites, and the Egyptians; they have married their daughters and married their sons to their daughters." When Ezra heard this, he rent his garments, tore his hair, and sat down aghast. At the evening offering he rose from his fasting, and spread out his hands to the Lord God, saying:

"O my God, I am ashamed, I blush to lift my face to thee; our guilt has mounted up to the skies. O our God, what shall we say? We have forsaken the commandments which thou didst send through thy servants the prophets, saying: 'The land which you are entering to possess is pol-

226

luted with the abominations of the peoples, who have filled it with their uncleanness from end to end. Therefore give not your daughters to their sons, neither take their daughters for your sons, that you may be strong and eat the good of the land.' O Lord God of Israel, here we stand guilty before thee; none of us can stand before thee because of this."

As Ezra prayed and made confession, weeping and prostrating himself before the house of God, he was joined by a very large gathering of men, women and children, who wept bitterly. Shecaniah said to Ezra: "We have broken faith with our God and have married foreign wives from among the natives. Still, there is some hope for Israel in spite of all this. Let us put away our wives and their children. Let us act according to the Torah. We are with you; be strong and take action."

Then Ezra withdrew from the house of God into a room of Johanan, where he neither ate bread nor drank water, for he was mourning over the faithlessness of the returned exiles. A proclamation was then issued throughout Judah that all should assemble at Jerusalem and, if anyone failed to appear within three days, all his property should be confiscated and he himself excommunicated.

Within three days all the men of Judah and Benjamin assembled at Jerusalem. They sat in the open square before the house of God, shivering from fear as well as from the chill of the heavy rain. Ezra, the priest, rose and said to them: "You have broken faith and married foreign wives. Now make confession to the Lord God of your fathers and do his will; separate yourselves from the natives and from your foreign wives." The assembly answered with a loud voice: "Truly, we shall do as you have said. But the people are many, and it is the rainy season; we cannot stand in the open; and this is not work for a day or two, for we have greatly transgressed in this matter. Let all in our towns who have married foreign wives come at appointed times before the judges and elders." Then the returned exiles took action and by the first day of the first month all had divorced their foreign wives.

Nehemiah

נְחֶמְיָה

These are the words of Nehemiah:

It happened in the month of Kislev, when I was in Shushan the capital, that one of my kinsmen came from Judah with a few men. I asked them about the Jews and about Jerusalem. They told me that the returned exiles were suffering great misery and shame; that the wall of Jerusalem was broken down and that the gates were destroyed by fire. When I heard this, I sat down and wept.

I was cupbearer to the king. He said to me: "Why is your face sad? You are not ill. This must be sadness of heart." I replied: "May the king live forever! Why should not my face be sad, when the city of Jerusalem lies waste and its gates have been destroyed by fire?" Then the king said: "What request have you to make?" I answered: "If it please the king, pray let me go to the city where my fathers are buried, that I may rebuild it." The king asked: "How long will you be gone?" I proposed a certain time to him, and it pleased him to allow me to go.

I also requested that letters be given me to the governors west of the Euphrates, permitting me to proceed to Judah and, also, a letter to Asaph, the keeper of the king's forest, to give me timber for the gates of the fortress of the temple, for the wall of the city and for the house in which I would live.

The king granted my request, for the good hand of my God was upon me. The king also sent with me some army officers and horsemen. When Sanballat the Samaritan and the Ammonite slave, Tobiah, heard of this, they were greatly incensed that a man had come to promote the welfare of the people of Israel.

After spending three days in Jerusalem, I got up during the night and inspected the broken walls and the gates. I came back and said to the people: "You see how Jerusalem lies in ruins. Come, let us rebuild the wall." "Let us start to build," they replied, and they set about their task with vigor. But when Sanballat heard that we were rebuilding the wall, he was furious. He said to his fellow Samaritans: "What are these feeble Jews doing? Will they restore things? Will they revive the stones out of the heaps of rubbish?" Tobiah, the Ammonite, added: "Let them build! If a fox stepped on that stone wall of theirs, he would knock it down!"

So we rebuilt the wall to half its height all round, for the heart of the people was in their work. But when Sanballat and Tobiah and the Ammonites and the Ashdodites heard that the walls of Jerusalem were being repaired, they were extremely angry. They then conspired to fight against Jerusalem. But we offered prayers to our God and posted guards to watch both day and night. I stationed men armed with sword and spear and bow and said to them: "Do not be afraid of them! Remember the Lord and fight for your sons, your daughters, your wives and your homes."

Half of my retinue worked on construction, and half held the spears, shields, bows, and coats of mail, protecting all those who were building the wall. The laborers were armed. Each of them worked with one hand, and held a weapon in the other. Each mason was girded with a sword. The bugler stood beside me. I said to the people: "The work is widely spread and we are far apart from each other on the wall; so, whenever you hear the bugle sound, rally to us there. Our God will fight for us." As for myself and my associates, none of us took off our clothes, and each of us kept his weapon in his hand at all times.

Then a loud outcry arose among the people. Some demanded: "Let us have food to keep us alive!" Others complained: "We are mortgaging our fields, our vineyards, and our houses to get food in the famine." Others cried: "We had to borrow money to pay the king's tax. We forced our sons and daughters to be slaves and we have no money to buy them back, for our fields and vineyards are in the hands of others."

When I heard their complaints, I was deeply moved. I brought charges against the nobles and officials, and said to them: "You are taking interest from your own people. We have done all we could to buy back our fellow Jews who have been sold to the heathens, and you would sell them back to us!"

They were silent, and could not find a word to say. So I went on: "The thing you are doing is not good. Come, let us stop taking interest from the people. Restore to them, this very day, their vineyards, their olive yards and their houses with the interest on the money and the food that you have been taking from them."

They replied: "We will do as you say." I summoned the priests, and took an oath of the money-lenders to do as they had promised.

From the time that I was appointed to be the governor in the land of Judah, for twelve years neither I nor my associates ate the food allowance of the governor. The governors who were before me had laid heavy burdens upon the people, and taken food and wine from them. Even the servants lorded it over the people. But I did not; I revered the Lord. I entertained at my table a hundred and fifty Jews who had come to us from the surrounding lands. My daily provision was one ox and six choice sheep. My God, remember all that I have done for this people.

Once the wall was built, I put Jerusalem in charge of Hanani and Hananiah. I said to them: "The gates of Jerusalem are not to be opened until the sun is high. Arrange guards from among the inhabitants of Jerusalem, each to be posted opposite his own house." The city was wide and large, but there were few people and houses had not been built.

On the first day of the seventh month, Ezra the scribe brought the Torah before the community, both men and women and all who could listen intelligently; he read from it, in the open space in front of the water gate, from early morning until noon, and all the people listened closely. Ezra stood on a wooden platform; and when he opened the book, all the people rose. Then Ezra blessed the Lord, and all the people answered "Amen, Amen," raising their hands; they bowed their heads and worshiped the Lord with their faces to the ground.

Chronicles

דִּבְרֵי הַיָּמִים

The first and second books of Chronicles count as one book. They contain a historical record dating from the creation of the world to the end of the Babylonian captivity. Unlike the book of Kings, which covers the history of the kingdoms of Israel and Judah, Chronicles is confined to the story of the kingdom of Judah only, and completely ignores the northern kingdom of Israel. The religious view presented by Chronicles is the conviction that history is not made by chance. Only those events are treated which illustrate a divine purpose and providence.

David defeated the Philistines and subdued them; he defeated Moab, and the Moabites became his subjects. He defeated the king of Zobah, and captured a thousand chariots. When the Syrians came to aid the king of Zobah, David slew twenty-two thousand of them, and then posted a garrison in Syria. This made the Syrians subject to David, and they brought him tribute. He posted garrisons throughout Edom, and all the Edomites became his subjects. Indeed, wherever David went, the Lord gave him victory.

Now David sent messengers to condole with Hanun, the Ammonite king, whose father had died. But the Ammonite princes said to Hanun: "Do you think that David is honoring your father by sending you comforters? His officers have come to explore and overthrow the country." So Hanun seized David's officers, shaved them, cut off their robes as far as their waists, and sent them away. When David was told what had happened to the men, he sent messengers to meet them, for they were greatly ashamed. "Stay at Jericho," he counseled, "until your beards are grown, and then return." In the spring, Joab besieged Rabbah, the capital city of Ammon; he stormed and overthrew it. Then the royal crown of the Ammonites was placed on David's head.

David told Joab to go and number Israel from Beersheba to Dan. So Joab went throughout all Israel and came back to Jerusalem. He reported to David that in all Israel there were one million one hundred thousand men-at-arms, while the tribe of Judah numbered four hundred and seventy thousand men-at-arms. Joab did not include the tribes of Levi and Benjamin in the numbering, for the king's order was detestable to him.

God was displeased with this action, so the seer, Gad, told David: "Thus says the Lord: Three things I offer you; choose one of them: three years of famine, three months of sweeping defeat by your foes, or three days of the Lord's sword and pestilence in the land." Then David said to Gad: "Let me fall into the hand of the Lord, for his mercy is very great; but let me not fall into the hand of man."

So the Lord sent a pestilence, and there fell seventy thousand men of Israel. Then the Lord said to the destroying angel: "It is enough; now stay your hand." When David raised his eyes, he saw the angel of the Lord standing between earth and heaven, holding a drawn sword over Jerusalem, so he said to God: "It was I who gave command to number the people. It is I who have sinned and acted wickedly. But these sheep, what have they done? Let thy hand, Lord my God, be against me and against my father's house, not against my people." Then the Lord commanded the angel, and the angel put the sword back into its sheath. And David said: "Here shall be the house of the Lord God."

David charged Solomon his son to build a house for the Lord God of Israel, saying: "My son, I myself intended to build a temple for the Lord my God. But the word of the Lord came to me: 'You have shed much blood, you have waged great wars; you shall not build a house to my name, because you have shed so much blood on earth. Behold, a son shall be born to you who shall be a man of peace. I will grant him peace from all his enemies round about, for his name shall be *Sh'lomoh,* Solomon, and I will give peace and quiet to Israel in his days. He shall build a house for my name. He shall be my son, and I will be a father to him; I will establish his royal throne over Israel.' Now, my son, may the Lord be with you, that you may succeed in building the temple of the Lord your God, as he has directed you. Be strong and of good courage. Fear not, be not dismayed. You have plenty of workmen, masons, carpenters, and all kinds of craftsmen. There is no end of gold, silver, bronze, and iron. Set to work, and may the Lord be with you!"

David blessed the Lord before all the assembly and said: "Blessed art thou, O Lord, God of Israel our Father, forever and ever. Thine, O Lord, is the greatness and the power, the glory and the victory and the majesty, for all that is in heaven and on earth is thine; thine, O Lord, is the kingdom, and thou art supreme over all. Riches and honor come from thee; thou rulest over all; in thy hand are power and might, and it is in thy power to make all great and strong. Hence, our God, we ever thank thee and praise thy glorious name."

Then Solomon began to build the house of the Lord in Jerusalem on Mount Moriah. When the temple was finished, Solomon brought in the things which David his father had dedicated, the silver and the gold, and all the other articles, and placed them in the treasuries of the temple of God. Then all the men of Israel assembled before the king at the festival in the seventh month. The Levites brought up the ark, the tent of meeting, and all the holy vessels that were in the tent. The priests brought the ark of the covenant of the Lord to its place, in the inner sanctuary of the house, in the most holy place, underneath the wings of the cherubim.

At the end of twenty years, in the course of which Solomon had built the house of the Lord and his own palace, he rebuilt the towns which Huram had given to him, and settled Israelites in them. He built Tadmor in the wilderness and all the store-towns, the towns for his chariots, the towns for his cavalry, and whatever he was pleased to build in Jerusalem, in Lebanon, and anywhere throughout his dominion. Then Solomon went to Ezion-geber and Eloth on the seacoast, in the land of Edom. Huram sent him ships and expert seamen, who accompanied Solomon's men to Ophir and brought back to King Solomon over nineteen tons of gold. The amount of gold that came to Solomon in one year was nearly twenty-nine tons, in addition to what was derived in taxes from traders and merchants. Arabian kings and princes, too, brought gold and silver to Solomon. In wealth and in wisdom King Solomon excelled all kings on earth.

After a period of nearly four hundred years, King Zedekiah did what was evil in the sight of the Lord his God. He would not humble himself before the prophet Jeremiah, and he rebelled against King Nebuchadnezzar; he hardened his heart and obstinately refused to turn to the Lord God of Israel. The leading priests and the people were likewise exceedingly unfaithful, copying the abominable practices of the pagans and defiling the temple which the Lord had hallowed in Jerusalem. They mocked God's messengers, despised his words, and scoffed at his prophets, until the wrath of the Lord burst upon the people, till there was no remedy. He brought down on them the king of the Chaldeans, who killed their young and old and had no compassion. All the treasures of the temple of the Lord, and the treasures belonging to the king and to his nobles, the Chaldean king took away to Babylon. The house of God and all the buildings of Jerusalem were burned; all the costly vessels were destroyed. The Chaldean king carried the survivors off to Babylon, where they became servants to him and to his sons until the establishment of the Persian empire. All this, in fulfillment of what the Lord had foretold through Jeremiah, that the land was to lie desolate for seventy years.

Then the Lord stirred up the spirit of Cyrus, king of Persia to issue a proclamation throughout all his kingdom, permitting reconstruction of the House of God at Jerusalem.